IEG
INDEPENDENT EVALUATION GROUP

WORLD BANK GROUP
World Bank • IFC • MIGA

I0105324

Brazil Country Program Evaluation, FY2004–11

EVALUATION OF THE WORLD BANK GROUP PROGRAM

RIGHTS AND PERMISSIONS

ISBN (paper): 978-1-4648-0216-4
ISBN (electronic): 978-1-4648-0217-1
DOI: 10.1596/978-1-4648-0216-4

Cover image: © Anton Balazh. Used with permission; further permission required for reuse.
Cover design: Crabtree + Company

Library of Congress Cataloging-in-Publication Data has been requested.

Contents

Boxes

Figures

Tables

Appendixes

Abbreviations

AAA	analytic and advisory activities
AES	Anhanguera Educational S.A.
APL	Adaptable Program Loan
ARPA	Amazon Region Protected Area Project
BRAVA	Brazil Evaluation Program
BNDES	National Bank of Economic and Social Development
BRASA	Brazil Analytic and Advisory Program for Social Assistance Program
CAR	Cadastro Ambiental Rural (nationwide rural environmental cadastre)
CAS	Country Assistance Strategy
CASCR	Country Assistance Strategy Completion Report
CDD	community-driven development
CPE	Country Program Evaluation
CPS	Country Partnership Strategy
DPL	development policy loan
ECD	early child development
EMBI	Emerging Market Bond Index
ESTAL	Energy Sector Technical Assistance Loan
FUNDEB	Fund for the Development of Basic Education and Appreciation of Teachers
FUNDEF	Fund for the Development of Primary Education and Appreciation of Teachers
GDP	gross domestic product
GDPL	Programmatic Loan for Sustainable and Equitable Growth
GTFP	Global Trade Finance Program
IBAMA	Brazilian Institute of Environment and Renewable Natural Resources
IBRD	International Bank for Reconstruction and Development
ICR	Implementation Completion and Results Report
IDB	Inter-American Development Bank
IEG	Independent Evaluation Group
IFC	International Finance Corporation
MIGA	Multilateral Investment Guarantee Agency
NHSFO	Non-Honoring of Sovereign Foreign Obligation
PAC	Growth Acceleration Program
PES	payment for environmental services
PPACAm	Action Plan for the Prevention and Control of Deforestation in the Legal Amazon
PPG-7	Pilot Program to Conserve the Brazilian Rain Forest
PPIAF	Public-Private Infrastructure Advisory Facility
PPP	public-private partnership
PPTAL	Rainforest Indigenous Lands Project
PSF	Family Health Extension Project
SEM DPL	Sustainable Economic Management Development Policy Loan
SME	small and medium-size enterprise
SWAp	sectorwide approach

Acknowledgments

This evaluation was prepared by an Independent Evaluation Group (IEG) team led by Jiro Tominaga. The evaluation was conducted under the guidance and supervision of Ali Khadr (Senior Manager) and Nick York (Director) and the overall direction of Caroline Heider (Director-General, Evaluation).

Members of the team included Jaime Biderman, Susan Caceres, Ken Chomitz, Corky de Asis, Kutlay Ebiri, Takatoshi Kamezewa, João Oliveira, Marcelo Selowsky (Senior Consultant), Tony Tyrrell, Carlos Eduardo Valez, Silvina Vatnick, and Cameron Wilson. William Hurlbut edited the report and Yasmin Angeles and Corky de Asis provided administrative support. Peer reviewers were Ariel Fiszbein (Chief Economist, Human Development Network), Thomas O'Brien (Country Program Coordinator: Kenya, Rwanda, Eritrea), and Sergei Soares (Chief of Staff, Instituto de Pesquisa Econômica Aplicada). The report also benefitted from the advice and review of an external panel composed of Armando Castelar (Coordinator of Applied Economic Research at IBRE/Fundação Gertúlio Vargas and Professor of Economics at the Federal University of Rio de Janeiro), Teresa Ter-Minassian (Former Director, Fiscal Affairs Department, International Monetary Fund), and Carlos Young (Associate Professor, Instituto de Economia, Universidade Federal do Rio de Janeiro and Senior Researcher at the Instituto Nacional de Ciência e Tecnologia—Políticas Públicas, Estratégias e Desenvolvimento).

The team is grateful to the numerous representatives of the government, private sector entities, and nongovernmental organizations who provided valuable insights into the World Bank Group's Brazil program. The team is also thankful to World Bank Group management and country team members, including both previous and current staff working on Brazil, who provided valuable time, information, and feedback to the evaluation team.

Overview | HIGHLIGHTS

Over 2004–11, the World Bank Group program in Brazil aimed to support the government's effort to achieve greater equity, sustainability, and competitiveness, underpinned by strong economic management and governance.

The major feature of the World Bank program was its adaptability as the government reallocated its lending capacity to achieve a combination of countercyclical and structural reform objectives. During the first years of fiscal consolidation, the program emphasized federal policy-based operations that would allow a smoother fiscal adjustment. As the federal fiscal situation improved, attention turned to subnational governments; during the period evaluated, the share of subnational lending increased from 19 percent to 78 percent of total commitments.

The International Finance Corporation's (IFC's) net commitment volume tripled during the period evaluated. The distinctive feature of IFC's Brazil portfolio compared to other Latin American countries was the relatively low level of equity investment and a very high share of short-term trade finance, which accounted for more than half of total net commitments during the period. The Multilateral Investment Guarantee Agency (MIGA) concentrated its activities on the electricity transmission subsector; the demand for MIGA's political risk guarantees declined as foreign investor confidence improved during the period.

The outcome of the Bank Group program is judged moderately satisfactory, although with some important variability across themes. The Bank Group made significant contributions when it served as a trusted advisor, providing analytical inputs and exchanging views on immediately relevant policy issues. Examples are support for *Bolsa Família*, improved student learning outcomes, pension reforms, and subnational results-based management systems. In addition, advisory support for structuring public-private partnership projects leveraged IFC's global expertise in project financing. The Bank Group's convening power provided diverse stakeholders with a platform to examine issues and trade-offs that cut across organizational boundaries in water resource management and in multisectoral operations at the subnational level. In the area of the environment, the Bank helped reduce deforestation in the Amazon through support for a major expansion of protected areas and indigenous territories, as well as for building the capacity of national and state environmental agencies.

Results were less satisfactory in addressing infrastructure bottlenecks, particularly in logistics and the cost of doing business, where the Bank Group was not able to make significant impact. These areas remained critical constraints to Brazil's growth and a key government concern. Given the already high tax burden and competing demand for public spending, particularly in the social area, it is important to improve public investment planning and execution and to enhance the regulatory framework and its predictability to attract private investment into infrastructure. In addition, the Bank Group was not able to advance the dialogue to enhance competition in the financial sector.

Given that the demand for Bank Group support remains strong, particularly in states, it is important that the Bank Group maximize its contribution per dollar loaned. Hence, in this evaluation, the Independent Evaluation Group recommends that the Bank Group make expected catalytic impact a major criterion in the design of its future strategy in Brazil. This means that in the selection of the programs and projects to support, the emphasis should be on those with benefits beyond the individual intervention. Support for reforms that create enabling environments and incentives for other actors, activities to enhance demonstration effects and replication of positive results, and engagements that leverage the Bank Group's knowledge base and its convening role to facilitate cross-sectoral dialogue are examples of activities that would fit this criterion. Collaboration among the World Bank, IFC, and MIGA to attract the private sector into infrastructure investment and to reduce the cost of doing business has a potential for high gain. It is also important for the Bank Group to continue promoting sustainable rural development.

This evaluation also recommends that the Bank Group further enhance dialogue with the Brazilian authorities and think tanks to identify the policy areas where it could provide the most effective knowledge support and undertake analytical work on selected issues with important long-term implications. Finally, IFC could expand its public-private partnership operations and sharpen its focus on supporting small and medium-size enterprises' increased access to long-term financing.

Country Context

Brazil made substantial achievements in fiscal adjustment and price stabilization in the late 1990s and early 2000s. But the resilience and continuity of that stabilization effort was tested in the early 2000s as a number of adverse events unfolded: a global economic slowdown, a domestic energy crisis, spillovers from the Argentine crisis, and uncertainties related to the 2002 presidential election. The subsequent macroeconomic stability and a favorable external environment allowed Brazil to resume moderate growth from 2004. The global financial crisis in 2008–09 led to a small and temporary contraction in gross domestic product (GDP), but the country's sound fundamentals and prompt response helped mitigate the decline.

Brazil has made substantial progress in reducing poverty and income inequality. Nonincome indicators of standards of living have also improved; for example, there have been reductions in child malnutrition and increases in primary school enrollment. Gender differences in enrollment have been eliminated. Progress has also been made in a major environmental objective to reduce the rate of deforestation.

Two challenges to further accelerating and sustaining growth remain: infrastructure bottlenecks and the cost of doing business *(Custo Brasil)*. Combining agricultural growth and poverty reduction with environmental and forest protection also remains a challenge. The quality of government expenditures and services remains low despite the high level of such expenditures—the tax burden in Brazil has reached 35 percent of GDP.

Evolution of the World Bank Group Strategy and Program: Continuity with Adaptability

This Brazil Country Program Evaluation (FY04–11) examines the relevance and effectiveness of the Bank Group program during the period covered by the FY04–07 Country Assistance Strategy (CAS) and FY08–11 Country Partnership Strategy (CPS). Both were jointly produced by the World Bank and the International Finance Corporation (IFC); the Multilateral Investment Guarantee Agency (MIGA) was expected to complement them. Because of the modest scale of Bank Group financial support in relation to Brazil's economy, the evaluation focuses on identifying the catalytic role of the Bank Group strategy and operations. The evaluation follows the standard methodology for the Independent Evaluation Group's (IEG) Country Program Evaluations.

Recognizing that broad-based poverty reduction requires continued improvement in economic growth, human capital development, and sustainable use of natural resources, the major goals of the CAS and CPS were to assist Brazil in achieving greater equity, sustainability, and competitiveness underpinned by strong economic management and governance. The engagement effort during the 2002 transition in administrations likely helped establish a durable framework for the Brazil program over the period evaluated. The Policy Note prepared by the World Bank's Brazil team (World Bank 2004) suggested priorities for the incoming administration and helped create an environment for dialogue.

The continuity of the country strategy objectives was complemented by flexibility. A major feature during the period was a significant shift from federal to subnational lending in FY08–11 to respond to emerging demand from subnational entities.

Trends and Patterns in IBRD, IFC, and MIGA Operations

WORLD BANK

The total IBRD (International Bank for Reconstruction and Development) lending commitment during the evaluation period was $16.8 billion. It grew constantly after FY04, except in FY07, when a significant dip resulted from the reconfiguration necessary to increase subnational lending.

A major feature of the program was its adaptability. It responded to the interest of the authorities in reallocating IBRD lending capacity over time to achieve a combination of countercyclical and structural reform objectives. During the first years of fiscal consolidation, the program emphasized adjustment operations at the federal level that would allow a smoother fiscal adjustment. As the federal fiscal situation improved, attention turned to subnational governments. During the global economic crisis in 2008–09, the Bank helped selected subnational entities cope with the adverse impact of the crisis while maintaining the discipline of the Fiscal Responsibility Law. As Brazil approached the IBRD exposure limits toward the end of the evaluation period, the authorities prepaid about $4 billion, about one-fourth of the exposure limit. This significant prepayment allowed the Bank to continue a high level of subnational support. It was also a signal from the authorities to keep a high level of overall engagement.

The Bank actively used the sectorwide approach (SWAp) in its subnational lending—it encouraged cross-sector dialogue and helped strengthen results-based management systems in the counterpart governments. Analytical and advisory work and nonlending technical assistance supporting dialogue and sharing lessons from experience complemented the lending. Many Brazilian counterparts noted that this was the most important contribution of the Bank. During the period evaluated, about $24 million (Bank budget and trust fund) was allocated to analytical activities.

IFC

IFC's Brazil operations were mainly related to the competitiveness pillar of the FY04–07 CAS and FY08–11 CPS. Specifically, IFC supported private sector activities that were expected to enhance Brazil's growth and competitiveness, such as agribusiness and infrastructure, and helped improve access to credit for Brazilian enterprises, particularly SMEs. Its strategic approach also recognized the importance of support for environmental sustainability and public-private partnerships (PPPs). During the FY08–11 CPS period, IFC sought a more direct role in reducing poverty and inequality by focusing on low-income groups and frontier regions. Its attention to second-tier companies and mid-size banks also increased over time.

During FY04–11, IFC's net commitment amounted to $5.01 billion. The distinctive features of the Brazil portfolio compared to that in other Latin American countries are the relatively low level of equity investment and the very high share of trade finance.

During the period, IFC's contributions through its advisory services on PPP were widely recognized. Most of these projects were supported by the Brazil Private Sector Partnership Program established by IFC, the National Bank of Economic and Social Development (BNDES), and the Inter-American Development Bank. This program provides advisory services to structure private concession projects with emphasis on establishing new standards and introducing innovative models for private sector participation in Brazil. During the period evaluated, the program successfully structured projects in transport, health, and education.

MIGA

Most of the 16 guarantees issued during the period evaluated were in the electricity transmission subsector. In the context of improving foreign investor confidence in Brazil, the demand for MIGA's political risk guarantees has declined. However, an expanded mandate, a new product, and changes in its Convention offer an opportunity for MIGA to rebuild its operations in Brazil.

Toward a More Equitable and Sustainable Brazil

The equity objective focused on reducing extreme poverty, enhancing skills formation, and improving health care for all communities. In some areas the Bank Group combined know-how, dialogue, and financial support to create synergies that were acknowledged by Brazilian counterparts. The best examples are the support to *Bolsa Família*—the main national program providing targeted income support to poor families contingent on actions by the family to improve the education and health status of their children—and the analytical work to improve the understanding of classroom dynamics to enhance students' learning outcomes.

Bolsa Familia reached a high percentage of poor families in Brazil and helped alleviate poverty at a sustainable fiscal cost while promoting human capital investment on children and youth. The Bank was strongly associated with the program from its inception through continuous technical and analytical support in monitoring progress, impact, and the quality of targeting. The Bank's sustained support has led to an exceptionally strong partnership with the government counterpart—a practice that should be examined further for replication elsewhere in the Bank.

In education, several analyses on the interaction between students and teachers in the classroom conducted during the FY08–11 CPS period became the basis for a significant amount of analytical work and dialogue. The studies provided policy makers with a benchmark on how teachers in Brazil use instructional time in comparison with other countries and offered insights about the incentive schemes relevant to a range of communities.

The Bank's advisory work to improve education funding for poorer municipalities and their capacity to finance early childhood development programs was also a notable contribution. In health, the Bank supported progress in eliminating communicable diseases, reducing transmission of HIV/AIDS, and expansion of the Family Health Program. In addition, IFC was instrumental in structuring an innovative hospital project in Bahia. Based on this evidence, the outcome of this pillar of Bank Group assistance is rated satisfactory.

The Bank Group strategy had three major objectives for sustainability: better water quality and water resource management; more sustainable land management, forestry, and biodiversity; and more equitable and integrated access to local services, particularly in poor urban and rural communities. These objectives are closely linked, and many of the Bank Group interventions address more than one of them. They are also closely related to efforts to reduce poverty.

The Bank made an important contribution to the dramatic reduction in deforestation in the Amazon by supporting a major expansion of protected areas and indigenous territories. The environment development policy loan (DPL) supported increased capacity at the Environment Ministry and the Brazilian Institute of Environment and Renewable Natural Resources (IBAMA), which undertook expanded and more effective enforcement of forest laws. The Bank has been most successful where it brought the long-term engagement of experts who understand local conditions and bring global knowledge. Goals of balancing development and poverty reduction with forest conservation proved more elusive.

A $1.3 billion DPL sought to support a wide range of policy actions to strengthen Brazil's environmental management system, including the effort for BNDES to adopt and apply a new environmental and social policy to project screening, approval, and monitoring. However, there is no documented impact on BNDES project selection, project design, or project supervision. The loan size was significant in relation to the total IBRD exposure in Brazil and a question emerges whether other avenues to mainstream effective implementation of environmental and social safeguards practice might have been more cost effective.

In water resource management, the Brazilian authorities recognized the value of the Bank's convening power to facilitate broad cross-sectoral dialogue on critical trade-offs. Its focus on water quality, coverage, effective management, and financial sustainability of water investments was also appreciated.

The Bank continued its support for the community-driven model that started in the 1980s with some positive effects in reaching the poor and other disadvantaged groups with key social services, such as access to water supply, sanitation, and electricity. Less clear effects were achieved in supporting farmer productivity and access to markets. In urban development, the Bank made important contributions in slum upgrading, but support for broader municipal development produced mixed results. There were substantial activities in the housing sector during the early phase of the evaluation period, but the scope of dialogue has diminished. Based on this evidence, the outcome of this pillar of Bank Group assistance is rated moderately satisfactory.

Growth, Competitiveness, and Economic Management

Accelerating and sustaining a high growth rate is a necessary condition for long-term poverty reduction. The Bank Group identified two areas to contribute to this objective. The first was the competitiveness and productivity of the Brazilian economy. The second was specific areas of fiscal management that could contribute to improving the quality of public expenditures and the sustainability of public finances.

COMPETITIVENESS

The main areas of support under the competitiveness pillar were addressing infrastructure bottlenecks and the regulatory framework, including for PPPs; the cost of doing business and the environment for competition; and the problem of high interest rates and the segmentation of the credit markets. Among these areas, relieving infrastructure bottlenecks remained a major priority in discussions with the Brazilian authorities throughout the period evaluated.

During the first CAS, the emphasis was on supporting federal-level reforms in many of these areas. Sustainable and Equitable Growth Programmatic Loans were the main operations supporting these reforms. These loans covered a wide range of areas, such as regulatory reforms and a framework for PPPs, reduction in logistics costs by improvements in customs and the operation of ports and roads, simplification of the process for starting a business and tax procedures for small and medium-size enterprises (SMEs), strengthening the corporate insolvency framework, and supporting measures to deepen financial intermediation.

These efforts were complemented by reviews of the cost of doing business and constraints to private participation in infrastructure. A pilot Doing Business in Brazil report (IFC 2006) examined various aspects of the cost of doing business in 13 states and detected large differences among them—an important benchmark study that could help identify factors behind the variability across states. The study "How to Revitalize Infrastructure Investments in Brazil: Public Policies for Better Private Participation" (World Bank 2007) examined constraints to private participation in infrastructure across several sectors and suggested several policy directions to address the problem—again, a useful benchmark for further work in this area. However, there were no major efforts to follow up these works during the period evaluated. Very recent initiatives to undertake a Doing Business report covering all 26 states and to assess the current status of PPP practices in Brazil are timely developments.

The FY08–11 CPS program focused on institutional improvements and regulatory reforms at the state and municipality levels by taking advantage of the new cohort of subnational SWAps and DPLs. Some of these operations included actions to streamline business registration; an operation in Minas Gerais supported steps to implement PPPs and achieved important progress.

The bulk of infrastructure lending took place during this period with an emphasis on roads and mass transit. In roads, the Bank Group's contributions through investments, analytical work, and technical assistance include support for output-based management and improved sector planning, as well as outsourcing of routine maintenance and rehabilitation.

A large share of loans to the transport sector was directed to metro and suburban rail system projects in Rio de Janeiro and São Paulo. Given the magnitude of urbanization challenges in Brazil, there was strong rationale for the Bank to engage in sustained dialogue on urban transport in these cities. These projects also succeeded in reducing commuting time, particularly for poorer households, as well as congestion and pollution. However, given the two cities' high levels of income, creditworthiness, and financial sophistication, as well as the cost recovery possibilities in these projects, these projects raise important issues of selectivity in the allocation of IBRD lending capacity: Could a larger part of these projects have been financed by other sources—including the private sector—while the Bank maintained its role in providing knowledge support?

In energy, the Bank supported key sector reforms, including development of a more competitive electricity market and regulation, access, and affordability for the poor, environmental licensing, and long-term expansion planning and coordination. IFC played an important role in improving trade logistics by developing rules for road concessions and helping mobilize resources for Port Santos. An issue that continues to affect Brazil's competitiveness is the need to strengthen the capacity of the public sector to plan and execute infrastructure investments. An Institutional Development Fund grant appeared to have had some positive impact, but challenges remain.

Reducing the cost of borrowing and improving SMEs' access to financing is a persistent concern in improving the competitiveness of the Brazilian economy. The Bank undertook several studies to understand the factors behind high interest rates and the extent to which they are influenced by macroeconomic factors or by a market structure in which directed credit crowds out private credit in the rest of the system, particularly for SMEs.

The predominant instrument for IFC in the financial markets has been short-term trade finance, which was valuable during the height of the global financial crisis, when trade finance lines from international corresponding banks dried up. However, trade finance has continued to be a dominant share of IFC's net commitments, even after much of the impact of the financial crisis had subsided and IFC's additionality had become less clear. IFC tried to reach SMEs through financial intermediation of medium-term lending via second-tier banks. However, because SMEs were defined very broadly in these projects, it is not clear whether more SMEs have been reached in these programs.

In summary, the Bank Group tried during the first CAS period to improve Brazil's countrywide competitiveness by supporting regulatory reforms at the federal level and undertaking relevant analytical work. During the FY08–11 CPS period, some progress on competitiveness was made through multisector operations to subnational entities and infrastructure operations. However, as the country program focus shifted to subnational entities, the direct channel for a countrywide catalytic effect in the competitive area was weakened. A considerable amount of financing was provided for building infrastructure in the southeastern states, which had positive project-level outcomes, but less obvious effects on helping relieve key infrastructure bottlenecks more broadly.

Taken as a whole, the Bank Group was not particularly effective in advancing the dialogue on regulatory reforms to enhance private participation in infrastructure investment, improve the quality of public investment spending, or reduce the *Custo Brasil*. This was also the case in other areas influencing competitiveness, such as investigating the role of the openness of the trade regime on the competitive environment and productivity and the impact of directed credit on the segmentation of credit markets and access to credit, particularly for SMEs. These are also the areas where the interest on the side of the counterparts to involve the Bank Group in a collaborative effort is limited.

Based on these results, the outcome of this pillar of the assistance strategy is rated moderately unsatisfactory.

SOUND MACROECONOMIC AND PUBLIC SECTOR MANAGEMENT

Bank assistance focused on areas where it has a comparative advantage because of its knowledge base, particularly through international experience. An example is the support for pension reform, consisting of a closely coordinated set of analytical work, technical assistance, and a policy-based operation. The background analytical work provided information on lessons from experiences in other countries and simulations of different scenarios that could be useful for the Brazilian authorities. The technical assistance helped in implementing the reforms at the state level beyond the lifetime of the DPL operation.

The second area of support was the budget and expenditure management system. Support was provided both at the federal and subnational level. Several analytic and advisory activities were undertaken on fiscal federalism and the challenges it presents in transfers, taxation, and indebtedness.

At the subnational level, DPLs and SWAps complemented the directions established by the Federal Responsibility Law regarding the rationalization and reallocation of expenditures. Because of their multisectoral nature, the loans proved ideal for addressing institutional reforms on state public finances that cut across sectors, particularly those involving difficult trade-offs and, hence, consensus across different agencies and stakeholders. These operations typically supported difficult areas of reform such as tax administration to reduce tax evasion, registry of pensioners (extension of the reform at the federal level), civil service census and certification, audit of payrolls, and improvements in procurement procedures. The convening role of the Bank in these operations was highly valued by Brazilian counterparts.

The objective of this pillar was very broad. In a country as large as Brazil, the outcomes are influenced by many factors that can predominate over the instruments that the Bank can deploy. The Bank's major contribution comes either from engaging in sustained dialogue, as in the pension reform, or fostering dissemination and replication, as in the work with selecting subnational governments. Replication and demonstration across states and municipalities will likely take time, although progress so far has been positive and the possibilities of replication may be significant. Based on these assessments, the contribution of the Bank Group in this area is judged satisfactory.

Emerging Messages and Recommendations

IEG rates the outcome of the Bank Group program in Brazil in FY04–11 as moderately satisfactory, although with some important synergies and variability across pillars. The Bank Group had significant impact when it served as a trusted partner in helping Brazilian counterparts think through real and evolving policy issues that they were trying to resolve. The Bank Group also made an important contribution by creating a platform where diverse stakeholders could examine issues and trade-offs that cut across organizational and sectoral boundaries. The SWAp model implemented in Brazil during the period evaluated made significant contributions to the development of the new Bank lending instrument, the Program for Results. However, one question that emerges regarding the overall strategy was whether the use of a few very large operations (metro and urban rail projects and a sustainable environmental management DPL totaling $3 billion), with opportunity cost relative to the IBRD exposure limit, was appropriate.

The focus on subnational clients will continue, given the strong demand for Bank financial and knowledge support among states and municipalities, limited needs for financing at the federal level, and the federal authorities' strong support for subnational lending by the Bank. During the period evaluated, the Bank supported the priorities defined in the dialogue involving the highest level of the subnational authorities—in some cases over many years, as in Ceará. The Bank coordinated with the federal authorities to ensure its support was consistent with the framework governing the relationship between the federal and subnational governments, most importantly the Fiscal Responsibility Law. Based on these considerations as well as the assessments of the commitment for and capacity to implement the agreed activity, the Bank developed its subnational portfolio.

The shift to subnational support has been a success for the Bank. It enabled the Bank to provide customized support for a wide variety of challenges across the country and helped it remain relevant in Brazil by establishing a mechanism to respond to strong demand for Bank financing and knowledge among subnational governments. The Bank and IFC, with support from the federal authorities, have also been working to direct their operational focus on the north and northeast regions during this period. Progress has been made, although the largest share of Bank commitments went to the richer southeast region because of the size of their economies and sustained dialogue with the Bank. The constraint in institutional capacity is particularly relevant in these regions. For IFC, identifying the right investment opportunities was challenging during the period evaluated.

The Bank Group could expand the focus on subnational entities by exploring ways to further facilitate and encourage the replication of positive results achieved in one subnational entity in others. In several areas, the Bank Group has been less effective in addressing the challenges, including infrastructure bottlenecks (particularly in logistics), the cost of doing business, and the environment for competition. Both the Bank and IFC have accumulated experience in different aspects of private participation in infrastructure investment, but apart from a few cases in the water sector, very little was done to explore potential synergies. Demonstrating the value of Bank Group collaboration remains a challenge for the future in Brazil.

Some of the findings of this evaluation may be relevant to Bank Group work in middle-income countries more generally. Many such countries have good access to the international financial markets and well-established fiscal or quasi-fiscal tools to finance their development activities. They also have advanced institutions and a high level of human capital.

In these countries, Bank Group financial contributions are marginal, and knowledge services add value only when they bring perspectives that are not available in the country. Based on the Brazil experience, the IBRD and IFC have a comparative advantage in sharing lessons from cross-country experiences in areas of interest to the authorities. Focusing on geographical areas that are less developed would also be relevant. A critical challenge is to combine the flexibility that allows responding to demands as they emerge and the medium-term strategy that encompasses issues with limited traction from the client in the short term. A difficult balance needs to be struck through strong, candid dialogue with the relevant authorities as well as candor in self-evaluation.

The nature of the engagement will also depend on the administrative links between the local and central government. Hence, the lessons in Brazil need to be interpreted in a particular context of countries with a federal system. For Bank Group engagement in federal states, the experience with multisectoral operations at the subnational level can be particularly relevant. Involvement by the highest authorities at the regional level, subnational government ownership, and strong institutional capacity for coordination and results monitoring are key. In Brazil, the Fiscal Responsibility Law provided an effective incentive framework for reform. Finally, given the large exposure to international capital flows, it is prudent for the Bank Group to maintain some lending space to respond to unanticipated shocks in the global capital flow.

As the demand for Bank Group operations remains strong, particularly with regard to subnational entities, and the IBRD's lending capacity is not without a limit, leveraging results from lending is more important than ever. The challenge is equally acute, if not more, for IFC and MIGA, given the volume of their operations relative to the size of private sector activities in Brazil. Priorities should be based on their externalities, knowledge sharing, and prospects for demonstration effects and replicability—proliferation of activities should be avoided. The Bank Group should focus on areas where it has comparative advantage—areas where a strong element of public good and collective action is particularly suitable.

As Brazil faces the possibility of lower growth and less favorable global economic conditions, the importance of ensuring the effectiveness of Bank Group operations is growing. Moreover, increased quality of public services and expenditures will remain priorities in coming years. For the Bank Group to remain a valuable partner in addressing these challenges, this evaluation makes the following recommendations.

▶ Use the potential for wider catalytic effects as one of the main criteria for selecting the sectors and subnational entities with which to engage.

Programs and projects should be selected on the basis of their expected ability to generate benefits beyond the individual intervention and where the Bank Group has a comparative advantage. The FY12–15 CPS already includes several such areas: continued focus on the northeast, support for social programs, and focus on the efficiency of public investment and incentives for private investments. Given the promising results from the multisectoral approach at the subnational level—most successfully demonstrated in Ceará and Minas Gerais—the Bank should continue pursuing opportunities for similar engagement, building on the lessons learned, such as the need for strong coordination capacity and a high degree of ownership within the counterpart agencies. To further enhance the leverage and the catalytic effect of subnational operations, the Bank Group should identify ways to encourage and facilitate the replication and demonstration of positive results achieved in one subnational entity or region in others.

▶ Enhance lending and nonlending support for improvement in the quality of public investment and the enabling environment for private sector investment.

This could be done through a combination of financial support as well as knowledge and advisory services. Because room for expansion in public spending is limited, it is important to intensify its analytical work to identify the constraints to private participation in infrastructure investments, reduce the cost of doing business, and explore ways to support improvement of public investment planning and execution. Given that both the IBRD and IFC have accumulated knowledge on relevant areas, synergies from Bank Group collaboration can be explored. The IBRD has been providing support for improving regulatory frameworks and IFC has extensive experience in advisory services for structuring specific projects. MIGA could also offer guarantees that would facilitate private sector participation in infrastructure investments.

▶ Continue to promote sustainable rural development, taking advantage of the opportunities presented by the new Forest Code.

Brazil's recently adopted Forest Code provides a new framework for strengthening the harmonization of conservation, development, and poverty reduction objectives. Brazil will face economic and institutional challenges in implementing the Code's provisions. These include completing a universal rural environmental cadastre in the near term and finding productive, cost-effective, and environmentally beneficial ways for private landholders to comply with forest reserve obligations under the Code. Building on past and ongoing work, the Bank and IFC should be prepared to offer technical and financial assistance to help meet the challenges of implementing the new Forest Code in a way that is cost-effective, poverty reducing, and environmentally sound.

▶ Enhance dialogue with authorities and think tanks to identify policy issues where the Bank Group could provide timely knowledge and advisory support.

Knowledge activities are areas where the Bank Group can have important positive externalities and catalytic effects per dollar loaned and per dollar of its budget resources. The Bank's managerial focus, incentives, and internal resource allocation need to reflect this potential and ensure that sufficient resources are allocated to these activities. This, however, should not mean undermining the role of lending, as experience shows that value often comes from a combination of lending and knowledge support.

The Bank Group was effective when it sustained close interactions during implementation as trusted partner and provided "how to" advice, as in *Bolsa Familia* and in multisectoral programs in Ceará and Minas Gerais, as well as in IFC's advisory support for PPP project structuring. The effort is rather in searching for an optimal mix of lending and knowledge support, acknowledging that the emphasis on knowledge may have to intensify over the medium term, given the strong demand for Bank Group support and the Bank's exposure limit.

Experience shows that the Bank Group can provide unique perspectives on issues that the authorities need to tackle in the short run. To provide useful and timely inputs on such issues, the Bank Group needs to identify the major policy areas where it can provide the most useful inputs and contribute most effectively. This requires active, ongoing dialogue with the federal and subnational entities as well as think tanks.

▶ Continue analytical work on selected topics with important long-term implications, even though traction with the authorities may be limited in the short term.

A challenge for the Bank Group in designing and implementing the Brazil country strategy is to maintain flexibility in responding to evolving client demand while ensuring a level of specificity that makes it a meaningful guide for operations. Achieving flexibility by defining very wide objectives over many areas works well in a rapidly changing environment; however, an excessively flexible strategy could result in pursuing only those outcomes that receive strong traction from the main counterparts, leaving out areas recognized to be important for overall long-term development. To avoid this risk, it is important to continue deepening the knowledge on critical medium- and long-term constraints to development in Brazil—even if some of these areas are not part of the immediate policy agenda. There may also be difficult political trade-offs involved in these areas. Given the medium- to long-term nature of this effort, resources that can realistically be allocated may be limited, and the choice of topics needs to be selective. Undertaking some minimum analytical work in these areas would help the Bank Group balance the flexibility in operational response with the stability in the strategic directions of the program.

This evaluation has identified several possible areas for consideration in the future country program. They include a review of Brazil's experiences with concessions in different sectors; an assessment of institutional and regulatory constraints affecting public agencies in the planning, selection, and execution of public sector investment; an analysis of the experience with direct credit; and the implications of different degrees of openness of the Brazilian trade regime for enhancing productivity.

IFC OPERATIONS

With regard to IFC operations, this evaluation recommends that the following two areas be pursued.

a. Expand IFC's work on PPPs.

IFC has added significant value in its support for PPP project structuring, and demand remains high for innovative projects that can be replicated and scaled up elsewhere in Brazil. Further expansion of the PPP collaboration with BNDES should be pursued. As the expansion of PPP projects in Brazil depends critically on the enabling regulatory environment and its predictability, this is an area for close collaboration between the IFC and the Bank, as noted earlier. IFC should also increase direct investments in infrastructure projects and project sponsors that have the potential to transfer IFC's knowledge on project financing as well as social and environmental standards.

b. Enhance the design and targeting of IFC activities to expand SMEs' access to long-term financing.

To make its SME support more effective, IFC's emphasis should be shifted from short-term trade finance guarantees toward expansion in the share of long-term loan and equity financing. IFC should also enhance its monitoring systems to examine whether SMEs that have relatively less access to long-term credit are reached. For that, IFC should sharpen the sub-borrower eligibility criteria in project and associated legal documents of IFC financial market investments aimed primarily to reach SMEs.

References

IFC (International Finance Corporation). 2006. *Doing Business in Brazil*. Washington, DC: World Bank.

World Bank. 2007. *How to Revitalize Infrastructure Investments in Brazil (Public Policies for Better Private Participation)*. FPSI/LAC Report #36624BR, World Bank, Washington, DC.

Management Action Record

Catalytic Effect

IEG FINDINGS AND CONCLUSIONS

World Bank Group financial contributions are highly valued by the government, but they are small compared to the size of Brazil's economy. Consequently, leveraging and having a catalytic effect from lending and nonlending support is particularly important. The challenge is equally acute, if not more, for IFC and MIGA, given the volume of their operations relative to the size of private sector activities in Brazil.

A major comparative advantage of the Bank Group is in examining policy options and trade-offs across several sectors and themes. The Bank Group can also be effective in facilitating the dialogue among stakeholders to discuss such trade-offs and identify solutions—the convening role of the Bank Group. Areas where there is an important element of public goods are particularly suitable. Given the size of Brazil, these activities are more manageable in the context of assisting subnational governments. In this context, multisectoral operations at a subnational level can effectively leverage the Bank Group's convening role to facilitate cross-sectoral dialogue.

IEG RECOMMENDATION

Use the potential for wider catalytic effects as one of the main criteria for selecting the sectors and subnational entities with which to engage. The Bank Group would focus in areas where it has comparative advantage and can expect to generate benefits beyond the individual intervention. In addition, the Bank Group should identify ways to encourage and facilitate the replication and demonstration of positive results achieved in one subnational entity or region in others. Given the promising results so far, the Bank should continue identifying opportunities for multisectoral approaches at the subnational level, while incorporating the lessons learned.

ACCEPTANCE BY MANAGEMENT

Agree

MANAGEMENT RESPONSE

While agreeing with the recommendation, the World Bank Group notes that transformational and catalytic engagements consist of a combination of advice, analysis, and lending over a period of many years and without knowing in advance whether an intervention or engagement will be truly catalytic. The Bank Group program in Brazil continues to seek catalytic interventions in a variety of ways: by pursing cutting-edge operations that bring sectors together to solve difficult development problems and in sharing lessons throughout the country and internationally, for example, through the World Without Poverty Knowledge Hub that shares lessons of experience in reduction of poverty and inequality within Brazil and internationally.

World Bank Group management is also seeking to draw on new instruments such as the MIGA Non-Honoring of Sovereign Foreign Obligation (NHSFO) Guarantee to draw in private resources as in the São Paulo Sustainable Transport Project. Management will continue to work with states and large municipalities on multisector projects, while incorporating lessons and seeking partnerships with other multilateral, bilateral and private partners (as in the case of the Third Minas Gerais Development Partnership DPL) so as to leverage resources from outside the Bank Group.

Private Participation

IEG FINDINGS AND CONCLUSIONS

To enhance Brazil's competitiveness, infrastructure bottlenecks and the high cost of doing business need to be addressed. There is a growing urgency to enhance private participation in infrastructure investments and to improve the quality of public investments.

Enhancing private participation is an area with potential for close collaboration and complementarities within the Bank Group, given the IBRD's experience in advising systemic regulatory issues and IFC's expertise in individual PPP project structuring in Brazil.

IEG RECOMMENDATIONS

Enhance lending and nonlending support for improvement in the quality of public investment and the enabling environment for private sector investment. This could be done through a combination of financial support and knowledge and advisory services. The Bank Group should intensify its analytical work to identify the constraints to private sector participation in infrastructure investment, reduce the cost of doing business, and explore ways to help improve the efficiency of public investment planning and execution. Synergies from Bank Group collaboration should be sought, building on IBRD's experience in supporting improvement in regulatory frameworks, IFC's expertise in PPP project financing and structuring, and MIGA's ability to offer guarantees that would facilitate private sector participation in infrastructure investments.

ACCEPTANCE BY MANAGEMENT

Agree

MANAGEMENT RESPONSE

The Group is already drawing on its lending, analytical, and advisory tools to advance the private sector agenda and the quality of public sector investment. Drawing on existing analytical work (Brumby, Mendes, and Velloso 2011), many of our state projects work to strengthen investment planning over the medium term. Management of IBRD/IFC has recently concluded a joint piece that looks at the experiences with concessions to date and the particular regulatory issues that need to be addressed. The IFC has augmented its support to the BNDES/IFC/IDB facility on PPPs, helping to structure innovative PPP arrangements, and we are working with BNDES to see how we may expend this work. IBRD has several Reimbursable Advisory Services under way providing up-front technical advice and guidance on PPPs in various sectors in Brazil, but particularly in infrastructure. There is approval at the federal level for a MIGA NHFSO guarantee that is expected to be drawn upon by other states in the future in order to further leverage private sector resources. The entities of the Group are working together to strengthen the synergies across the work program.

Conservation, Development, and Poverty Reduction

IEG FINDINGS AND CONCLUSIONS

Brazil's recently adopted Forest Code provides a new framework for strengthening the harmonization of conservation, development, and poverty reduction objectives. Brazil will face economic and institutional challenges in implementing the Code's provisions. These include completing a universal rural environmental cadastre in the near term and finding productive, cost-effective, and environmentally beneficial ways for private landholders to comply with forest reserve obligations under the Code.

IEG RECOMMENDATION

Continue to promote sustainable rural development, taking advantage of the opportunities presented by the new Forest Code. Building on past and ongoing work, the Bank and IFC should be prepared to offer technical and financial assistance, as required, to help meet the challenges of implementing the new Forest Code in a way that is cost-effective, poverty reducing, and environmentally sound.

ACCEPTANCE BY MANAGEMENT

Agree

MANAGEMENT RESPONSE

We agree with the need to continue to support sustainable rural development by supporting implementation of the Forest Code. However, the Group notes and does not agree with the finding of the IEG review that group efforts to balance "development and poverty reduction with forest conservation proved more 'elusive.'"

The Bank Group continues to engage strongly with both the Ministry of Environment and state governments on the implementation of the land cadastre, drawing on a variety of analytical tools, loans, trust funds, and partnerships with others to support implementation of the Forest Code.

Our program in the state of Acre is an example of how we are helping to support service delivery in remote areas, implementation of cadastres, protection of the environment, and development of sustainable economic activities in environmentally sensitive zones.

Knowledge Services

IEG FINDINGS AND CONCLUSIONS

Knowledge activities can have important externalities and catalytic effects per dollar loaned and per dollar of the Bank Group's budget resources. Experience in Brazil shows that value often comes from a combination of lending and knowledge, so the two need to go together.

The Bank Group is highly valued when it serves as a trusted partner in examining policy options, including sharing lessons from other experiences.

IEG RECOMMENDATION

Enhance dialogue with authorities and think tanks to identify policy issues where the Bank Group could provide timely knowledge and advisory support. The Bank Group should conduct active, ongoing dialogue with the federal and subnational entities as well as think tanks to identify the major policy areas where timely Bank Group inputs would be most useful.

ACCEPTANCE BY MANAGEMENT

Agree

MANAGEMENT RESPONSE

Conducting active, ongoing dialogue with the federal and subnational entities as well as think tanks to identify the major policy areas where timely Bank Group inputs would be most useful activities is among the guiding principles of World Bank Group engagement in the country, and will continue to be so in the future. The Bank Group team engages with government authorities and a wide number of think tanks in Brazil to assess where our involvement could have the most impact. In addition to a partnership with the Ministry of Social Development, IPEA (Brazil's main think tank), and the UN International Poverty Center on lessons from Brazil in reducing poverty and inequality (the World Without Poverty Initiative), the Bank team has begun an intensive dialogue with the Secretariat of Strategic Subjects and IPEA, as well as others, on productivity and competitiveness in Brazil, including work on skills and jobs and a subnational Doing Business survey with SEBRAE in all 25 states as a Reimbursable Advisory Service.

Management is also working with the federal government and several think tanks on issues related to water management—climate change, irrigation, water usage plans, and so forth—to assist governments in understanding better how to deal with drought and how to prepare for the effects of climate change especially in the Northeast.

Flexible Country Strategy

IEG FINDINGS AND CONCLUSIONS

A challenge for the Bank Group designing and implementing the Brazil country strategy is to maintain flexibility in responding to evolving client demands while ensuring a level of specificity that makes it a meaningful guide for operations. Achieving flexibility by defining very wide objectives over many areas serves well in a rapidly changing environment; however, an excessively flexible strategy could result in pursuing only those outcomes that receive strong traction from the main counterparts, leaving out areas well recognized to be important for overall long-term development. To avoid this risk, it is important to continue deepening the knowledge on critical medium- and long-term constraints to development in Brazil—even if some of these areas are not part of the immediate policy agenda. Given the medium- to long-term nature of this effort, the resources that can realistically be allocated may be limited, and the choice of topics needs to be selective. Undertaking some minimum analytical work in these areas would help the Bank Group balance the flexibility in operational response with the stability in the strategic directions of the program.

IEG RECOMMENDATION

Continue analytical work on selected topics with important long-term implications, even though traction with the authorities may be limited in the short term. Possible areas for consideration include a review of Brazil's experiences with concessions in different sectors; an assessment of institutional and regulatory constraints affecting public agencies in the planning, selection, and execution of public sector investment; an analysis of the experience with direct credit; and the implications of different degrees of openness of the Brazilian trade regime for enhancing productivity.

ACCEPTANCE BY MANAGEMENT

Agree

MANAGEMENT RESPONSE

Finding avenues to support improved productivity and competitiveness is probably the single most important long-term issue for Brazil, which incorporates many of the issues mentioned here. The PPP study mentioned above looks at the experience with concessions, as well as institutional and regulatory issues with PPPs. The recent Financial Sector Assessment Program (2012) addressed issues related to direct credit. There are, however, a number of areas related to issues that affect firm productivity from the outside (logistics, trade, rent-seeking, tax structure); issues related to firm management; and issues related to how to improve the productivity of individual workers, which will be brought together to advance the agenda. Although a difficult and complex area, productivity and competitiveness has become and will continue to be central to our engagement.

IFC Work

IEG FINDINGS AND CONCLUSIONS

IFC has provided valuable support for PPP project structuring. Demand remains high, especially in subnational entities, for innovative projects that can be replicated and scaled up elsewhere in Brazil.

IFC has pursued its strategic objective of supporting SMEs through financial intermediation via second-tier banks. The impact of such operations is difficult to identify, given how the eligibility criteria for sub-borrowers are defined. Also, the trade finance program relative to long-term financing increased dramatically during the 2008–09 crisis period and has remained high, even though one would expect the additionality of trade credit programs to have diminished as the immediate impact of the crisis has waned.

IEG RECOMMENDATION

a. Expand IFC's work on PPPs. Pursue further expansion of the PPP collaboration with BNDES, increasing direct investments in infrastructure projects and project sponsors that have the potential to transfer IFC's knowledge on infrastructure and project financing as well as social and environmental standards. Also, seek collaboration with IBRD and MIGA, as noted.

ACCEPTANCE BY MANAGEMENT

Agree

MANAGEMENT RESPONSE

The Bank Group agrees that IFC's work on PPPs has had a strong impact in Brazil, and management agrees on the recommendation to continue expanding work in this area. Going forward, the focus on the expansion of the partnership with BNDES should be at the subnational level, where IFC could add more value to the process. As the PPP partnership program with BNDES involves direct engagement with a government agency, the Bank Group also agrees that increased collaboration between IBRD, IFC, and MIGA would improve synergies and program effectiveness. The Brazil model can be one that could be replicated in other large middle-income countries.

IEG RECOMMENDATION

b. Enhance the design and targeting of IFC activities to expand SMEs' access to long-term financing.

- Shift emphasis from short-term trade finance guarantees toward expansion of long-term loan and equity financing.

ACCEPTANCE BY MANAGEMENT

Disagree

MANAGEMENT RESPONSE

While the Bank Group team understands the report's conclusions and agrees that long-term financing to SMEs is key for Brazil's development, it believes that short-term trade finance had and continues to have an important impact on Brazilian SMEs and thus should not have decreased as the immediate impacts of the crisis waned.

IEG RECOMMENDATION

- Sharpen the sub-borrower eligibility criteria in the project and associated legal documents of IFC financial market investments aimed primarily to reach SMEs that have relatively less access to long-term credit.

ACCEPTANCE BY MANAGEMENT

Agree

MANAGEMENT RESPONSE

The Bank Group welcomes IEG 's comments on sharpening the sub-borrower eligibility criteria for future projects, but as this recommendation has corporate-wide implications beyond Brazil, it will be addressed in more detail in the context of the upcoming IEG SME report.

Reference

Brumby, James A., Marcos Mendes, and Tarsila Velloso. 2011. "Public Investment Management in Brazil." Mimeo, World Bank, Washington, DC.

1 Purpose and Country Context

This Country Program Evaluation (CPE) evaluates World Bank Group (International Bank for Reconstruction and Development [IBRD], or the Bank, International Finance Corporation [IFC], and Multilateral Investment Guarantee Agency [MIGA]) operations in Brazil from FY04 through FY11. It seeks to answer two questions:

- To what extent was the Bank Group program relevant to Brazil's development needs?

- How effective were Bank Group operations in helping to accelerate economic growth and making growth more inclusive and environmentally sustainable?

The period reviewed was covered by two country strategies, one for FY04–07 and the other for FY08–11. The evaluation comments on aspects of the Country Partnership Strategy (CPS) FY12–15 with particular reference to its relevance and design. The report aims to extract lessons relevant to future Bank Group operations in Brazil.

Country Context Prior to the Evaluation Period (1995–2003)

The development challenges and accomplishments of the 1990s and early 2000s are the setting for this evaluation. Substantial achievements in fiscal adjustment and price stabilization during the Cardoso administration helped shift the public sector primary balance from a deficit to a surplus, reaching about 3.5 percent of gross domestic product (GDP) in 2000. Starting in 1997, 25 of Brazil's 27 states signed debt-restructuring agreements with the federal government, significantly improving their fiscal position. The passage of the Fiscal Responsibility Law in 2000 provided a general framework for budgetary planning, execution, and reporting for the three levels of government. It prohibited the federal government from financing state and local governments beyond the yearly transfers, effectively guaranteeing that debt-rescheduling agreements would be respected. The sustained effort to tighten fiscal policies helped control inflation, which decreased from about 2,076 percent in 1994 to 3.2 percent in 1998 (Figure 1.1).

FIGURE 1.1 Substantial Achievement in Fiscal Adjustment and Price Stabilization in the Late 1990s

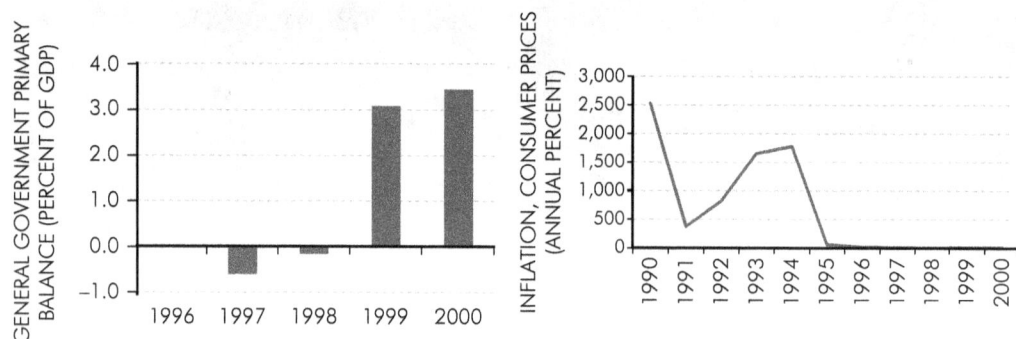

SOURCE: International Monetary Fund, International Financial Statistics and data files.
NOTE: GDP = gross domestic product.

Efforts to improve education and health standards resulted in progress on most social indicators. In education, enrollment was improved through policy changes and federal initiatives such as *Fundescola* and the FUNDEF. Conditional cash transfer programs tied to school attendance, such as *Bolsa Escola*, started during this period. The net enrollment rate in primary education increased from 84 to 96 percent during the 1990s.

Various public policies for health also were implemented, including the *Programa de Atendimento Básico*, as were focused programs for AIDS and malaria, decentralization, and greater participation of communities. Infant mortality declined from 47 to 31 per 1,000 live births between 1991 and 2000. The administration also implemented structural reforms that abolished state monopolies, launched land reform, restructured and privatized some state banks, and initiated reforms in various infrastructure sectors.

The resilience of Brazil's stabilization effort was severely tested in the last two years of the Cardoso administration. Adverse events during this period included a global economic slowdown, a domestic energy crisis, spillovers from the Argentine crisis, and uncertainties related to the 2002 presidential election. The reduction in capital inflow and the resulting depreciation led to an increase in debt to GDP ratio from 52.2 to 60.6 percent during 2002, as a significant part of public debt was linked to the exchange rate. As market expectations about Brazil's economic performance worsened and uncertainty regarding the future of fiscal discipline and economic reform after the election grew, the market began to price into Brazilian bonds a risk of default. The Emerging Markets Bond Index (EMBI) spread[1] moved from 700 basis points in the spring to 2,400 at the end of July.

Under these circumstances, the International Monetary Fund extended Brazil a $30 billion standby in August 2002, on the basis of maintaining sound policies in such areas as primary surpluses, inflation targeting, a floating exchange regime, and respect of contracts, including the public debt. Various signals and statements from leading candidates in favor of the fiscal stance required to stabilize debt dynamics followed. Supported also by a proactive monetary policy, the economy rapidly stabilized: the EMBI spread had fallen to 1,500 basis points by the end of December and to 463 basis points in December 2003.

During this tumultuous period, the main objective of the Bank Group strategy was alleviation of poverty,[2] with an intermediate objective of sustained growth—including some attention to environmental issues. The Bank expanded its lending to Brazil between 1995 and 2003 with a noticeable shift toward adjustment lending. The success in stabilization led to improvement in the quality of the portfolio and a stronger rationale for increased lending. The government became progressively more engaged in the elaboration of the assistance strategy, and the decentralization of the Country Management Unit to Brasilia in 1997 facilitated policy dialogue. Since 1997, the country strategy has been prepared jointly by the IBRD and IFC.

In 2003, the Independent Evaluation Group (IEG) undertook an evaluation of World Bank assistance in Brazil between 1990 and 2002 (IEG 2004). That evaluation rated the program satisfactory. It concluded that the Bank made important contributions to improvements in social indicators and access of the rural and urban poor to basic infrastructure. In addition, the Bank's self-assessment of the FY00 Country Assistance Strategy (CAS) Completion Report covered operations through the end of FY03. The main success area was poverty reduction through interventions in health and education. The major area where outcomes were below expectations was growth. The report acknowledges that the Bank program had failed to mobilize growth. It states that the authorities and the Bank expected that private investment would meet infrastructure needs, which did not materialize (see Appendix A for Bank Group operations in 1995–2003).

Brazil's Development Challenges during the Evaluation Period (FY04–11)

Brazil has enjoyed political and economic stability during the period evaluated. A single party has been in power throughout, first under President Luiz Inácio Lula da Silva (January 2003–December 2010) and then under President Dilma Rousseff (since January 2011). At the start of his administration, President Lula maintained continuity of the macroeconomic framework, aimed at fiscal responsibility and a primary surplus, inflation targeting, and a flexible exchange rate. Inflation declined sharply, and reforms in the public sector balance sheet substantially reduced domestic debt indexed to foreign currencies. Public sector net debt fell over the decade, from about 60.2 percent in 2002 to 36.4 percent in 2011. Countercyclical measures adopted during the global financial crisis raised the net debt ratio in 2009 to 42.8 percent, but it declined to 39.7 percent in June 2011.

The macroeconomic stability and a favorable external environment allowed Brazil to resume moderate growth from 2004. GDP grew by nearly 5 percent per year between 2004 and 2008, with some fluctuations. The global financial crisis led to contraction in GDP in the fourth quarter of 2008 and the first quarter of 2009. But the country's sound fundamentals and prompt response to the crisis helped mitigate these declines. Brazil was one of the last nations to fall into recession in 2008 and among the first to recover; after experiencing a −0.3 percent growth in 2009, Brazil grew at 7.5 percent in 2010. Brazil has also made considerable progress in its long-term foreign currency sovereign credit ratings. Standard & Poor's rating for Brazil improved by four notches, from noninvestment grade BB− in 2003 to above investment grade of BBB in 2011.

Poverty was also reduced during the period, reflecting the strong emphasis the government placed on social programs. Poverty declined from 35.8 percent of the population in 2003 to 21.4 percent in 2009 (representing an escape from poverty for about 22 million people); and extreme poverty fell from 15.2 percent in 2004 to 7.3 percent in 2009 (representing an escape from extreme poverty for about 13 million people).[3] Between 2001 and 2011, the income of the poorest 10 percent of the population grew by 6.7 percent per year, whereas

FIGURE 1.2 Poverty and Inequality Declined Steadily

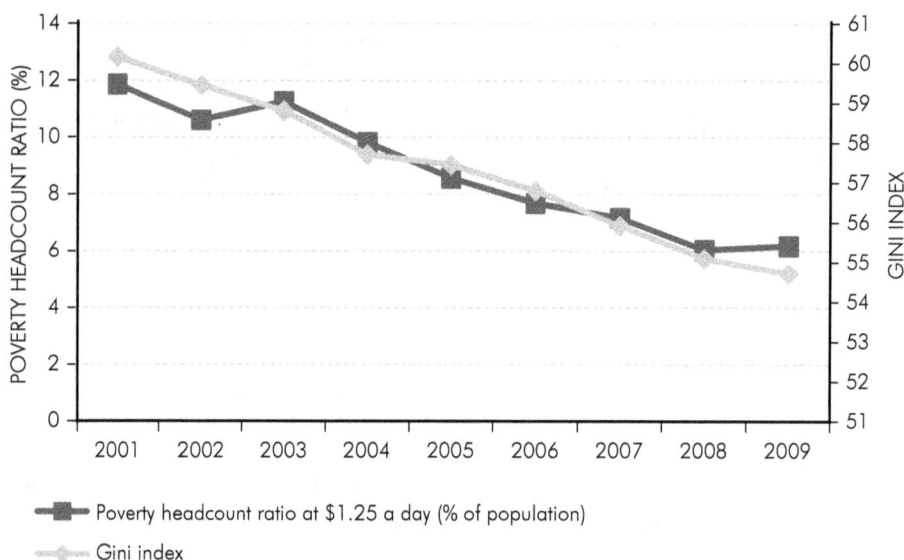

Poverty headcount ratio at $1.25 a day (% of population)
Gini index

SOURCE: World Bank data.
NOTE: Brazil does not have an official poverty line. In recent years, the R$70 and R$140 per capita per month, which are administrative poverty lines defined for the *Bolsa Família* program and the *Brasil Sem Miseria* plan, have been increasingly used in place of official poverty lines. The international $1.25 per day poverty line is also used on occasion, notably in relation to the Millennium Development Goals. As a result of methodological differences in the computation of lines and income aggregates, there are sometimes small differences between government and World Bank estimates. However, trends are broadly consistent across methodologies.

that of the richest 10 percent grew by 1.55 percent. This helped reduce income inequality (measured by the Gini index) to 0.527 in 2011, down from 0.594 in 2001[4] (Figure 1.2).

A range of nonincome indicators has also improved. For example, malnutrition among children under five has been halved since the 1990s, and 98 percent of children aged 7–14 are enrolled in education. Gender differences in access to education have been nearly eliminated, although the participation rate among boys is now lower than that of girls, particularly in the later stages of secondary schooling (World Bank 2011b).

Although Brazil's growth rate during the evaluation period was higher than that in preceding two decades, it was lower than major emerging countries (Figure 1.3). Much of the literature on this topic maintains that accelerating Brazil's economic growth requires sharp increases in investment rates, particularly in infrastructure, which was low relative to comparator emerging markets over the past decade. Key issues seem to be weak incentives to invest, particularly for the private sector, and low savings rates. Regulatory frameworks to encourage private investment in infrastructure and reforms to reduce the cost of doing business are also important to increase productivity and competitiveness. Other key development challenges discussed with the authorities during the CAS preparation include:

FIGURE 1.3 GDP Growth Rate: Brazil and Major Emerging Countries

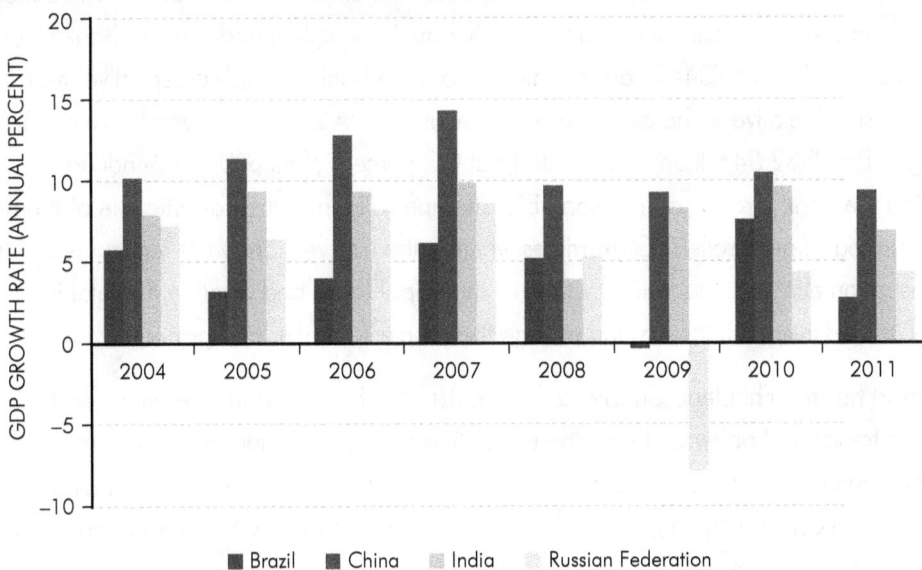

SOURCE: World Bank data.
NOTE: GDP = gross domestic product.

- Extreme regional differences, especially in social indicators such as health, infant mortality, and nutrition, with the richer south and southeast regions far outperforming the poorer north and northeast

- Reduced but still significant poverty in absolute numbers

- The quality of government services in relation to expenditures, which remains relatively low compared to other middle-income countries

- A variety of environmental challenges associated with deforestation and the need to combine agricultural growth, environmental protection, and sustainable development.

Evaluation Issues

This evaluation examines the relevance and effectiveness of the Bank Group program during FY04–11. The question on relevance "To what extent was the assistance of the Bank Group relevant to Brazil's development needs?" involves examining how well the Bank Group exercised selectivity to maintain the program's relevance to Brazil's evolving priorities; how realistic the country program objectives and the results frameworks were; and how well the Bank Group adapted to the changing external environment. The study also examines the synergies between lending and knowledge services and the effectiveness of collaboration within the Bank Group and with external development partners. This evaluation follows the standard methodology for IEG's CPEs described in Appendix B.

The modest scale of Bank Group financial support in relation to the size of Brazil's economy presents some special evaluation challenges. Although the extent and scale of Bank Group activities in Brazil over FY04–11 are significant from the Bank Group's perspective, that support is small relative to the overall Brazilian economy. In 2011, for example, World Bank lending in Brazil ($2.54 billion) represented just 0.3 percent of all public expenditure. In assessing the Bank Group contribution, IEG attempts to identify the catalytic role of the Bank Group strategy. Specifically, IEG examines whether the interventions were replicable or had demonstration effects at the federal, state, or municipal levels and whether the total impact of a set of related interventions was larger than the simple sum of its components.

This report has five chapters. Chapter 2 summarizes the Bank Group operations and examines trends and patterns during the evaluation period. Chapters 3 and 4 assess the relevance and contributions of these operations to the objectives stated in the country strategies. The concluding chapter draws lessons and recommendations for the Bank Group's future engagement in Brazil.

Endnotes

[1] The Emerging Market Bond Index spread shows the difference between the yield on dollar-denominated bonds issued by Brazil and that on equivalent U.S. Treasury bonds.

[2] See the Country Assistance Strategies of 1995, 1997, and 2000.

[3] Based on the poverty and extreme poverty lines calculated by the *Instituto de Pesquisa Econômica Aplicada*.

[4] The CPS FY08–11 notes that about half of the reduction in poverty is explained by *economic growth*. The other half is due to reduced inequality, mostly due to the particularly high growth of labor incomes as well as government transfers (in equal proportions), indicating the important role played by the safety net programs and other social transfer programs.

Reference

IEG (Independent Evaluation Group). 2004. *Brazil: Forging a Strategic Partnership for Results: An OED Evaluation of World Bank Assistance*. Washington, DC: World Bank.

2 Continuity and Evolution of the World Bank Group Program

World Bank Group Strategy: FY04–11

Brazil is one of the major middle-income countries where the Bank Group has sustained policy dialogue and a strong operational program on a wide range of development issues. The major goal of the program throughout the evaluation period was to help Brazil achieve greater equity, sustainability, and competitiveness, underpinned by strong economic management and governance.

The Bank Group strategy recognized that poverty reduction requires continued improvement in multiple dimensions of development and attempted to capitalize on the interlinkages between them. For example, better learning and targeted social programs would lead to greater opportunities and smaller income inequalities. Improved water supply would lead to healthier children and better learning outcomes. Enhanced competitiveness would lead to higher economic growth that creates jobs. Sustainable use of natural resources would attract investment while ensuring long-term growth. Both the FY04–07 CAS and the FY08–11 Country Partnership Strategies (CPSs) were produced jointly by the World Bank and IFC. MIGA, as a member of the World Bank Group, was expected to complement these country strategies.

STABILITY OF FOUR STRATEGIC PILLARS AND THE 2002 POLICY NOTE

Equity, sustainability, competitiveness, and foundations for economy and governance form the pillars of both the FY04–07 CAS (World Bank 2003) and the FY08–11 CPS (World Bank 2008) (see Figure 2.1). The specific operational areas included in the FY04–07 CAS remained broadly stable throughout the evaluation period.

The intense engagement effort during the transition from the Cardoso administration to the Lula administration in 2002 helped establish the durable framework of the Brazil country program. The dialogue involved Bank staff across all sectors and Brazilian authorities on both sides of the transition. The Bank had established a strong relationship with the outgoing administration, but the scope for policy alignment with the new administration was uncertain.

FIGURE 2.1 CAS/CPS Pillars with FY04–07 Subpillars

A More Equitable, Sustainable, and Competitive Brazil		
More Equitable: Human Capital and Social Development	**More Sustainable: Natural Capital and Local Services**	**More Competitive: Investment and Productivity**
• Reducing extreme poverty, vulnerability, and social exclusion • Better knowledge and skills • Living longer, healthier lives	• Better water quality and water resource management • More sustainable land management, forests, and biodiversity • More equitable access to local services	• Improved infrastructure, investment climate, and competition • Broader and more efficient financial sector • More modern innovation climate
Foundations of Economy and Governance • Sound economic management and fiscal reform • More efficient public sector management • Good governance		

SOURCE: World Bank 2003.
NOTE: CAS/CPS = Country Assistance Strategy/Country Partnership Strategy.

The Bank had started the outreach and engagement with the teams of key presidential candidates during the election period, and these meetings proved instrumental in building relationships with the team that eventually formed the new administration.

In particular, the Policy Note prepared by the World Bank's Brazil team during in 2002 (World Bank 2004) was instrumental in creating an environment for meaningful dialogue. The note suggested priorities for the incoming administration, underpinned by a strong knowledge base on diverse subjects. The proposals were in five thematic categories: investing in people, growing through productivity, stabilizing the economy, delivering government services to all, and managing Brazil's natural inheritance.

The underlying vision in the Policy Note was a more equitable, sustainable, competitive Brazil—the three pillars of the next two country strategies. Most of the main authors of the Policy Note were based in Brazil and continued their involvement with the country program for a sustained period. This allowed for continuity and facilitated subsequent policy dialogue. The strategic directions set in the Policy Note also helped enhance multisectoral activities oriented toward development results. From the outset, the Policy Note established cross-cutting priorities that required collaboration among Bank sector staff. It emphasized the need to achieve macroeconomic stability and make it compatible with strong growth and equity.

ADDRESSING EVOLVING NEEDS: AGILITY AND FLEXIBILITY IN THE COUNTRY PROGRAM

The stability in the country strategies was complemented by flexibility. Each strategy emphasized the need for increased agility and flexibility by Bank Group institutions to adapt to emerging priorities and realities. The FY04–07 CAS cites the need to use "programmatic selectivity" and the FY08–11 CPS suggests a need for "principled opportunism."

The high level of flexibility in the program was demonstrated most notably by the significant shift in operational focus from federal to subnational entities. The consolidation of macroeconomic stabilization and marked improvement in the foreign exchange and fiscal position of the federal government led the authorities to increasingly focus the Bank's assistance at the subnational level. The Fiscal Responsibility Law provided the framework for that assistance.

Engagement with subnational governments was a focus area in the FY04–07 CAS, but the federal-subnational balance shifted significantly during FY08–11. More than three-fourths of total commitments went to states and municipalities during this period. The largest part of the lending was in the southeast, because of the size, income, and interest in transforming those states. In the second half of the period the Bank enhanced its operations in the north and the northeast (Figure 2.2). In this mode of operation, governors and mayors interested in working with the Bank had to define their priorities.

FIGURE 2.2 Share of Subnational Lending under the FY08–11 CPS

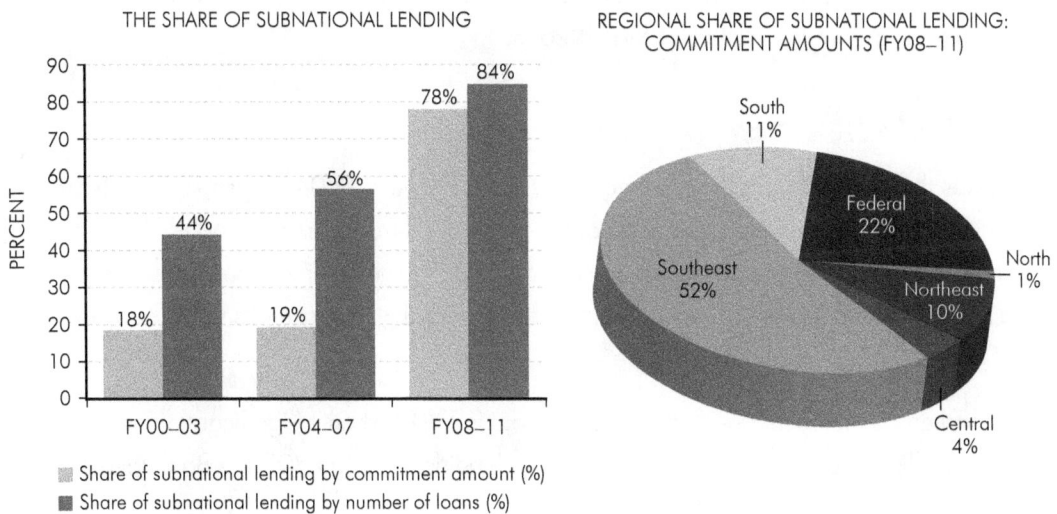

THE SHARE OF SUBNATIONAL LENDING

REGIONAL SHARE OF SUBNATIONAL LENDING: COMMITMENT AMOUNTS (FY08–11)

Share of subnational lending by commitment amount (%)
Share of subnational lending by number of loans (%)

SOURCE: World Bank.
NOTE: The data only include IBRD lending. Global Environment Facility and other grants are excluded. CPS = Country Partnership Strategy.

The Bank, for its part, offered its analytic work and experience in Brazil and elsewhere and provided customized support to state-specific issues. The direct involvement of subnational leaders ensured strong political backing, which helped overcome many longstanding implementation barriers. The process also helped shorten the project preparation period from 30 to 11 months during the FY08–11 CPS period.

Operational Trends and Patterns: Bank Group Products and Services

The Bank and IFC significantly increased the volume of operations, especially during the last three years of the evaluation period. Much of the Bank's increase can be attributed to accelerated uptake of subnational lending. Development policy loans (DPLs) accounted for a larger share of total commitment amount in FY04–07 than in FY08–11, although there was significant year-to-year fluctuation (Figure 2.3.A). IFC's commitments more than tripled between the FY04–07 CAS and FY08–11 CPS periods. An increase in short-term trade finance was the major contributor to this expansion. The shift is particularly pronounced in the last three years of the period (FY09–11), reflecting the rapid increase in demand after the global financial crisis (Figure 2.3.B).

During the evaluation period, MIGA issued 16 guarantees in Brazil with a gross exposure of $314.6 million; most of these were in the power sector ($246 million in gross risk exposure). At the beginning of the evaluation period, Brazil was one of the largest host countries for MIGA, but new guarantees have not been issued in Brazil since FY09. MIGA does not have outstanding exposure in Brazil as of March 2013.

WORLD BANK OPERATIONS

Brazil was the second largest borrower of IBRD loans between FY04 and FY11 in both the commitment and gross disbursement amounts (Table 2.1). Transport received the largest share of lending during the period, and economic policy and the environment also accounted for a substantial portion of the program. Health considerably increased its share between the FY04–07 and FY08–11 periods (Figure 2.4).[1]

Bank lending commitment grew after FY04, except in FY07, when a significant dip was caused by the reconfiguration that increased subnational lending. During FY07, the Bank focused

FIGURE 2.3 IBRD and IFC Commitments

A. IBRD Commitment Amount

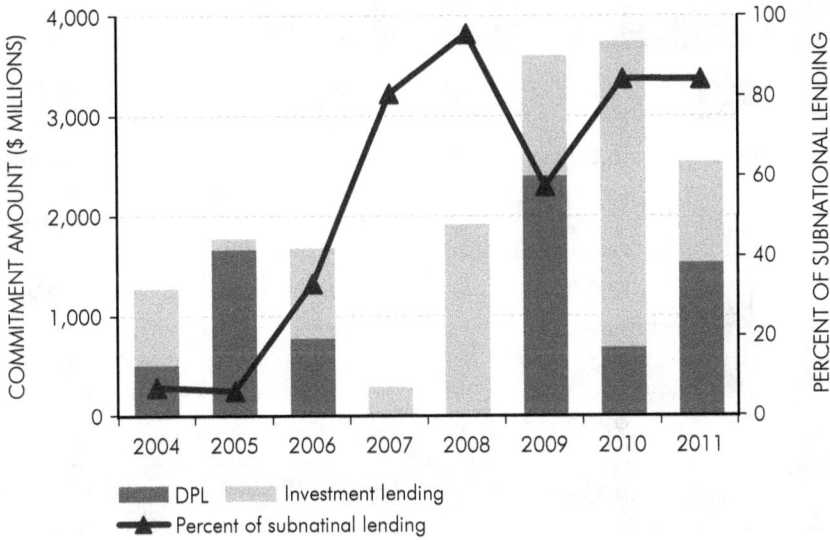

DPL Investment lending
Percent of subnatinal lending

B. IFC Annual Commitment

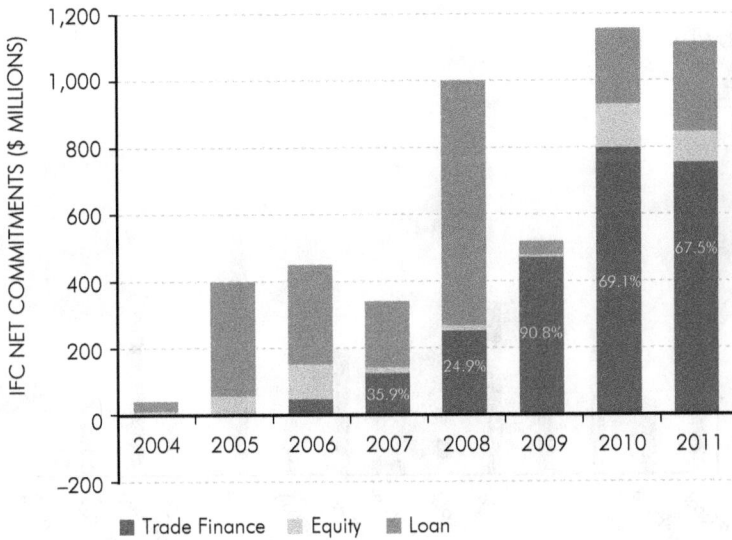

Trade Finance Equity Loan

SOURCES: World Bank and IFC.
NOTE: DPL = development policy loan; IBRD = International Bank for Reconstruction and Development; IFC = International Finance Corporation.

TABLE 2.1 IBRD Lending and Disbursement, FY04–11

Country	Commitment Amount ($ Millions)	Country	Gross Disbursed Amount ($ Millions)
India	17,314	Mexico	14,200
Brazil	16,801	Brazil	13,614
Mexico	16,358	India	10,484
Indonesia	12,570	China	9,968
China	12,371	Indonesia	8,485
Argentina	9,400	Argentina	5,298
Peru	3,768	Peru	2,107

SOURCE: World Bank.
NOTE: IBRD = International Bank for Reconstruction and Development.

FIGURE 2.4 Lending by Themes

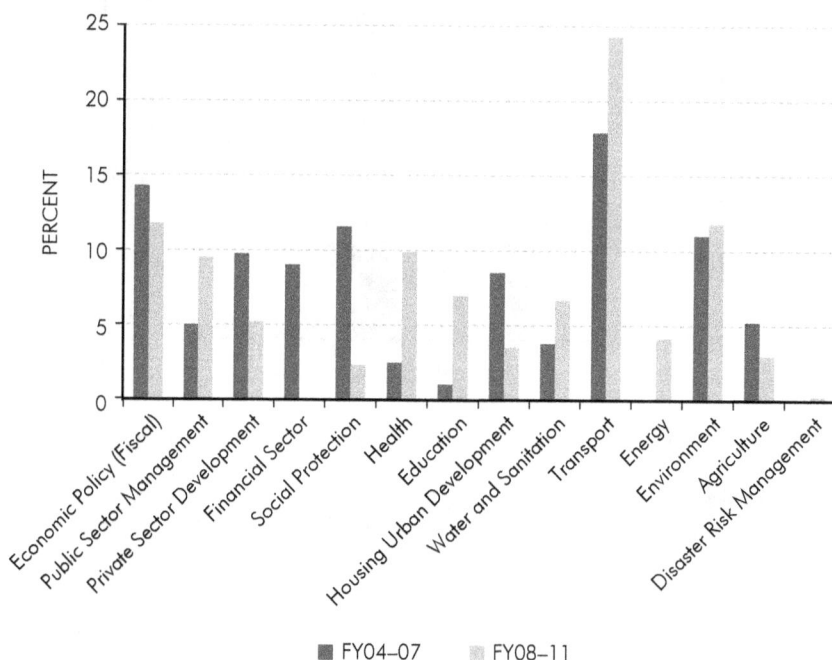

SOURCE: World Bank data and staff calculation.

on building a pipeline of lending to subnational entities. In this process, many planned operations, primarily intended for federal entities, were dropped—53 percent of the projects planned for the first two years of the FY04–07 CAS materialized, but only 15 percent of those planned during the second two years reached the implementation stage.

The global economic crisis in 2008–09 increased demand for Bank lending. Although the federal government mitigated the impact of the crisis through prompt action, the reduction in revenues caused by the slowdown was felt more severely in states and municipalities. As their ability to undertake countercyclical fiscal measures was constrained by the Fiscal Responsibility Law, many had to cut discretionary spending, mainly investments. The Bank was asked to support selected subnational entities to address this challenge while maintaining the discipline of the Fiscal Responsibility Law.

The Brazilian authorities reallocated the IBRD lending capacity over time to achieve a combination of countercyclical and structural reform objectives. As Brazil approached the IBRD's single borrower limit, the authorities exercised the prepayment option for existing loans—a strong sign of their interest in continuing engagement with the Bank. The prepayment was significant and relaxed the overall exposure to the IBRD. Between December 2009 and June 2011, Brazil prepaid about $4 billion—about one-fourth of the IBRD single borrower limit of $16.5 billion. That allowed new lending to flow to subnational programs, including important structural and fiscal reform programs consistent with the Fiscal Responsibility Law. However, as of March 31, 2013, the disbursed outstanding balance is $11.5 billion, and Brazil is again approaching the single borrower limit. Addressing the lending capacity limit will likely remain a medium-term challenge.

As for knowledge support, the Bank engaged in a total of 114 analytic and advisory activities (AAA), with economic and sector work and nonlending technical assistance constituting 60 percent and 40 percent of this figure respectively. Between FY05 and FY11, approximately $23.6 million in Bank budget and trust fund finance was allocated to economic and sector work and nonlending technical assistance products.[2] In the FY09–11 period, trust fund finance constituted an increasing portion of total knowledge product costs (Figure 2.5). Each CAS claims that AAA has a transformative role in the implementation of Bank Group strategy. Some of the knowledge support activities, for example, in education, fiscal management, health, infrastructure, and social programs, have had important impacts in Brazil, as discussed in Chapters 3 and 4.

The Bank has also been supporting South-South dialogue that involves sharing knowledge accumulated through experience in Brazil with other countries that are facing similar

FIGURE 2.5 ESW and NLTA Activities, FY04–11

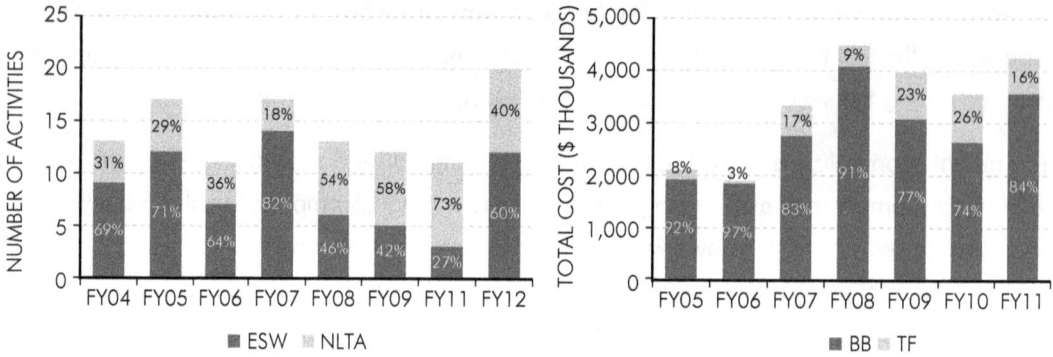

SOURCE: World Bank.

NOTE: BB = Bank budget; ESW = economic and sector work; NLTA = nonlending technical assistance; TF = trust funds.

challenges. The Bank has assisted this process in various areas, including tropical agriculture, health, community-driven development, conditional cash transfers, and fiscal management, among other areas. The Bank helped organize and has facilitated visits to Brazil by a large number of foreign delegations to learn about the experience in Brazil and to exchange views.[3]

During FY04–11, 78 Bank-financed projects exited the active portfolio in Brazil and were reviewed by IEG. The outcome of 87 percent of those closed projects was rated moderately satisfactory or better.[4] Based on net commitment amounts, 92 percent were rated moderately satisfactory or better. These shares are higher than the average for the Latin America and the Caribbean Region, which are 78 percent of the number of projects and 91 percent of the net commitment amounts (see Appendix Tables C.7 and C.9 for more detail). The outcome ratings for all 10 policy-based lending operations rated by IEG were moderately satisfactory or better. Though most investment projects reviewed largely achieved their objectives, many experienced delays, and in a number of operations.

Sectorwide Approach to Address Multisectoral Challenges

Innovative use of the sectorwide approach (SWAp), particularly in multisectoral projects in states, left a mark on the Brazil country program. In a typical SWAp arrangement, the Bank disburses against evidence that at least 70 percent of the budgeted expenditure in each of the agreed priority expenditure programs have been attained. The sector diagnostics and subsequent plans also identify disbursement-linked indicators (defined for each sector) to be attained before the Bank will disburse. In Brazil, the linkages between this 70 percent rule and the indicators helped the government manage its fiscal resources and allocations while forging a partnership between the central secretaries and the line secretaries who were responsible for meeting disbursement conditions. It also helped the discussions within the government and the dialogue between the Bank and the government focus on achieving results, as specified in the disbursement-linked indicators.

The SWAp model in subnational lending drew attention and support from the federal government and was replicated across Brazil. The first multisectoral SWAp was extended in the Ceará Multi-Sector Inclusion Development Project. It was quickly replicated in the Second Minas Gerais Development Partnership Loan and in several other state-level projects (Bahia, the Federal District, and Pernambuco). The Ceará project also included the indicators related to three ongoing Bank-financed projects in the state of Ceará as disbursement conditions. The implementation of two of three such projects was unsatisfactory, but the cross-linkage with the SWAp project helped turn around their performance.

The SWAp model implemented in Brazil also made significant contributions to the development of the new Bank lending instrument, Program-for-Results. The lessons learned from the experience in Brazil, particularly in Ceará and Minas Gerais, provided an important analytic base for the design of this instrument.

However, multisectoral projects can also be risky because of their highly complex designs. These projects need to interlink multiple components and implementing agencies, which requires significant efforts for conducting cross-sectoral coordination both within the Bank and in the country, as well as for resolving intersectoral trade-offs. The multisector SWAp approach also has administrative implications. The budgetary resource required per multisectoral project tends to be higher than for a single sector project, as participation by experts from diverse sectors is essential. The country program budget is not likely to increase significantly, so the challenge is to identify the appropriate mix of multisectoral and single-sector operations as well as to determine how many sectors should be part of the project.

IFC PROGRAM

IFC's Brazil operations were mainly related to the competitiveness pillar of the FY04–07 CAS and the FY08–11 CPS. Specifically, it supported private sector activities that were expected to enhance Brazil's growth and competitiveness, such as agribusiness and infrastructure, and helped improve access to credit for Brazilian enterprises, particularly small and medium-size enterprises (SMEs). Its strategic approach also recognized the importance of support for environmental sustainability and public-private partnerships (PPPs). During the FY08–11 CPS period, IFC sought a more direct role in reducing poverty and inequality by focusing on low-income groups and frontier regions. Its attention to second-tier companies and mid-size banks also increased over time.

During FY04–11, IFC's net commitment totaled $5.01 billion for 113 investments, making Brazil one of its largest investment portfolios. A significant share was represented by financial sector investments (Figure 2.6), mostly because of a rapid increase in short-term trade finance operations after the global financial crisis in 2008–09.

The long-term nature of IFC loans and equity financing offers important value for the banking and corporate sectors in Brazil, as they face constraints in accessing long- to medium-term financing. IFC long-term investments had particular added significance when Brazil's country risk was considered high after major market volatility in 2002–03. However, IFC's commitments for long-term investments did not grow to the extent the short-term trade finance program did during the period evaluated (Figure 2.7). IFC complemented financing from its own account by mobilizing funding from development finance institutions and commercial banks mainly through the B-loan program. Cofinancing of $2.36 billion was mobilized, in addition to a net loan commitment of $2.15 billion (excluding trade finance) on IFC's own account, doubling the resources available for investments (see Appendix D for more information on operations in FY04–11).

High Share of Trade Finance and Limited Equity Investment

The composition of IFC commitments (own account) to Brazil differs from that of comparator Latin American countries and IFC overall. The distinctive features of the Brazil portfolio are the relatively low level of equity investment and the very high share of trade finance. Equity

FIGURE 2.6 IFC Net Commitments, FY04–11

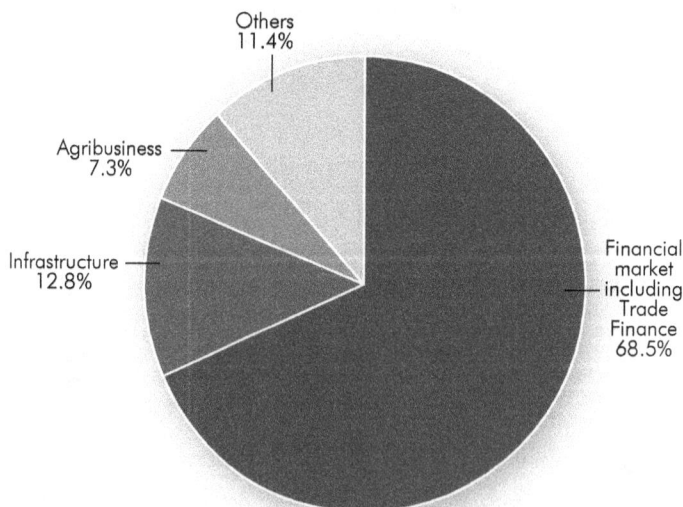

Others
11.4%

Agribusiness
7.3%

Infrastructure
12.8%

Financial
market
including
Trade
Finance
68.5%

SOURCE: IFC.

FIGURE 2.7 Growth of Long-Term Investments and Trade Finance

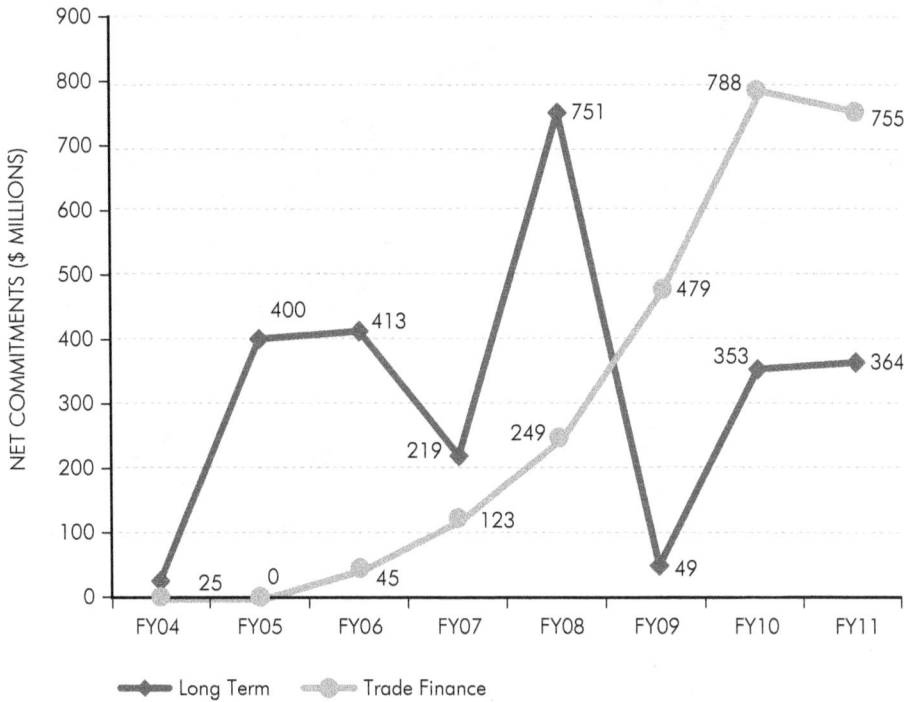

SOURCE: IFC.

investment in Brazil accounts for 8 percent of IFC commitments; the figures for Mexico and Colombia are more than 30 percent, and 20 percent for IFC overall. Equity investments are also relatively low in relation to the Brazilian economy. Brazil's volumes are below Mexico's and about equal to Colombia's, despite the Brazilian economy being 40 percent and 5 times larger, respectively. Equity investments in Brazil are about 2.7 times larger than in Peru, but its economy is 7.5 times larger (Table 2.2).

Short-term trade finance accounts for about 50 percent of IFC's total net commitments in Brazil and almost 25 percent of the trade finance provided to all countries during the period. A large part of the trade finance in Brazil started during the global crisis, whereas in other Latin American countries—also very open economies and affected by the crisis—trade finance was almost nil.[5]

These differences raise two questions that this evaluation cannot answer but that are important to reflect on for the future. First, given that equity investment and trade finance are at the extreme of the risk-taking spectrum, why do IFC operations seem to have taken so much less

TABLE 2.2 IFC Net Commitment, FY04–11

Instrument	Brazil		Colombia		Mexico		Peru		All IFC	
	$ millions	%	$ millions	%	$ millions	%	$ millions	%	$ millions	%
Equity investment	418	8.3	408	33.1	479	32.0	154	14.8	12,690	20.4
Trade finance	2,438	48.7	90	7.3	20	1.4	57	5.5	12,953	20.8
Loan	2,155	43.0	735	59.6	1,000	66.7	831	79.7	36,593	58.8
Total	5,012	100.0	1,234	100.0	1,499	100.0	1,043	100.0	62,237	100.0

SOURCE: IFC.
NOTE: Numbers by IFC's own account.

risk in Brazil than in the other countries? Second, what factors have determined this pattern and what are the implications, given the significant needs for mobilizing private resources into long-term investments, particularly in infrastructure?

Geographically, IFC has been increasing its emphasis on the north and northeast regions, in line with the Bank Group's country strategies. IFC financed 10 operations in these regions during the FY08–11 CPS period for a total of $389 million in infrastructure, financial services, and manufacturing. However, significant challenges existed in identifying the right investment opportunities in these regions. Based on discussions with the top audit firms in Brazil in 2008, four companies in the frontier regions of Brazil have been audited by major international audit firms, making it difficult for IFC to find business opportunities there.

Enhancing Catalytic Effect through Advisory Services

During the evaluation period, IFC committed approximately $12.7 million for 30 advisory service engagements in Brazil. These activities supported, among other areas, sustainable business advice to soya producers and forestry companies and PPP transactions in infrastructure and health and education facilities. IFC also advised federal and state agencies on ways to improve business climate. In connection with the CAS/CPS emphasis on frontier regions, IFC undertook regional initiatives in Amazon, Para, and Northeast (supported by specific investment programs). Toward the end of the evaluation period, PPPs became the most important component of advisory services, with the total dollar amount spent on them doubling in FY11 (Figure 2.8).

IFC worked as transaction advisor in PPP advisory projects and helped set new standards for subsequent transactions in the relevant areas. Most of these projects were supported by the Brazil Private Sector Partnership Program established by IFC, the National Bank of Economic and Social Development (BNDES), and the Inter-American Development Bank (IDB). This partnership program provides advisory services to structure PPP and private concession projects. To maximize its catalytic impact, it focuses on sectors and themes where the private sector has not participated before. During the evaluation period, the program successfully structured the first PPP projects in the transport, health, and education sectors in Brazil. The contributions of these transactions in setting a standard for subsequent projects are widely recognized. For example, the *Hospital do Subúrbio* project in Bahia and the Belo Horizonte School project were included among KPMG's 100 most innovative projects in 2011.[6] Specific contributions of individual projects are discussed in Chapters 3 and 4.

MIGA PROGRAM

During the evaluation period, MIGA concentrated its activities on the electricity transmission subsector (see Appendix E for more on MIGA operations in FY04–11). Given the importance of transmission capacity in Brazil—connecting the major energy production area in the north Amazon and the consumption centers in the southeast—these activities are consistent with the CAS and CPS objectives of helping Brazil increase its competitiveness. The transmission projects guaranteed by MIGA have developed about 2,600 kilometers of high-tension

FIGURE 2.8 IFC Advisory Services Total Cost by Business Line, FY05–11

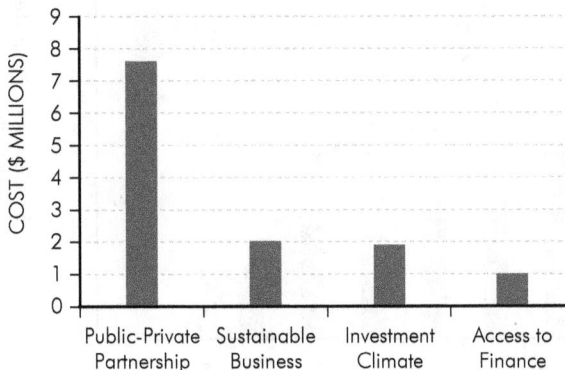

SOURCE: IFC.

transmission lines and associated facilities such as substations.[7] The concentration on transmission helped consolidate MIGA's leverage within the subsector, but it also increased vulnerability to changes in the overall subsector environment.

MIGA's overall exposure to Brazil declined throughout the evaluation period, because of cancellations and the absence of new business after FY09 (Figure 2.9). The market environment for MIGA operations in Brazil has become more difficult because of positive improvements in Brazil's country risk. During the period evaluated, Brazil's sovereign credit rating improved significantly and foreign direct investment flows soared. In the context of improving foreign investor confidence, the demand for MIGA's political risk guarantee has declined.

However, MIGA can potentially rebuild its operations in Brazil. An expanded mandate, a new product, and changes in its Convention will allow MIGA to engage in risk underwriting, in particular for the infrastructure sector. MIGA can now cover subsovereign credit risk without a federal government guarantee. It can also offer political risk insurance for freestanding debt coverage as well as for certain types of existing investments. The beneficiaries of the new product—nonhonoring of sovereign foreign obligation coverage (NHSFO)—are commercial lenders that provide loans to public sector entities for infrastructure and other productive investments. MIGA can protect the lender against losses from a nonpayment by the government caused by an inability or unwillingness to pay. It also covers a government

FIGURE 2.9 MIGA Outstanding Gross Exposure

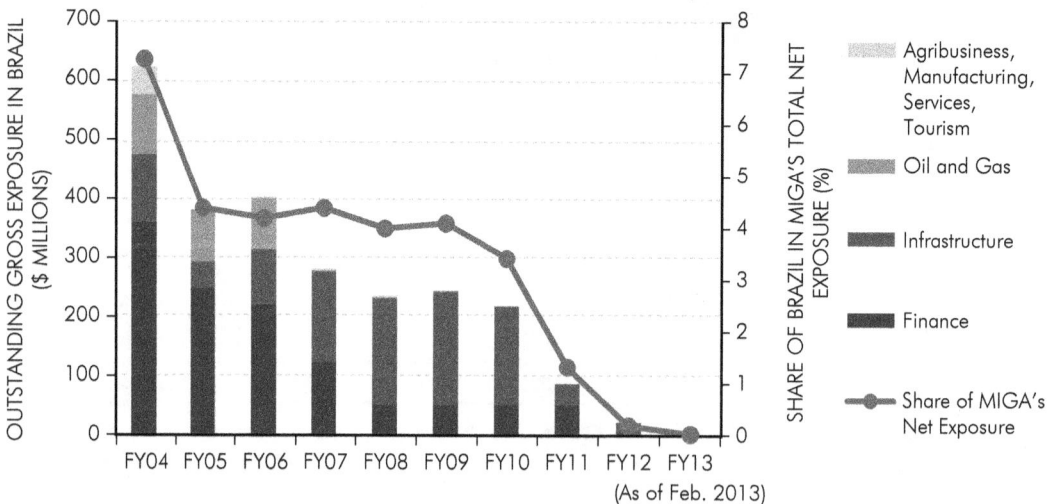

SOURCE: MIGA.

guarantee obligation of a state-owned enterprise or PPP joint venture. Furthermore, MIGA can extend the tenor of the commercial infrastructure loans with its NHSFO coverage combined with its new capability to offer coverage for freestanding debt.

Collaboration with Development Partners and within the World Bank Group

During the evaluation period, the largest sources of external development finance were the Bank Group, with $22.6 billion, and the IDB, with $10.7 billion in total approved commitments (including private investments). Brazil also benefits from diverse bilateral donor finance, with Norway, Germany, and Japan accounting for the bulk of those bilateral operations.

The federal government led the coordination of external financing institutions. It supported informal consultations and helped facilitate a division of labor among various development partners, minimizing the need for a formal mechanism of regular coordination among external financing institutions. Although the Bank and the IDB share the emphasis on subnational lending and operate largely independently of one another, no major difficulties have been caused by duplication and overlap. The two institutions have several channels of communication, and dialogue between them has increased in recent years, particularly in the field.

IFC, and to some extent MIGA, participated in broad strategic discussions associated with the FY04–07 CAS and FY08–11 CPS. However, their operations do not fall under the government's formal coordination mechanism, which focuses on public sector borrowing. There have been successful cases of Bank Group collaboration in Brazil, but the efforts to promote intra-Bank Group synergies were not systematic during the evaluation period. Government agencies generally have had little experience in interacting directly with IFC and MIGA. As a result, government knowledge about their operations is limited. The combination of the lack of systematic demonstration of Bank Group synergies and the government's limited familiarity with IFC and MIGA operations is possibly hampering the opportunities for strategic dialogue to maximize the potential that the Bank Group as a whole could offer.

Endnotes

[1] Allocation of lending resources across 14 themes was reviewed. This is not based on the sector or thematic coding.

[2] Accurate Bank budget and trust fund finance figures exist for the FY05–11 period for economic and sector work and nonlending technical assistance knowledge products.

[3] According to the Bank's Brazil Country Team, in FY10, the Bank helped organize and facilitate visits from 37 countries, often involving multiple visits. In FY11, visits from 31 countries were facilitated.

[4] These figures are based on the information available as of June 17, 2013.

[5] It is likely that IFC played an important role in finding international corresponding banks for IFC's client mid-size banks when trade finance lines from international corresponding banks dried up at the height of the crisis. However, trade finance remained the major product for IFC operations in Brazil after the global financial market largely stabilized. In FY11, it represented a dominant share of the net commitments at about 79 percent (55 percent after adjusted for risk).

[6] These projects are included in *Infrastructure 100: World Cities Edition* (KPMG International 2012).

[7] MIGA provided political risk coverage for a portion of investments, so MIGA's contribution to the entire project output of 2,600 kilometers of transmission line needs to be considered in context.

References

KPMG International. 2012. *Infrastructure 200: World Cities Edition*. Geneva: KPMG.

World Bank. 2003. *Country Assistance Strategy 2003–2007 for the Federative Republic of Brazil in Support of a More Equitable, Sustainable, and Competitive Brazil*. Washington, DC: World Bank.

———. 2004. *Brazil: Equitable, Competitive, Sustainable--Contributions for Debate*. Washington, DC: World Bank.

———. 2008. *International Bank for Reconstruction and Development and International Finance Corporation Country Partnership Strategy for the Federative Republic of Brazil for the Period FY2008–2011*. Washington, DC: World Bank.

3

Toward a More Equitable and Sustainable Brazil

The equity and sustainability pillars of the country strategy primarily address the quality of growth. They reinforce each other and interact through many channels. Poverty and inequality can threaten the sustainability of exhaustible resources, whereas sustainable use of exhaustible resources can affect poverty reduction in many contexts. This is particularly relevant in a rural economy, where water and forests are key resources. Interventions to reduce poverty in the short term may be critical to help human capital formation, which is vital for sustainable long-term growth.

This chapter first examines the relevance and effectiveness of Bank Group assistance on inclusiveness and equity, with an emphasis on social protection, education, and health. It then discusses the achievement of sustainability objectives through the management of exhaustible resources, in particular forests, land, and water. It also discusses the sustained access of poor local communities to land and housing and to services such as electricity, water supply, and sanitation. In rural communities, all these activities are closely linked and are related to the management of natural and human resources for overall community development.

Toward a More Equitable Brazil

The equity-related activities of the Bank Group focused on three subobjectives: reduce extreme poverty and social exclusion, enhance skills formation, and improve health care for all communities. These objectives were maintained throughout the period, though the details and specifics for achieving them changed.

REDUCE EXTREME POVERTY

The most important and successful intervention in this area was the Bank's support to *Bolsa Familia*, a program that provided income support to poor families contingent on some actions by the family to improve the education and health status of their children (see Box 3.1). *Bolsa*

Familia started in 2004 and expanded quickly. By 2010, it had provided income transfers to 11.8 million families and more than 50 million beneficiaries—22 percent of the Brazilian population.

The Bank was strongly associated with the program from its inception. During the initial phase of the Lula administration, the Brazilian authorities tried to develop a program that simultaneously addressed economic growth and income distribution in a practical manner. In this context, the Bank helped organize a seminar where there was focused discussion about global experience with social assistance programs. The meeting was attended by President Lula, most of his cabinet members, the World Bank President and Chief Economist, and international experts on conditional cash transfers. The idea of *Bolsa Familia* gained momentum in this seminar and in associated dialogue.

The Bank's sustained support through close dialogue with the relevant counterparts in all the phases of *Bolsa Familia*'s evolution is acknowledged by a wide range of Brazilian counterparts—it may be the most valued contribution of the Bank across all its assistance strategy. The Bank helped in the efforts to consolidate existing social programs,[1] establish a

BOX 3.1 Conditions for *Bolsa Familia* Assistance

"The program also helps keep the kids in school because they know how important it is for us to get the money and that this depends on them attending school."
—Ms. Dinalva Pereira de Moura, *Bolsa Familia* beneficiary, Vila Varjão (slum), Brasília

The conditions of the *Bolsa Familia* program are intended to break the intergenerational transmission of poverty by promoting human capital investment among children born in poor households. These conditions also constitute an implicit pact between society and poor households: society transfers cash to poor households, which ensure that they invest in their children. By monitoring compliance with the conditions, providers of social services such as education and health can verify whether *availability* of services has transformed into *real and equitable* access to those services.

Benefits are targeted to families that are extremely or moderately poor. The benefits are set according to the number of children (capped at three) and to whether the mother is pregnant or lactating. Monthly transfer amounts range from R$29–218 ($16–118) per family per month; the average was R$75 in 2011[a] (Soares 2012). Transfers can be temporarily or permanently suspended if targeting requirements are not satisfied or there is repeated noncompliance. The table below describes the conditions associated with various beneficiary types.

continued on page 27

Bolsa Familia: Menu of Conditions for Assistance

Sector and Beneficiary Type	Conditions for Assistance
Health: Pregnant or lactating women***	• Prenatal and postnatal checkups • Participate in educational health and nutrition seminars offered by local health teams
Health: Children 0–7 years old	• Vaccine schedules • Regular health checkups and growth monitoring of children
Education: Children 6–15 years olds Adolescents 16–17 years old	• Enroll in school and attend daily (minimum 85 percent attendance)* • Enroll in school and attend daily (minimum 75 percent attendance)**

*Parents must explain reasons for missing school and must inform the *Bolsa Familia* program coordinator when the child changes schools.
**Benefit started in 2008.
***Benefit started in November 2011.

SOURCES: Lindert and others 2007; World Bank 2010.
a. The Secretaria Nacional de Renda da Cidadania (the National Secretariat for Citizens' Income) in the Ministry of Social Development and Fight Against Hunger reports that the cash transfer could vary from R$32 to R$306, and the average benefit awarded, starting April 2011, was R$115.

unique register of beneficiaries (*Cadastro Único*), improve targeting, and enhance monitoring and evaluation systems. This was done through two Adaptable Program Lending (APL) operations in FY04 and FY11.

The Bank's most significant contribution was its technical and knowledge assistance, as its financial support was marginal to the overall scope of the program.[2] The APLs were complemented by a technical assistance loan aimed to strengthen government capacity to monitor the progress, impact, and targeting of social policies. An extensive AAA program also provided flexible means for analytical support. The multiyear BRASA[3] provided support to improve the design and implementation of the *Bolsa Familia*'s targeting as well as the monitoring and evaluation system. The BRAVA helped strengthen technical capacity for monitoring and impact evaluation at the Ministry of Social Development.[4] As a result, lessons from global experiences with conditional cash transfers, both in Brazil (Bolsa Escola) and in other countries (such as Colombia and Mexico), were incorporated into Bolsa Familia's design, implementation, and operation.

The target performance indicators for the first APL were either achieved or surpassed for coverage of the poor, targeting accuracy, and school attendance (Table 3.1). Targeting accuracy was exceptional: 68 percent of benefits were received by those in the bottom quintile; the outcome target was set at 40 percent.

Intermediate outcome indicators were achieved as well: the four federal programs that preceded Bolsa Familia had been integrated and included in the Cadastro Único, targeting instruments had been strengthened, and Cadastro Único had been updated and purged of duplicates. By 2009, nearly all municipalities had online access to the Cadastro Único database.[5] The economic analysis and simulations undertaken to quantify the expected impact of Bolsa Familia on poverty, inequality, and educational attainment helped enhance the credibility and robustness of the results framework.[6]

TABLE 3.1 Outcome Achievement during the Bolsa Familia APL 1

Outcome Indicator	Status
At least 2/3 of extreme poor families receiving Bolsa Familia transfers	Achieved—11.1 million families receiving benefits (100 percent of target)
At least 40 percent of total transfers going to bottom quintile	Surpassed—68 percent of Bolsa Familia benefits were received by those in the poorest quintile (and 90 percent by those in the poorest two quintiles)
At least 80 percent of primary-age school-age children in extremely poor beneficiary families attending school	Surpassed—87.4 percent attending school had a monthly attendance rate above 85 percent (2009)
At least 95 percent of beneficiary children with health cards	Partially achieved—reporting of compliance improved in recent years, although information is only available for about 64.48 percent of families; 67.7 percent of children of beneficiary families have their vaccinations monitored

SOURCE: World Bank 2010.
NOTE: APL = Adaptable Program Loan.

Several studies document the positive impact of the program (Figure 3.1). Extreme poverty declined, and an attribution analysis finds that about 35 percent of that reduction is due to the program (Soares 2012). A study finds that school attendance was raised with much larger effects for females and in the poorer northeast region.[7] On health, the evidence indicates that pregnant women have more prenatal visits with health care professionals (De Brauw and others 2012).

The Bank is starting to assist a second-generation program that evolved from *Bolsa Familia*—the *Brasil Sem Miséria* program, which focuses on extreme poor families. The second *Bolsa Familia* APL, the implementation of which started in 2012, includes support for creating the secretariat responsible for coordinating the *Brasil Sem Miséria* Program.

FIGURE 3.1 Impacts of *Bolsa Familia*

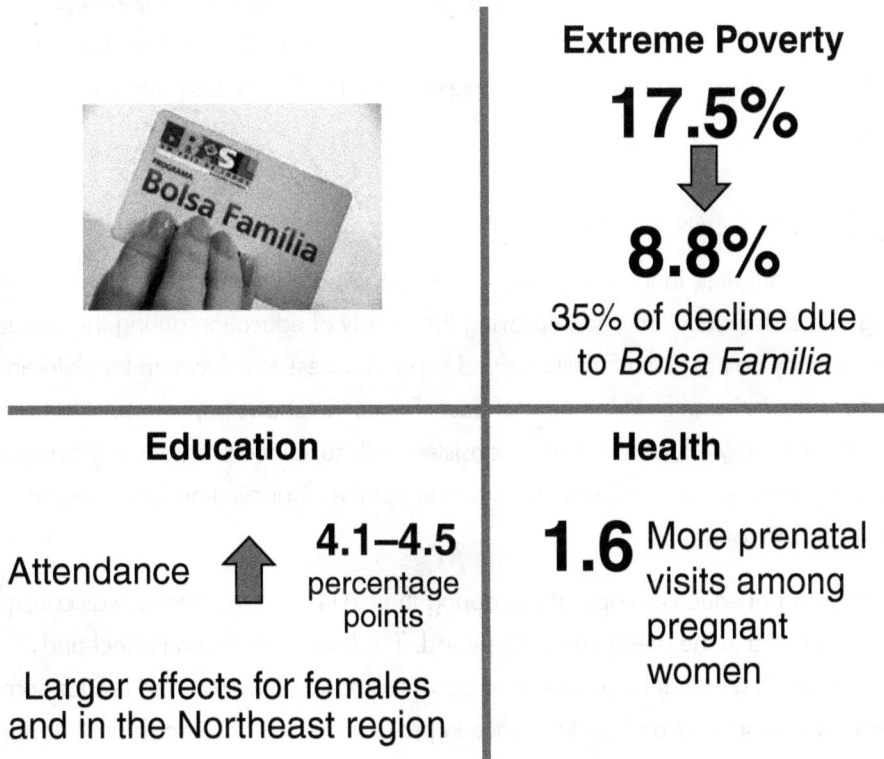

Extreme Poverty

17.5%

⬇

8.8%

35% of decline due to *Bolsa Familia*

Education

Attendance ⬆ **4.1–4.5** percentage points

Larger effects for females and in the Northeast region

Health

1.6 More prenatal visits among pregnant women

SOURCE: Soares 2012 (poverty), De Brauw and others 2012 (education and health).

In sum, *Bolsa Familia* has been successful to the extent that it expanded quickly and reached a high percentage of the extreme poor and a large share of the moderate poor in Brazil. It also helped alleviate poverty and inequality of those families at a moderate fiscal cost, while promoting human capital investment in children and youth. The Bank helped the government achieve these results primarily through technical and analytical support, as its financing of cash transfers was limited, relative to the total size of the program. The Bank effectively leveraged its analytical strengths, particularly its ability to consolidate and package global knowledge on relevant issues to be applied in the Brazilian context, to generate a large-scale impact.

The FY04–07 CAS also included other subobjectives, such as reducing youth unemployment and decreasing wage and service gaps for indigenous populations. These objectives were ambitious and complex, and the issues they addressed were influenced by many factors beyond the control of instruments available to the Bank. The CAS Completion Report (CASCR), a self-evaluation by Bank staff, acknowledges that the Bank did not have a comparative advantage in these areas. In consequence, it achieved very little on these objectives.

IMPROVE KNOWLEDGE AND SKILLS

The Bank's main activities in this area were in the education sector. Brazil made progress in expanding access to education and improving the quality of education during the evaluation period. As already noted, *Bolsa Familia* helped expand access to education for children in poor families. The Index of Development of Basic Education shows improvement in both primary and secondary education. This is consistent with sustained progress in Brazil's score in the Program for International Student Assessment of the Organisation for Economic Co-operation and Development.

An important part of education operations during the FY04–07 CAS period was continuation of projects approved in the preceding CAS period. The Bahia Education Project and *Fundescola* series (II and IIIa) helped expand access to basic education and reduce some of the disparity of resources and performance in project schools in the north and Northeast Brazil. They also contributed to establishing pedagogical models used in subsequent lending operations. Schools were encouraged to develop their own development plans as a way to strengthen their autonomy and to improve management efficiency in the *Fundescola* series, the Bahia education project, and the Ceará basic education project. They were given grants to implement the activities included in their development plans. An evaluation of *Fundescola*'s school planning and grants found that schools that received more grant funding from *Fundescola* performed better in student learning, although there was no clear effect on achievement from schools' development planning (Carnoy and others 2008).

Early work toward developing learning assessment systems began with *Fundescola* and informed the subsequent refinement by the Ministry of Education. IEG rated the outcomes of these education projects—except for *Fundescola II*—less than satisfactory because of limited evidence of the impact on student learning. A considerable population of the newly enrolled students came from poorer backgrounds, which may have affected how quickly the learning outcomes improved. In addition, students who in the past had dropped out were staying in school (World Bank 2007b), putting more pressure on schools and teachers.

The Bank's approach during the FY04–07 CAS seems to have been more sporadic in comparison. Many of the lending and AAA tasks foreseen in the CAS were dropped, including activities in early child development (ECD), a topic that could be highly complementary to the assistance to *Bolsa Familia*.[8] Most of the AAA addressed broad aggregative issues of human development, innovation, and growth, with less policy relevance for educational reform at the micro level. Despite the ambitious CAS objectives for improvements in the quality of ECD and primary education, and enhancing access and quality of secondary education, few instruments were deployed to help the authorities reach these objectives.

One notable knowledge contribution of the Bank was its provision of advice to the National Institute for Education regarding reforms to a funding mechanism that equalized primary education resources across states. The Bank analysis helped show the positive impact of this policy and of its expansion to include ECD (Box 3.2). This policy has provided incentive to expand enrollment, particularly in states with low tax revenues, such as those in the north and northeast.

The Bank activities in education gained renewed impetus under the FY08–11 CPS. The Bank made a major contribution to knowledge in the sector toward the end of the evaluation period, when it shifted emphasis to the quality of learning on the basis of observing the interaction between students and teachers in the classroom. This provided the basis for a significant amount of analytical work and dialogue that also took into account international experiences. The contribution of the Bank in this area has been recognized by several key stakeholders in Brazil.

One example of this analytical work was the study *Different Paths to Student Learning* (World Bank 2008a). The study was requested by the Ministry of Education to identify policies that would enable some municipalities and schools to obtain higher scores on standardized tests

Prior to the FUNDEF, education spending varied across regions, with schools in the northeast having the lowest level. Under the reform, a minimum per student funding was guaranteed, which created an incentive for school systems to expand enrollment. Funding was equalized by sharing resources across municipalities within a state, as well as redistributing federal funds to those states that could not reach the minimum threshold with their own revenues. Six of 26 states have typically received the additional federal resources.

In 2007, this reform was expanded (and renamed FUNDEB) to provide resources to municipalities for ECD (infancy to six years old) and secondary education, based partly on Bank advice. This is one reason for the rapid increase in access, with gross secondary enrollment rates in 2008 exceeding 100 percent and in 2009 preschool (age four to six) and crèche (infancy to three years) enrollments reaching 81 percent and 18 percent, respectively. The Bank has suggested that reallocating resources for ECD nationally, rather than within states, would facilitate further enrollment increases, considering the varying abilities of municipalities to make additional investment.

SOURCE: Evans and Kosec 2012; Bruns, Evans, and Luque 2012.

despite low student socioeconomic status. It led the ministry to provide municipalities with additional resources to adopt particular practices.

Analysis of observations of classrooms and teacher practices, summarized in *Achieving World Class Education* (Bruns, Evans, and Luque 2012), has provided policy makers with a way to benchmark how teachers in Brazil use instructional time in comparison with other countries. The Bank also evaluated teacher and school performance bonuses linked to improved student learning in the Pernambuco Education Quality Improvement Project.[9] This work offered new insights about the conditions under which bonus schemes can improve student outcomes— bonus systems have now been established in 20 states and municipalities. These findings have helped shift the policy dialogue toward teachers and their effectiveness. Policy makers are now examining issues such as how to recruit, support, and motivate teachers.

Also during this period, the Bank reestablished interest in ECD. By the end of the FY08–11 CPS period, the Bank focused its support for ECD with analytic work and lending. The study *Early Childhood Education: Making Programs Work for Brazil Most Important Generation* (Evans and Kosec 2012) showed that there were stark disparities in coverage and quality across states. It stressed that future investment in ECD need to be adaptable and creative and to reach and benefit the poorest children. One example where this knowledge was incorporated was a large DPL to the Municipality of Rio de Janeiro to help improve the delivery of services in poor areas. It helped improve ECD interventions for the disadvantaged in slum areas in the city. The Acre Social Economic Inclusion Project also employed new models for ECD, including nonformal services and home-based visits.

On the lending side, most of the activity was concentrated during the FY08–11 CPS period. The instrument of choice was multisector SWAp operations to subnationals, with education as one of the sectors. These operations typically focused on early literacy, accelerated learning programs for over-aged students, early childhood development, school and teacher performance bonuses, and spending efficiency.

Progress in the sector is often measured by a few indicators, such as reduction in the illiterate population 15 years and older, improved learning achievement, improved score on the Index of Development of Basic Education, reduction in age-grade distortion, increase in completion rate, and increase early childhood enrollment. Most of the operations approved during this period have not been completed,[10] so it is too early to assess their impact. But experience points to the growing importance of strong analytic and policy dialogue that would deepen understanding of each state's education sector with these types of operations.

Brazil was IFC's largest education sector portfolio at the end of FY11, with $135.6 million in commitments. During the review period, IFC invested in six projects in the education sector for a total net commitment of $189 million. The major counterpart in these investments is Anhanguera Educacional S.A (AES), a major vocational training company in Brazil. Since FY06, IFC has been supporting AES through various instruments. With the growing middle class in Brazil, AES increased its student enrollments from 10,800 in 2005 to 435,000 in 2012, with a compound annual growth rate of 64 percent by implementing its aggressive acquisition strategy. However, given that AES has raised over $1.6 billion from the capital market from 2007 to 2012 and that IFC's financing to AES was $40.6 million, IFC's financial contribution to this expansion is small.[11]

INCREASE ACCESSIBILITY TO QUALITY HEALTH CARE FOR ALL COMMUNITIES

Over the past 20 years health outcomes in Brazil have improved significantly. Data indicate early or imminent achievement of such Millennium Development Goal indicators as halving the number of underweight children and attaining a two-thirds reduction in mortality rate of children younger than five. These improvements have been underpinned by such factors as economic growth, reduction in income disparities, improved education of women, and decreased fertility rates. Several interventions outside the health sector—conditional cash transfer programs and improvements in water and sanitation—have likely helped, too. Success has also been facilitated by Brazilian authorities' efforts in health systems development, spearheaded by the 1990 establishment of a constitutionally mandated, tax-funded unified national health service (Sistema Único de Saúde).[12]

During the evaluation period and the preceding decade, the Bank Group was active in the majority of key reforms in health in Brazil. It has also been involved in many of the interventions outside the health sector that contributed to improved health outcomes. Feedback from interviews points to the particular value of the Bank's involvement for discipline in planning, monitoring, evaluation, and performance review.

A number of projects approved in the FY99–02 CAS period (Family Health Extension Project [PSF], HIV/AIDS Control Project II, and Vigisus) continued their implementation during the evaluation period.[13] The PSF, a flagship project that pioneered the sectorwide pooled lending approach in Brazil, was perhaps most significant. It emphasized the reorganization of primary care so that primary health care clinics and teams focused not just on maternal and child health, but on families and communities more broadly. It integrated medical care with health promotion and public health actions and provided incentives to municipalities—the main players in the organization and delivery of a highly decentralized system—to adopt relevant reforms and practices.

Through this project, the Bank contributed to the development of systems for monitoring and evaluation as well as performance management. The pooled lending approach, which disbursed against qualified expenditures in the program, brought the Bank to the heart of this major policy initiative. The main FY08–11 CPS outcome measure for investment in health was the proportion of people covered by the PSF. The target of 55 percent was almost reached (52.7 percent), meriting a rating of substantial progress in the CASCR.

During the period evaluated, the Bank's engagement shifted through various issues that span the breadth of the health system in Brazil. Between FY04 and FY11, 17 operations containing health-related components were approved, totaling about $1.3 billion dollars,[14] with most of the activity concentrated in FY08–11. Five operations, accounting for half of the financing, were freestanding federal-level operations. They sought to address systemic and countrywide issues, such as communicable diseases, disease surveillance, reforms involving federal-subnational coordination, and reforms at the tertiary level, with particular reference to medical education and research.[15]

The remaining 12 operations were subnational multisector DPLs or SWAps that addressed resource allocation, efficiency, and management practices across a number of sectors, including health.[16] This emphasis on multisectoral lending was designed to help subnational entities build their own fiduciary and public sector management systems and to help build synergies across sectors. Health sector issues in these operations varied, depending on local factors. In some poorer and more rural states, projects focused on infant and maternal mortality by targeting improvements in maternal and neonatal services and access to clean water. In wealthier states, projects focused on consolidating emergency care and transfer systems between municipalities and the state, implanting standardized costing systems in hospitals, and encouraging PPPs.

AAA activities during the period evaluated appear to have matched evolving country priorities and pointed the way to a new generation of challenges. These challenges include noncommunicable diseases (World Bank 2005), achieving efficiencies in the health system, and better management of resources (World Bank 2007a). A major report, *Hospital Performance in Brazil* (La Forgia and Couttolenc 2008), analyzes Brazilian hospital performance on several policy dimensions, including regulatory issues, resource allocation, and payment mechanisms. The report was sponsored by the Ministry of Planning. It supported much of the policy dialogue in this area and also in relation to specific operations.

Hospital do Subúrbio—a PPP project structured by the Brazil Private Sector Partnership Program among BNDES, IFC, and IDB—offers an interesting model for efficient hospital management. The hospital serves the poor community of Salvador in Bahia, providing health care services using performance standards that apply to a private hospital operator. IFC's involvement was critical in structuring this first PPP hospital transaction in Brazil. IFC provided global experience in the health sector PPPs, played "honest broker," and mobilized private sector funding. This project served as a model for hospital projects in seven other states and municipalities in Brazil.

RATING OF THE EQUITY PILLAR

In the three areas discussed above, the Bank Group seems to have made important contributions when know-how, dialogue, and financial support were combined to create synergies. The best examples are the support to *Bolsa Família* and the analytical work and dialogue that improved understanding of the classroom dynamics. The advisory work to improve education funding for poorer municipalities and their capacity to finance ECD programs is also a notable achievement.

In health, the Bank has made valuable contributions through sustained efforts to support progress in eliminating communicable diseases, reducing transmission of HIV/AIDS, and expansion of the PSF. The PSF project also pioneered the sectorwide pooled lending approach in Brazil. In addition, IFC was instrumental in structuring an innovative hospital project in Bahia. Although challenges in further improving the effectiveness of public services remain, the Bank's sustained support for the *Bolsa Família* has led to an exceptionally strong partnership with the government counterpart—a practice that should be examined further for replication elsewhere in the Bank. Based on this evidence, this pillar of Bank Group assistance during the period evaluated is rated satisfactory.

Toward a More Sustainable Brazil

The Bank Group strategies for sustainability had three major objectives: better water quality and water resource management; more sustainable land management, forestry, and biodiversity (including improved land access and protection of indigenous communities); and more equitable and integrated access to local services, particularly in poor urban and rural communities. These objectives are closely linked, and many of the Bank Group interventions address more than one of them. They are also highly relevant to the objective of reducing extreme poverty.

BETTER WATER QUALITY AND WATER RESOURCE MANAGEMENT

The Bank has had a sustained engagement with water resource management and water supply and sanitation in Brazil at both the federal and subnational levels. During the FY04–07 CAS period, the emphasis was on the regulatory and management aspects of water systems at the national, regional, state, and municipal levels, with continuing support for investments in relevant infrastructure. Projects at the federal level, such as the Federal Water Resources Management Project, focused on priority water resource management investments as well as on improving the planning, regulation, and management of water systems at the state and river basin levels. Similarly, the Water Sector Modernization Project and the earlier Low-Income Sanitation Technical Assistance Project focused on improving the efficiency of water and sanitation utilities; strengthening the weak institutional and regulatory framework for water supply and sanitation; increasing private sector participation; and providing technical assistance for slum upgrading and water supply services to the urban poor.

In the FY08–11 period, state and municipal projects were the main vehicle to enhance the water management system and to reach underserved communities. State-level integrated water resource management projects that address systemic water management issues were extended to Rio Grande do Norte, Pernambuco, Espírito Santo, and Ceará. Two operations in São Paulo addressed these issues in a densely populated metropolitan region. Of particular interest were the multisector operations, which provided considerable additional support for water, especially the SWAp series in Ceará—a state with severe scarcity of water resources.

These SWAps focused on key water sector issues in addition to financing major investments, which led to increased coverage and efficiency.

One feature of the Bank water portfolio in Brazil is its close integration with both sanitation objectives and urban development projects and slum upgrading. A number of city-based operations approved in FY04–11 included considerable support for water investments and related issues. In fact, projects containing important water components were targeted to municipalities in both rural and urban areas, while some activities are part of community-driven development (CDD) projects addressing many cross-sectoral challenges. The CDD projects have special features and will be discussed separately.

In the water sector, IFC and the Bank demonstrated an interesting model of collaboration. Under the Subnational Financing Program, IFC extended loans to water utility companies in Sergipe and Santa Catarina to improve their operational efficiency. This involved close collaboration with a Bank specialist, who was instrumental in linking the IFC team with potential subnational clients, supporting coordination with the federal government, and contributing to analyses on sector-specific technical issues during the project development phase as the coleader of the joint IFC-Bank team. Sector expertise from the Bank proved to be particularly valuable, given IFC's relative unfamiliarity with the water sector in Brazil.

These engagements in the water sector have made significant contributions in some areas. According to IEG's reviews of completed projects, Bank support helped enhance water resource management in priority river basins—in the northeast in particular—and strengthen the National Water Agency. It also helped expand access to water supply and improve the efficiency of service delivery by encouraging a more competitive and better regulated environment. However, the impact of operations in states varied. There was limited progress on implementing bulk water supply cost recovery systems and enhancing water quality, though there was significant improvement in the provision of water supply to households.[17]

Government counterparts view the Bank as a key partner helping tackle diverse challenges, ranging from environmentally sensitive river basins to deteriorating water quality, sewerage coverage and treatment, utility management, and financial sustainability. The Bank's convening power was recognized as useful in promoting and providing a platform for a multidisciplinary deliberation across different levels of government—an essential component for water resource management in the federal system. More recently, the Bank approved the Federal Integrated Water Sector Project (FY11, $107 million)—a large technical assistance loan to help address the persistent challenges in Brazil's complex water resource management system, including interagency coordination, weak planning and portfolio of projects, and limited institutional capacity. Though the project has just gotten started, a senior official observed that the preparation process has had positive effects by strengthening links between different federal entities and subnational levels.

MORE SUSTAINABLE LAND MANAGEMENT, FOREST, AND BIODIVERSITY

A prominent component of the sustainability pillar of the FY04–07 CAS and FY08–11 CPS addresses the "paradigmatic" challenge of reconciling growth, poverty reduction, and conservation of forest environmental values. Forests have been cut down mostly to create large, low-productivity ranches, but also small plots of subsistence farming, highly profitable soy plantations, and hydropower reservoirs. Against these gains is the widespread damage caused by deforestation: biodiversity loss, global climate change as a result of forest burning, hydrological and local climate impacts, and loss of land and livelihoods by forest dwellers.

The Bank has long struggled with optimizing these trade-offs, shifting from a problematic development emphasis in the 1980s to a conservation emphasis in the 1990s. The first CAS reemphasized the need for a sustainable balance. It set "more sustainable land management, forests and biodiversity" as a priority goal to be achieved through land use zoning, promotion of certified logging, and increased forest protection. This CAS coincided with the initiation of the Brazilian government's vigorous Action Plan for the Prevention and Control of Deforestation in the Legal Amazon, also known as PPCDAm.

The FY08–11 CPS treated forests more prominently than its predecessor, signaling increased attention to conservation/development balance. It outlines an approach that supports forest protection, indigenous lands, "the power network and logistical corridors in sensitive biomes" (meaning hydropower and roads in the Amazon),[18] payment for environmental services, certification of "sustainable agribusiness and forestry," and "improving the environmental and social quality of infrastructure lending." It also promised to boost income, health, and educational outcomes in the Amazon region. Appendix Table F.1 summarizes the relevant indicators of the FY08–11 CPS.

Outcomes at the National Level

Amazonian deforestation declined dramatically over 2004–12 (Figure 3.2), surpassing the most optimistic views at the beginning of the period. This reduction, *if maintained*, could be considered one of the great turnarounds of environmental destruction in the modern era. Deforestation also declined in the Atlantic Forest and in the *cerrado*. Although general economic factors played some role, deforestation decline is strongly related to Brazilian policy interventions, including some supported by the Bank.

FIGURE 3.2 Amazonian Deforestation by Year and State, 2000–12

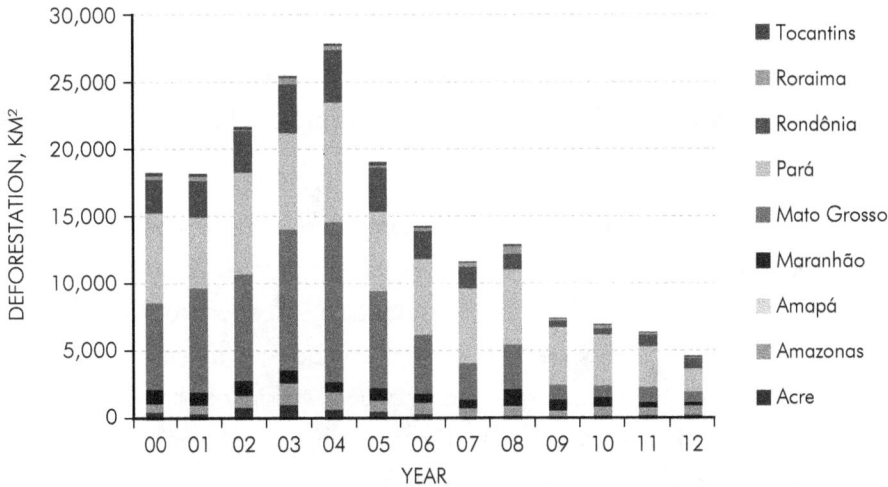

SOURCE: http://www.obt.inpe.br/prodes/prodes_1988_2012.htm
NOTE: 2012 is a preliminary estimate.

Although the goal of *improving* relative household incomes in the Amazon was not met, the deforestation crackdown at least did not *reduce* incomes. It decelerated but did not halt the formerly rapid growth of the Amazonian cattle herd.

Tracing Channels of Bank Group Action

This section traces the links from Bank Group action to government policies and programs, and from those to impacts on the ground. First is regulating large infrastructure—dams and major roads—that carries the potential both for large gains and large damages. Second is promoting sustainable land use and poverty reduction through conservation, regulation, incentives, and technical assistance. Third is mainstreaming climate change in public and private sector investments.

INFRASTRUCTURE LICENSING AND SAFEGUARDS: Brazil's environmental licensing system needs to grapple with complex and difficult trade-offs. Notably, the government plans a massive expansion of hydropower in the Amazon, offering a potentially large supply of nonfossil energy but requiring careful attention to the risks of social and environmental damage. The existing system of environmental impact assessment and licensing was diagnosed by the Bank as doubly inadequate. On one hand, a Bank study[19] found that such assessments were often of poor quality and that the licensing authorities had limited capacity to evaluate them. On the other hand, the FY08–11 CPS characterized the licensing system as slow moving and an impediment to rapid implementation of needed infrastructure. Three strands of Bank involvement relate to this challenge.

First, the National Environment Project II focused on improved licensing. The first phase of this APL helped establish environmental licensing in 7 states and improved the licensing system in 12 more. It was credited by the Brazilian Institute of Environment and Renewable Natural Resources (IBAMA), the federal environmental enforcement agency, with support for its public information system on licensing. The second phase of this project, however, has made little progress since its initiation in 2009.

With regard to hydropower licensing, a Bank-sponsored study called for better delineation of federal versus state licensing responsibilities, which was subsequently accomplished through a complementary law (World Bank 2008b). The study also called for more attention to river basin level planning of hydropower and systems-level power planning, as did a Bank-supported section of a key hydropower guidance manual (Ministry of Mines and Energy 2007). However, there is still no requirement for a comprehensive strategic environmental assessment of hydropower options at the river basin level.

The $1.3 billion Sustainable Economic Management Development Policy Loan (SEM DPL, 2008) tried to encourage further actions in this area. A target outcome of the DPL and the CPS was for BNDES to adopt a new environmental and social policy and to use it to screen and monitor all projects. The program self-evaluation (World Bank 2011) states that by June 2011, all projects submitted directly to BNDES were screened, approved, and monitored according to the new environmental and social institutional policy. However, the extent to which it improved the quality of projects approved for financing, enhanced BNDES's monitoring and supervision, and resulted in improved environmental and social compliance is not fully known at this time.[20]

The SEM DPL also had as an outcome indicator the increased issuance of licenses by IBAMA. IBAMA added staff and improved systems during this period, and license issuance continued its post-2003 growth trend (Figure 3.3). However, effectiveness of the implementation of safeguards and license conditions has yet to be verified, as the increased number of licenses issued does not necessarily lead to improvement in environmental outcomes. These issues merit continued attention, given the FY08–11 CPS emphasis on reconciling conservation with development in the Amazon, including reengagement in energy and transport infrastructure; the program's goal of "improvement of the environmental management framework for infrastructure and natural resource-based productive chains"; and BNDES's role in financing activities in environmentally sensitive sectors, including large-scale infrastructure in the Amazon. It is also highly relevant to the FY12–15 CPS focus on sustainable management of natural resources.

FIGURE 3.3 Licenses Issued by IBAMA, 2001–12

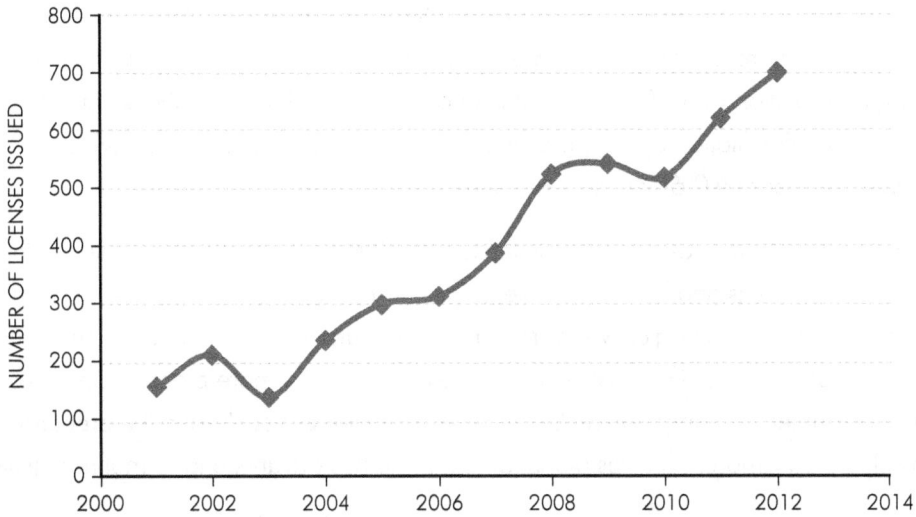

SOURCE: Sistema Informatizado de Licenciamento Ambiental Federal, http://www.ibama.gov.br/licenciamento.

FOREST PROTECTION: The most obviously attributable contributions of the Bank to reduced deforestation were in forest protection. The Rain Forest Indigenous Lands Project (PPTAL) supported demarcation and recognition of 87 indigenous territories encompassing 37 million hectares of lands—a major advance in securing indigenous rights and in regularizing Amazonian land. It developed useful operational methodologies that have been incorporated into the procedures of FUNAI, a government body that establishes and carries out policies relating to indigenous peoples procedures. There was no Bank loan for a follow-up project to improve indigenous peoples' livelihoods.[21]

The Amazon Region Protected Area Project (ARPA) created 24 million hectares of new conservation units, about equally divided between strict protection and those allowing sustainable use by forest dwellers. Overall, about 47 percent of protected areas in existence in 2010 were created under ARPA. The program helped create a strategic bulwark against the advance of the agricultural frontier, while also securing large tracts in more remote areas (Santos, Pereira, and Veríssmo 2013). It innovated by using FUNBIO, a quasi-official nongovernmental organization created by a prior Bank project to funnel grant funds directly to conservation unit managers. However, the program was less successful at setting up effective management plans for the conservation units. By 2012, 32 of 98 ARPA-supported areas had completed management plans;[22] many are viewed as overly academic and lacking practical guidance. Forty-seven areas had management councils that incorporate local representatives.

Together, ARPA and PPTAL put 610,000 square kilometers under protection, roughly the size of Germany and the United Kingdom combined. A recent rigorous analysis of the impact of Brazilian protected areas looked at the overall impact of protected areas created in or before 2005 on deforestation over 2006–10 (Nolte and others 2013). It found that strict protected areas reduced deforestation by 1.8 percentage points, indigenous territories by 1.2, and sustainable use areas by 0.6 percentage points.

Attempts to mainstream protected area establishment into statewide road-planning in the *cerrado* states of Goias and Tocantins have made less rapid progress. In Goias, a project succeeded in mapping biologically sensitive areas and put 1 million hectares under a very weak form of protection (IEG 2009). Overall, the project made more progress on roads than on environmental management. In Tocantins, a similar project began the preparation of 18 protected areas (more than was planned), but none has advanced to formal recognition.

LAND AND FOREST USE REGULATION AND ENFORCEMENT: Brazil has deployed a set of approaches to prevent illegal seizure of public lands, regularize land tenure, and increase private landholders' compliance with land and forest law. These include a *policing-type approach to detection and punishment of illegal deforestation by IBAMA*. This activity became much more effective after 2004, because of a series of government policy actions.[23] According to an econometric analysis by Assunção, Gandour, and Rocha (2013), the result was a 75 percent reduction in deforestation, without a reduction in economic output. The Bank's contribution to this was indirect. The Programmatic Reform Loan for Environmental Sustainability (2004) has been credited with boosting the profile and capacity of the Environment Ministry and of IBAMA, arguably bolstering IBAMA's ability to carry out this program.

A parallel track has been to *assist state environmental agencies to monitor and enforce private landholders' compliance with the Forest Code*. The Code requires private landholders to maintain part of their property under forest as a "legal reserve," in addition to maintaining forest on streambanks and hillsides—requirements that have been widely flouted. In 2000, the Bank, via the Pilot Program to Conserve the Brazilian Rain Forest (PPG-7), supported what has turned out to be a catalytic approach to this: Mato Grosso's SLAPR licensing system. SLAPR required landholders to register property boundaries and conservation commitments in a state-run geographic information system. The state uses this information to license the landholder's logging and agriculture. Compliance is monitored via remote sensing, which drastically reduced monitoring costs. In practice, the system has worked imperfectly. After 9 years, just 30 percent of nonprotected areas had been enrolled, and deforestation continued on licensed properties (Rajão, Azevedo, and Stabile 2012; Bastos, Micol, and Andrade 2009).

Nonetheless, Mato Grosso's SLAPR system became a reference for a nationwide rural environmental cadastre (*Cadastro Ambiental Rural*, or CAR) program. This evolving program aims to become the first comprehensive, systematic, transparent registry of landholdings in the Amazon and nationwide. As such, it has been used as a tool for a variety of command and control and incentive mechanisms, including some that have been effective in reducing deforestation (see below). CAR registration is mandatory under the new Forest Code and will serve as a first step in the states' environmental regularization and licensing procedures in rural areas. The CAR is explicitly not designated as a land titling mechanism,[24] but in practice the cadastre will serve as a kind of rough draft of an eventual universal land registry and will facilitate land titling efforts.

In addition, each of the 46 municipios "blacklisted" by the government for high deforestation rates needs to enroll 80 percent of its area in the CAR to be taken off the blacklist. This requires an intensive grassroots effort to enroll and georeference properties and a coordinated effort to assemble remote sensing imagery and maps. With a small PPG-7 grant, the Bank partially funded a Nature Conservancy-led effort to implement CARs in blacklisted *municipios*. These have been successful at the local level and are welcomed by local environmental authorities as a powerful tool for management. The CAR could also support the implementation of two important deforestation control measures developed by Brazil without direct Bank support: the cutoff of agricultural credit to noncompliant landholders (Assuncão, Gandour, and Rocha 2013) and the requirement that meatpackers buy from compliant suppliers.

Complementing the licensing and cadastre efforts is a *long-standing effort to support ecological-economic zoning*, which continues under the ongoing CPS. There is a sound theoretical argument for zoning as a tool for optimizing conservation and development trade-offs. For example, some areas are favorable for sustainable agriculture, some contain irreplaceable endemic species, and some need large contiguous areas to ensure the survival of ecosystems. Yet in Brazil—and globally—zoning exercises have had little impact on the ground. That appears to be generally the case to date with the Bank-sponsored plans, with two exceptions and a caveat. First, zoning builds on Bank-supported efforts to identify and demarcate protected areas. These are enshrined in zoning and influence licensing and infrastructure decisions. Second, observers in and out of the government point to Acre's zoning plan as one that was developed in a participatory fashion and incorporated in policy processes and that has the best prospects for effective implementation.

Finally, the new Forest Code contains incentives for states to institute and apply zoning.[25] Ultimately the impact of zoning will depend on Brazil's political will and administrative ability to implement CAR and enforce the new Forest Code.

SUPPORT FOR SUSTAINABLE PRIVATE SECTOR LAND MANAGEMENT: The Bank Group supported several avenues for making private sector actions more environmentally friendly. *Payment for environmental services* (PES) featured prominently in the FY08–11 CPS. The idea is to reward those who conserve or plant forests for the environmental benefits that they provide.

Global Environment Facility–funded projects have supported two nascent PES systems, in Espírito Santo and São Paulo. Both have helped establish state-level regulations on PES, but actual implementation is only beginning. In Espírito Santo, Bank staff helped the state adopt an ambitious plan to reforest 320,000 hectares by 2025 by introducing to policy makers relevant programs from New York City and Costa Rica and by linking PES to the Bank's longstanding dialogue with the state on water supply.[26] If it succeeds, it could advance biodiversity, carbon storage, poverty reduction, water quality, legal compliance, and municipal cost savings. But it faces challenges: devising payment schemes that balance equity and efficiency, developing appropriate technologies for the state's highly diverse agroecosystems, and convincing farmers of the financial viability of the promoted agroforestry systems.

The Bank's ProManejo project assisted in the set-up of *forest concessioning rules for the national forests*. The idea was to institute sustainable logging on vast tracts of forest, providing a profitable and socially acceptable alternative both to forest conversion and to strict protection. However, the area successfully bid out for concession has been below expectations. Hypothesized reasons include red tape, inherent lack of profitability given management rules, and competition from illegal suppliers. An IFC Advisory Services project is currently helping the Brazilian forest service diagnose the issues and prescribe a solution.

IFC has been active in promoting *more responsible cattle and soy production*. This was done initially through engagement with producers. Engagement with Bertin, a cattle producer, was unsuccessful, but loans to Amaggi, a soy producer, helped promote improved practices. IFC has also been active in the soy and beef roundtables of producers. The soy roundtable is helping define criteria for certification, including identifying sensitive areas from which purchase would be prohibited. Certified soy is beginning to be produced in response to demand from foreign buyers, but does not command a price premium. Because domestic beef consumers express little demand for certification, IFC efforts are directed at support for Brazilian initiatives to promote good practices.

In terms of market impact, IFC efforts have been overshadowed by the soy moratorium and by a federal agreement compelling meatpackers to buy beef from legalized properties. Both of these factors have had powerful effects on producers and indirectly stimulate demand for certification-like services.

POVERTY REDUCTION IN FOREST AREAS: The final piece of conservation-development balance—poverty reduction in remote forest areas—faces huge challenges, including low capacities, sparse population density, and remoteness from markets. These are difficult and unsolved problems, as discussed in the section, Community-Drive Development and Reaching the Rural Poor.

MAINSTREAMING CLIMATE CHANGE: Brazil has made progress in reducing its overall level of greenhouse gas emissions. This is due primarily to the sharp decrease in deforestation, particularly in the Amazon, to which Bank support has made attributable contributions as noted earlier. In other areas of climate change, low-key Bank support may have helped build consensus within a government and society that had diverse views on engagement with the carbon market and on climate policy. The Prototype Carbon Fund supported some of the first Brazilian carbon projects and helped catalyze follow-on projects in part by developing the validation methodologies and demonstrating the procedures necessary for project registration. The Low Carbon Study (De Gouvello and others 2010), a major piece of analytic work, did not directly contribute to Brazil's national plan on climate change but has been credited with supporting dialogue, building networks among researchers, and sponsoring research that provided building blocks for ongoing work.

Emerging Challenges

Over the past decade, Brazil has mustered political will and regulatory creativity to accomplish a remarkable reduction in deforestation, with global and domestic benefits. The Bank significantly contributed through support for a major expansion of protected areas and indigenous territories and for capacity building of national and state environmental agencies. Global Environment Facility and PPG-7 grant funding has been important for protected areas. The Bank has been most successful where it brought the long-term engagement of experts who understand local conditions and bring global knowledge. Relatively small, sustained efforts such as ARPA have had far more impact than the $1.3 billion SEM DPL, which—although it had deforestation reduction as an outcome—was not related to the key policy drivers of the deforestation slowdown. In addition, the SEM DPL loan size was significant in relation to the total IBRD exposure in Brazil, and a question emerges whether other avenues to mainstream effective implementation of environmental and social safeguards practice might have been more cost effective. The effectiveness of this loan is currently being evaluated by IEG, and the results will be made available in a forthcoming Project Performance Assessment Report.

Brazil's challenges now have two critical aspects where the Bank Group may be able to offer assistance. First is the challenge of implementing the new Forest Code. This gives states a two-year deadline to enroll all landholders in the CAR, the institutional platform for command and control, incentive systems (including payment for environmental services and eligibility for loans), and potentially for land titling. The states will need considerable help in setting up relevant systems. An even bigger challenge is to convince landholders to register, as this will oblige them to reconstitute missing forest, at large expense. In Mato Grosso alone, compliance costs are estimated at $12 billion (Stickler and others 2013). The credibility and effectiveness of the Forest Code may depend on rapidly finding ways to reduce this burden, for instance, by supporting tradeability of legal reserve obligations.

Second, the relation between deforestation and poverty is changing. In the early 2000s, Amazonian deforestation was driven by capital-intensive largeholders, as evidenced by the size of forest clearings. But with the success of enforcement, credit restriction, and other policies targeted at largeholders, there has been rapid growth in the proportion of deforestation associated with small clearings (IPEA and others 2011). The share of deforestation taking place in land reform settlements has also grown (Brandão, Barreto, and Souza 2012). This suggests that residual Amazonian deforestation is now increasingly the domain of poor, often subsistence-oriented farmers and ranchers, with limited skills, finance, and market access. A fresh look at how to deal with this poverty/deforestation nexus at scale is needed. Meanwhile, attention is also turning toward deforestation in the cerrado—often driven by large-scale farm and pasture expansion—where the poverty-growth-environment dynamics are different.

MORE EQUITABLE ACCESS TO LOCAL SERVICES

More equitable access to local services was thought to be an important element for both a more sustainable and equitable Brazil. The emphasis was in two areas. First, the Bank sought to improve access to housing and key social services by the urban poor, focusing on housing finance, slum upgrading, and integrated urban development projects. Second, increasing access to land and credit to poor rural families, particularly in the northeast, and availability of key social services were pursued in integrated CDD programs.

Housing and Urban/Municipal Development

Brazil has become highly urbanized—84 percent of its population and half of the poor live in urban areas. Facilitating access to housing and critical services to the urban poor in a context of fiscal sustainability and improved management capacity of cities is a major challenge. To assist government efforts in this area, the Bank approved 13 housing and urban operations in FY04–11, amounting to $1.3 billion in lending commitments.[27] The Programmatic Loan for Housing (federal; $502 million) and the Rio de Janeiro Metropolitan Urban and Housing DPL

(Rio de Janeiro state; $485 million) dominated the overall urban lending program in terms of commitments.

There are also a number of water sector projects that include investments in housing, urban upgrading, and urban land regularization. The Housing Sector Loan (FY05), accompanied by a technical assistance loan and a number of related AAA, supported efforts to improve access of the poor to housing and was consistent with the government's *Minha Casa Minha Vida* (My House, My Life) program. It aimed to assist the development of a national housing policy, promoting incentives to expand housing finance, providing a scheme of transparent housing subsidies for the poor, and reducing urban land development costs through regularizing property registration.

These were ambitious long-term objectives, particularly given the high interest rates still prevailing in Brazil. The loan helped consolidate the institutional framework for housing policy in the Ministry of Cities. Housing finance expanded significantly, partly helped by the greater use of the trust deed supported by the loan, but evidence of increased access to housing by the poor and the lower costs of urban land provision was limited (IEG 2010).

Progress in implementing up-front subsidies for social housing has also been limited with some initiatives taken as part of the *Minha Casa Minha Vida* program. Overall progress fell short of rationalizing the housing subsidies embedded in the below-market interest rates in the dominant mortgage funding windows. The Bank continued to work on some of the critical sector issues through AAA, which focused on a housing policy and plan as well as new instruments to raise long-term funds from the capital markets. However, the momentum of policy dialogue waned after the Housing Sector Loan closed without the second-phase DPL envisaged in the original program design.

The Rio Metropolitan Urban and Housing Project (FY11) focused on planning and managing of territorial growth in the Rio metropolitan region. It also aimed to help promote the affordable housing and create integrated social development programs for the urban poor. It supported a wide range of issues, including creation of the *Bilhete Único* (consolidated fare) to improve convenience and affordability of urban transportation; strengthening capacity for protecting environmental assets; introducing a fee for water rights holders for watershed management; enhancing the framework for land titling programs; and piloting social programs, including a citizen security initiative. Although technical assistance was available for some components, feedback from the interviews conducted by IEG suggests that a stronger technical assistance program would have been useful in view of the complexity in program scope. Support from a companion technical assistance loan to complement the reform effort as originally envisaged did not materialize. Project development objective achievement has been mixed according to the Implementation Completion and Results Report (ICR) in May 2013.

Beyond the housing and Rio metropolitan engagements, the Bank was involved in several statewide or metropolitan operations focused on slum upgrading and citywide infrastructure and institutional improvements. Statewide operations in Ceará and Bahia approved in the 1990s and closed during the period evaluated included significant slum upgrading and water components. The Recife Urban Upgrading Project and the Bahia Poor Urban Areas Integrated Development Project supported slum upgrading in poor urban areas as well as related efforts to strengthen municipal infrastructure institutions.

The design and implementation of these projects was complex because of the multiplicity of components, implementing agencies, and jurisdictions, as well as the need to operate in socially sensitive areas. Despite the challenges, some projects made significant contributions. The Ceará and Bahia operations benefitted a large number of low-income people in poor urban areas and municipalities. The Bahia integrated slum upgrading experience was instrumental in the preparation of national guidelines (Cities Alliance 2012).

The Bank was also engaged in projects supporting city-specific programs in a number of urban areas. The Betim Integrated Municipal Project (FY05) focused particularly on sewerage and wastewater treatment, with mixed results.[28] After this, urban projects were approved for a number of cities as part of a horizontal APL operation (FY08),[29] Recife (FY08), and Santos (FY10). There was also an urban project focusing on nine small municipalities in Ceará (FY09) and two separate operations addressing solid waste management.

The large number of broad, integrated urban projects has required considerable implementation support and coordination efforts by the Bank. Several Bank managers and staff interviewed for this evaluation observed that the series of municipal projects linked to the horizontal APL may not have been the most strategic approach, given that its demonstration effects are not clear.[30] This raises a question for future projects—whether the Bank's comparative advantage could be deployed more effectively in projects that addressed slum upgrading and infrastructure and institutional issues in the larger urban and metropolitan areas.

Overall, the Bank has made important contributions to the urban development and housing agenda, but the effectiveness of its lending operations has been modest compared to its sometimes ambitious objectives. Various approaches have been applied with emphasis on the urban poor, and some of these have been relatively successful in upgrading their living conditions. However, the Bank has yet to consistently achieve intended results in a cost-effective manner.

Given the significance of the urban agenda in Brazil, it is vital that the Bank remain engaged. The experience during the evaluation period points to the need to revitalize its strategy that would further leverage its comparative advantage and promote catalytic effects through demonstration and replication among cities.

Reaching the Rural Poor

Brazil and the Bank have a longstanding partnership in fostering rural development and family farming, particularly in the northeast. This relationship has evolved and supported a variety of projects that made important contributions to improvements in access to basic services in rural communities (Bhatnagar and others 2003; Tendler 1993). Of particular significance is the support through a CDD approach that emerged from successful implementation of a small component in the Northeast Rural Development Program in 1985. That project funded small-scale, demand-driven investment in poor rural communities and relied on communities' ability to identify priorities and execute subprojects. Over time, the CDD approach was expanded to several north and northeastern states.

During the evaluation period, 14 CDD projects were approved, totaling $630 million in commitments. The development objectives of the CDD projects approved during and prior to the evaluation period were very similar. They typically focused on the provision of basic infrastructure (water, sanitation, electricity) in line with local demand, reflecting the highly participatory CDD model.

Several studies have examined the outcomes of the CDD approach. Coirolo and Lammert (2009) and a companion volume (Binswanger and others 2009) find that CDD projects in the northeast have benefitted approximately 11 million people, primarily through the provision of electricity and domestic water supply. The studies find the interventions cost effective and well targeted to the very poor. They have also avoided local elite capture, and minorities and disadvantaged groups have been included.

An important share of the community associations have been headed by women (30 percent in a specific survey), and some of the investments in water and electrification have lightened women's workloads and greatly improved their quality of life. IEG (2005) found that results on social capital formation were mixed based on surveys of around 1,000 households in

Northeast Brazil, whereas other studies (Corriolo and Lammert 2009; Binswanger and others 2009) found CDD to be operating as fora to discuss alternative programs facilitating citizen participation, including issues of transparency and accountability of public resources.

Finally, results are inconclusive regarding the sustainability of impact for complex productive projects that depend on markets outside the community. The need to develop local economies and employment opportunities represents an ongoing and pressing challenge for the traditional CDD model whose success to date is largely located in meeting basic needs.

Many of the CDD projects were complemented by the Land-Based Poverty Alleviation Project (*Credito Fundiario*; $202 million), approved in FY00 and closed in FY08. The project focused on access to land and productive inputs by the rural poor. It helped extend loans on favorable terms to community groups for land purchase, and it provided matching funds for complementary investment and technical assistance to increase productivity. The households benefitting from the projects were below the poverty line. The average income of families remaining in the project was reported to have significantly increased, although concern about the sustainability of development outcomes has been noted due to high turnover among the settlement group membership.[31]

The scope and quality of the challenges to reaching the rural poor in remote forest areas in the Amazon are different from those in northeast states. In these areas, extremely sparse population density makes service delivery expensive, and remoteness from markets makes many agricultural and forest products commercially unviable. The Bank, however, has been slow to learn how to address these challenges. The Amapá Sustainable Communities Project was designed to "learn lessons about Amazon-specific approaches to reduce urban and rural poverty through measures that are environmentally sustainable, economically efficient and socially equitable." It did not achieve these objectives, and its outcome was rated highly unsatisfactory. The Maranhão Integrated Program: Rural Poverty Reduction Project, with an unsatisfactory outcome, was faulted for neglecting in its design to take account of the lessons of earlier CDD projects and of the state's weak capacity. The local implementing agency was slow to process subprojects and ran into procurement issues.

Implementation problems have also plagued the ongoing Pará Rural Project, which has fallen short of its goals. The ongoing Alto Solimões Project, in some of the remotest regions of the Amazon, sought to boost incomes through productive chains and to support urban and rural water supply and sanitation. These goals have proved more costly and difficult than anticipated. Both of the ongoing projects had unrealized plans for thorough, informative monitoring and evaluation systems. In both cases, baseline data are being collected only as the projects near their planned conclusion dates. In contrast, the Tocantins Sustainable Regional Development Project included a rigorous impact evaluation for rural roads construction.

However, the $150 million ProAcre project (approved in 2008), instituted in a state noted for its progressive environmental stance, is making good progress on health and education service delivery. Progress on productive activities has run into implementation bottlenecks similar to the other projects'. Impressive efforts are being directed toward helping indigenous groups prepare land management plans, despite the difficulty in training and recruiting extension agents, in an efficacious and culturally respectful manner.

Challenges differ in the more densely populated forest/farm landscapes of the southeast, where the Bank has a history of working on sustainable land management and conservation. For example, the Santa Catarina Natural Resources Management and Rural Poverty Reduction Project (2002–09) concentrated on management of small watersheds. It used an unusually good monitoring system to show that participating farmers boosted incomes by 10 percent to 18 percent, compared to a control group, and that the project had an economic rate of return of 45 percent. Although improved land management practices were adopted, actual impacts on erosion and sedimentation were not measured—a lost opportunity to inform the subsequent PES projects.

Available analyses indicate that CDD programs in Brazil are a qualified success.[32] They have been carefully targeted and reached the poor and other disadvantaged groups (women, minorities, and indigenous populations). Design improvements have been built in over time to maximize participation. The bulk of the investment has been in water supply, sanitation, and electricity, which has likely helped improve the quality of life and health conditions in rural communities.

However, effects have been ambiguous for more complex productive or entrepreneurial activities and for the capacity to ensure sustainability of project outcomes.[33] Enhancing support to develop the productive sector—the emerging challenge in rural development— would likely require a more customized approach that recognizes the heterogeneity of regions, states, municipalities, and localities. As for the Bank's Amazonian poverty projects, working on a small, "retail" scale, fared poorly against the ambitious FY08–11 CPS goals for reducing poverty among the 23 million residents of Amazonia, although ProAcre shows promise.

RATING OF THE SUSTAINABILITY PILLAR

The Bank significantly contributed to a dramatic reduction in deforestation through support for a major expansion of protected areas and indigenous territories. It supported increased capacity at the Environment Ministry and IBAMA, which undertook more effective enforcement of forest laws. Harmonization of development and forest conservation remains a challenge, however. Attempts to promote poverty reduction in remote forest areas have had limited success; hydropower planning and assessment is not yet on a basinwide basis; and the SEM DPL's impact to further improve Brazil's environment management system is hard to detect despite the size of the loan.

In water resource management, the value of the Bank's convening power facilitating broad cross-sectoral dialogue on trade-offs was well recognized. Also, Bank-supported investments and technical assistance contribute to a greater focus on water quality, efficiency, and sustainability, though challenges in the water sector persist.

The Bank continued its support for the community-driven model that started in the 1980s, with some positive effects in reaching the poor and other disadvantaged groups, providing access to water supply, sanitation, and electricity. Less clear effects were achieved in supporting farmer productivity and access to markets. In urban development, the Bank made important contributions in slum upgrading, but the support for broader municipal development has produced mixed results. There were substantial activities in the housing sector during the early phase of the evaluation period, but the scope of dialogue has diminished. On the basis of this evidence, this pillar of Bank assistance is rated moderately satisfactory.

Endnotes

[1] The existing programs consolidated under *Bolsa Familia* are *Bolsa Escola* (schooling), *Bolsa Alimentação* (health care), *Cartão Alimentação* (food stamps), and *Auxilio Gas* (compensating for adjustments in fuel costs).

[2] At appraisal the cash transfer component of the first adaptable program loan represented less than 10 percent of the total cost of $6.2 billion. Fast and successful expansion of the cash transfer program reduced the share of Bank loan in the total program even further.

[3] The Brazil Analytic and Advisory Program for Social Assistance Program comprises three AAA activities—Social Protection Phases 1, 2, and 3.

[4] Two AAA activities—Labor Markets and Jobs (FY07) and Labor Programmatic AAA Phase 2 (FY09)—examined the impacts of transfers on labor supply and found labor market programs could improve employability of at-risk groups and promote graduation from welfare programs.

[5] Only 7 of the 5,560 municipalities in Brazil have no online access to the *Cadastro Único* webpage version 7, launched in December 2010.

[6] Based on the estimates of Bourguignon, Ferreira, and Leite (2003).

[7] More than double for children age 15–17 and nearly triple in the Northeast region. For instance, a 15-year-old girl is 19 percentage points more likely to attend school if her family is a *Bolsa Familia* program beneficiary. See also Gilligan and Fruttero (2011) and the synthesis of impact evaluation results in Lindert and others (2007) and Soares (2012).

[8] During this period, the envisioned support for ECD did not occur except for its support to municipalities in the state of Ceará to expand nonformal ECD.

[9] The work was supported by the Spanish Trust Fund for Impact Evaluation.

[10] The Ceará Multisector Inclusion and Rio State DPL are the only two closed projects. They were rated moderately satisfactory for outcome and modest for the education objective by IEG.

[11] Anhanguera completed its initial public offering in 2007 and raised a total of R$2,462 (around $1.2 billion) from the Brazilian capital market. It also issued three debentures of R$770 million (around $385 million).

[12] Paim and others (2011) suggest a defining characteristic of health sector reform in Brazil is that it was driven by civil society (healthcare as a right) rather than government or international organizations.

[13] IEG reviews rated all of them satisfactory.

[14] The amount includes the allocation for health sector components in loans.

[15] For example, the Health Network Formation and Quality Improvement Project (FY09) supports efforts to provide subnational entities with the flexibility to design and organize delivery systems in line with local conditions.

[16] Relevant operations include support for Rio de Janeiro state, Rio de Janeiro municipality, Ceará, Minas Gerais, Amazonas, Acre, and Bahia.

[17] The issues of bulk water supply cost recovery systems and water quality are being addressed in such recent operations as the Rio de Janeiro State Urban development policy loan as well as the Sergipe and Pernambuco states water projects. Two ongoing operations in São Paulo are building on earlier operations that initiated new approaches to water quality in dense urban watersheds, improving the quality of life of poor populations while promoting integrated water management in a metropolitan area.

[18] "Amazon" and "Amazonia" are here used to refer to the Brazilian Amazon forest. The "Legal Amazon" encompasses some states that are partly outside the Amazon forest biome.

[19] *Licenciamento Ambiental de Empreendimentos Hidrelétricos no Brasil: Uma Contribuição para o Debate,* 2008.

[20] IEG's detailed evaluation of SEM DPL is ongoing to examine the effectiveness of this loan in more depth.

[21] There are differing explanations on the absence of Bank loan for the follow-up project. Several stakeholders interviewed by the IEG team indicated that the Bank withdrew promised support with little explanation. The Bank team, on the other hand, notes that it supported the preparation of a large grant with PPG7 funds to be financed by KfW and additional assessments to improve FUNAI's capacity; the federal government declined to go ahead and support a project to improve FUNAI's capacity.

[22] Dados-UCs-ARPA-21-set-1.xls, downloaded from programaarpa.org.br, May 5, 2013. Data as of September 21, 2012.

[23] The government introduced a new, near-real time remote sensing system for detecting deforestation, allowing rapid and strategic targeting of enforcement efforts. It also published remote sensing data, so that nongovernmental organizations could serve as an independent check on the progress of enforcement activities. Under the PPCDAm, coordination was improved among the many government agencies involved in forest law enforcement. Finally, IBAMA was granted new legal powers allowing them to instantly seize the property (timber, cattle) of suspected offenders—this being a much more effective deterrent than instigating court actions that could take years or levying fines that might never be collected.

[24] No presumption is made that the person who is registering the landholding has legal title.

[25] Amazonian properties in appropriately zoned areas need only recover their legal reserves to 50 percent, rather than 80 percent. In principle, zoned areas with excess forest can qualify as suppliers in a tradeable permit scheme for legal reserve.

(That is, a forest deficit property can pay a forest-surplus property to set aside forest in order to meet the buyer's legal reserve requirement.)

[26] The PES scheme focuses on reforestation of riverbanks to intercept the storm-driven pulses of sediment that clog and occasionally shut down the water filtration plants that serve the capital city of Vítoria. Reforestation will be done with fruit, coffee, and rubber trees intended to boost smallholders' income. Funding will come from a windfall—royalties from offshore oil—together with a levy on water users. The scheme would solve the problem of how the state's smallholders will come into compliance with the Forest Code—because the riverbanks should never have been deforested in the first place.

[27] The number excludes the Betim Integrated Municipal Project (FY05), which was technically mapped to the environment sector.

[28] This project was mapped to the environment sector.

[29] Includes five cities in Rio Grande do Sul, and São Luis, Teresina, and Uberaba.

[30] These operations have not been completed and have not been evaluated by IEG.

[31] During the period up to 2006, about 35 percent of the initial settler families left the settlement and in almost a quarter of the settlement, the exit rate was 50 percent.

[32] As of March 2013, IEG had reviewed nine CDD projects that closed during the period evaluated and rated eight of them satisfactory (the ninth was rated moderately satisfactory).

[33] In their analysis of the literature on CDD, Mansuri, and Rao (2013) contend that donors, especially the Bank, often adopt an overly ambitious approach to CDD, characterized by a lack of acknowledgment of the complexity of context (for example, culture, politics, geography, social structure).

References

Assunção, Juliano, Clarissa Gandour, Romero Rocha, and Rudi Rocha. 2013. "Does Credit Affect Deforestation? Evidence from a Rural Credit Policy in the Brazilian Amazon." Rio de Janeiro: Climate Policy Initiative.

Bastos, Yandra, Laurent Micol, and João Andrade. 2009. Transparência Florestal Mato Grosso: Análises do Desmatamento e da Gestão Florestal. Ano II, n.2, 2008/2009. Cuiabá: ICV, 2011.

Bhatnagar, Deepti, Ankita Dewan, Magui Moreno Torres, and Kanungo Parameeta. 2003. FUMAC—Municipal Fund for Community-Driven Development Projects, Northeast Brazil. Empowerment Case Studies. World Bank, Washington, DC.

Binswanger, Hans, Fatima Amazonas, Tulio Barbosa, Alberto Costa, Naercio Menezes, Elaine Pazello, and Claudia Romano. 2009. An Evaluation of Community-Driven Development (CDD). Vol. 2 of Rural Poverty Reduction in Northeast Brazil. Washington, DC: World Bank.

Bourguignon, François, Francisco H. G. Ferreira, and Phillippe G. Leite. 2003. "Conditional Cash Transfers, Schooling, and Child Labor: Micro-Simulating Brazil's Bolsa Escola Program." World Bank Economic Review 17 (2): 229–54.

Brandão, Jr., Amintas, Paulo Barreto, and Carlos Souza, Jr. 2012. Análise do Desmatamento em Assentamentos. Belem: IMAZON.

Bruns, Barbara, David Evans, and Javier Luque. 2012. "Achieving World-Class Education in Brazil: The Next Agenda. Directions in Development Human Development Network." Report No. 65659, World Bank, Washington, DC.

Carnoy, Martin, Amber Gove, Susanna Loeb, Jeffery Marshall, and Miguel Socias. 2008. "How Schools and Students Respond to School Improvement Programs: The Case of Brazil's PDE." *Economics of Education Review* 27: 22–38.

Cities Alliance. 2012. *Cities without Slums, Annual Report.* Washington, DC: Cities Alliance.

Coirolo, Luis, and Jill Lammert. 2009. *Achieving Results through Community Driven Development (CDD).* Vol. 1 of *Rural Poverty Reduction in Northeast Brazil.* Washington, DC: World Bank.

De Brauw, Alan, Daniel O. Gilligan, John Hoddinott, and Shalini Roy. 2012. *The Impact of Bolsa Família on Child, Maternal, and Household Welfare.* Washington, DC: International Food Policy Research Institute.

De Gouvello, Christophe, Britaldo S. Soareas Filho, Roberto Schaeffer, Fuad Jorge Alves, and Joao Wagner Silva Alves. 2010. "Brazil Low-Carbon Country Case Study." World Bank, Washington, DC.

Evans, David K., and Katrina Kosec. 2012. "Early Child Education Making Programs Work for Brazil's Most Important Generation." Report No. 69307, World Bank, Washington, DC.

Gilligan, Daniel, and Anna Fruttero. 2011. "The Impact of *Bolsa Família* on Education and Health Outcomes in Brazil." PowerPoint presentation at Second Generation of CCTs Evaluations Conference, World Bank.

IEG (Independent Evaluation Group). 2005. *The Effectiveness of World Bank Support for Community-Based and -Driven Development.* Washington, DC: World Bank.

———. 2009. "Project Performance Assessment Report: Brazil Goias State Highway Management Project, First Phase." World Bank, Washington, DC.

———. 2010. "Project Performance Assessment Report: Brazil Programmatic Loan for Sustainable and Equitable Growth: Housing Sector Reform (Loan 7306)." World Bank, Washington, DC.

IPEA, Cepal, et al. 2011. Avaliação do Plano de Ação para a Prevenção e Controle do Desmatamento da Amazônia Legal. Technical Report.

La Forgia, Gerard M., and Bernard F. Couttolenc. 2008. *Hospital Performance in Brazil: The Search for Excellence.* Washington, DC: World Bank.

Lindert, Kathy, Anja Linder, Jason Hobbs, Bénédicte de la Brière. 2007. "The Nuts and Bolts of Brazil's *Bolsa Família* Program: Implementing Conditional Cash Transfers in a Decentralized Context." World Bank, Washington. DC.

Mansuri, Ghazala, and Vijayendra Rao. 2013. *Localizing Development: Does Participation Work?* Washington, DC: World Bank.

Ministry of Mines and Energy. 2007. "Manual for Hydropower Inventory Studies of River Basins: 2007 Edition." Ministry of Mines and Energy. Secretariat of Planning and Energy Development, CEPEL, Rio de Janeiro.

Nolte, Christoph, Arun Agrawal, Kristen M. Silvius, and Britaldo S. Soares-Filho. 2013. "Governance Regime and Location Influence Avoided Deforestation Success of Protected Areas in the Brazilian Amazon." *Proceedings of the National Academy of Sciences* (doi: 1 0.1073/pnas. 1 214786110).

Paim, Jairnilson, Claudia Travassos, Celia Almeida, Ligia Bahia, and James Macinko. 2011. "The Brazilian Health System: History, Advances, and Challenges." *The Lancet* 377 (9779): 1778–97.

Rajão, Raoni, Andrea Azevedo, and Marcelo C. C. Stabile. 2012. "Instisional Subversion and Deforestation: Learning Lessons from the System for the Environmental Licencing of Rural Properties in Mato Grosso." *Public Administration and Development* 32(3): 229–44.

Santos, Daniel, Denys Pereira, and Adalberto Veríssimo. 2013. *O Estado da Amazonia: Uso da Terra*. Belem: IMAZON.

Soares, Sergei Suarez Dillon. 2012. "Bolsa Família, its Design, its Impacts and Possibilities for the Future." Working Papers 89, International Policy Centre for Inclusive Growth.

Stickler, Claudia M., Daniel C. Nepstad, Andrea A. Azevedo, and David G. McGrath. 2013. "Defending Public Interests In Private Lands: Compliance, Costs and Potential Environmental Consequences of the Brazilian Forest Code in Mato Grosso." *Philosophical Transactions of the Royal Society B: Biological Sciences* 368 (1619).

Tendler, Judith. 1993. "New Lessons from Old Projects: The Workings of Rural Development in Northeast Brazil." Operations Evaluation Department, World Bank, Washington, DC.

World Bank. 2005. *Brazil: Addressing the Challenge of Non-Communicable Diseases in Brazil*. Washington, DC: World Bank.

——. 2007a. *Brazil—Governance in Brazil's Unified Health System: Raising the Quality of Public Spending and Resource Management*. Washington, DC: World Bank.

——. 2007b. "Implementation Completion and Results Report (IBRD-71860) on an Adaptable Program Loan in the Amount of US$60.0 million to the State of Bahia with the Guarantee of the Federative Republic of Brazil for a Bahia Education Project in Support of the Second Phase of the Bahia Education Program." World Bank, Washington, DC.

——. 2008a. *Different Paths to Student Learning: Good Practices and Student Performance—Identifying Success from Municipal School Systems in Brazil*. Public Expenditure Review. World Bank, Washington, DC.

——. 2008b. "Environmental Licensing for Hydroelectric Projects in Brazil: A contribution to the Debate. Volume I (of 3 volumes): Summary Report." Washington, DC: World Bank.

——. 2010. "Implementation Completion and Results Report on a Loan in the Amount of US$572.2 million to the Federative Republic of Brazil for a *Bolsa Família* Project in Support for the First Phase of the *Bolsa Família* Program." World Bank, Washington, DC.

——. 2011." Implementation Completion and Results Report on a First Programmatic Development Policy Loan for Sustainable Environmental Management in the Amount of US$1.3 billion to the Federative Republic of Brazil." World Bank, Washington, DC.

4 Growth, Competitiveness, and Economic Management

Accelerating and maintaining a high rate of growth is a necessary condition to achieve long-term reductions in poverty and improvements in equity and to provide incentives for human capital formation. It also facilitates the implementation of policies to support the sustainability of exhaustible resources. Thus, growth complements the objectives set in Chapter 3. The government of Brazil and the Bank Group agreed at the beginning of the evaluation period that constraints to growth would be a key organizing principle to identify areas of assistance by the Bank Group's program—and this was reemphasized by the authorities at later points during the evaluation period.

Two broad areas for Bank Group support were identified. The first was enhancing competitiveness of the Brazilian economy, particularly by raising infrastructure investments and overall productivity. Improving the investment climate and the environment for competition in product and factor markets, including capital markets, was deemed critical to competitiveness. It was also supported by growing evidence from various studies on sources of growth showing that infrastructure bottlenecks and the cost of doing business—Custo Brasil—were important constraints to growth.

Growth also depends critically on the quality of public expenditures. And for growth to be sustained and not be interrupted, macroeconomic vulnerabilities need to be reduced and carefully managed. Thus, the second area of support was to strengthen public sector management, in particular fiscal sustainability, and to improve the allocation of public spending and investment as well as the overall efficiency of resource use in the public sector at both the federal and subnational levels.

A More Competitive Brazil

The FY04–07 CAS was conceived in a period of relatively low annual GDP growth, about 1.75 percent during 1999–2003. It was influenced in part by temporary factors, such as external shocks and the efforts to stabilize public debt and reduce inflation. But it was also affected by low levels of investment, particularly in infrastructure. Public investment in infrastructure had continued to fall, reaching levels of about one percent of GDP—much lower than the levels of comparator countries. Since 2007, the Growth Acceleration Program has been the most prominent response from the federal government to increase infrastructure investments. A slight increase in investments during the initial years of the program has been reported, but it has yet to significantly affect aggregate investment in infrastructure as a proportion of GDP.

The CAS projected a gradual recovery of growth to 4.0 percent and emphasized the need for coordinated actions in several areas that historically had been constraints to sustained growth. The focus on growth was also triggered by evidence in previous evaluations of weak Bank performance in this area. The Country Assistance Evaluation (IEG 2004) and the CASCR on the assistance during the 2000–03 period concluded that the Bank program had not succeeded in removing key bottlenecks that constrained public and private investment. They also acknowledged that the expectation that private investment would meet infrastructure needs did not materialize and concluded that the Bank program had not mobilized growth-generating reforms at an adequate pace.

During preparation of the FY08–11 CPS, the projected growth rates remained in the range of 4.5 percent. Sound macroeconomic management and improvements in debt sustainability were considered to have helped reinvigorate growth. But it was also recognized that part of the fiscal primary surplus had been financed by high levels of taxation and compression of public spending on infrastructure, which had fallen to less than one percent of GDP in 2007 (World Bank 2008). However, taxes could not increase much more without negative effects on private investment. The ratio of taxes to GDP today is estimated to be about 35 percent of GDP (World Bank 2011).

There was, however, an important difference in the approach to competitiveness between the two strategies. The FY04–07 CAS tried to address systemic countrywide regulatory issues that would improve the overall enabling environment for investment. The emphasis was on lending operations and dialogue at the federal level, including countrywide and cross-sectoral AAA on the constraints to mobilizing private investment in infrastructure. With the significant shift in focus to subnational entities, the FY08–11 CPS saw the challenge partly as that of the competitiveness of large Brazilian cities, given increased urbanization and their large share in GDP. The share of lending for major urban infrastructure investments grew substantially, while engagement on countrywide regulatory reforms was reduced. Independently of this difference in emphasis, and on the basis of discussion with the Brazilian authorities, four areas for improving Brazil's competitiveness were identified during the evaluation period:

• Infrastructure bottlenecks and the regulatory framework for infrastructure, including for PPPs

• The business climate and the environment for competition

• High interest rates and segmentation of the financial markets

• Innovation policy.

ADDRESSING INFRASTRUCTURE BOTTLENECKS AND IMPROVING THE REGULATORY FRAMEWORK, INCLUDING FOR PPPS

The overall objective of the Bank assistance in infrastructure was to help relieve major infrastructure bottlenecks in selected areas, improve the institutional and management capabilities of agencies and subnational governments in managing infrastructure, and enhance the incentives for private sector participation in infrastructure, with a particular emphasis on PPP arrangements. IFC played an important role in this last area.

The Bank used a combination of instruments to achieve its objective. First, policy-based lending formed an important part of the effort. It initially consisted of a series of federal DPLs—the Sustainable and Equitable Growth Programmatic Loans (GDPLs)—and technical assistance operations supporting policy and regulatory changes at the federal level. Later, it consisted of subnational SWAps and DPLs. Second, a program of investment operations in various infrastructure sectors was approved, usually accompanied by extensive technical assistance. Third, a major piece of AAA in 2007 consolidated learning from three years of nonlending technical assistance activities in the area of private investment in infrastructure in Brazil. The report (World Bank 2007) provided an overview of pending issues across several sectors and identified major areas of systemic reform.

Federal and Subnational Policy Operations

The GDPL series was originally defined in very general terms in the FY04–07 CAS—and it was the main vehicle of support to the competitiveness objective, not only infrastructure. The GDPL series was envisaged as several loans, the emphasis to be developed depending on reform progress. GDPL loans were approved in 2004 and 2006, supporting several areas of the competitiveness objective. A technical assistance loan accompanied the 2004 operation, supporting the custom reform program, work on port reform, and reforms in the regulatory framework for transport.

As seen by IEG's review of the ICR (IEG 2009b), the results of the program related to infrastructure reforms were mixed (Table 4.1). Progress was generally good in lowering logistic costs, particularly in customs, ports, and federal roads. However, progress in the rail sector was modest.[1] In the critical area of overall regulatory reforms to encourage PPP and the entry of the private sector, progress at the federal level was also modest.

The Bank tried to complement the passage of the federal law regulating PPPs through a grant to the government unit in charge of implementation. The Bank also supported some PPP activities at the state level, for example, in Minas Gerais and Rio de Janeiro.

The CASCR for FY04–07 acknowledged that public infrastructure investments remained low—below one percent of GDP—and that regulatory uncertainty was high among the risks facing private investors. Overall progress in infrastructure regulation and maintenance was judged as modest. Weak regulatory capacity and contract renegotiation affect private sector confidence in investing in infrastructure. Lack of modern cross-border links and the continuing poor condition of ports constrained Brazil's integration in international trade. Although PPP legislation created high expectations, PPPs have proven lengthy and cumbersome to prepare, and management capacity exacerbates the risk for private investors.

The FY08–11 CPS had a different strategy for dealing with infrastructure bottlenecks. Given the shift in Bank assistance from federal to subnational entities, the options for vehicles to achieve country-level effect on the regulatory side were more limited than in the earlier CASs. The lending strategy focused on multisector SWAp and DPL operations and direct lending to states and municipalities for roads and mass transit, in particular the large urban centers of Rio de Janeiro and São Paulo. A federal road transport project approved in FY06 remained active throughout the period, and related AAA activities continued the dialogue at the federal level, notably "How to Decrease Freight Logistics Costs in Brazil" (Rebelo 2012).

A significant emphasis of the state DPL and SWAp operations was to improve states' capacity for expenditure prioritization and public sector management across sectors (see the next section). Agreement on steps to improve the regulatory framework for private sector entry and PPPs became more limited—they were components of a larger reform agenda, though with some exceptions. In the DPL to the Municipality of Rio (FY10), the establishment of a legal

TABLE 4.1 Infrastructure: Results of the Reforms Supported of the Programmatic Growth Series as Seen in IEG's ICR Review (FY04–07)

Objectives	Achievements
Strengthen infrastructure regulation	• Sixteen independent regulatory agencies were established and Congress approved the PPP law for infrastructure in 2004 • Government approved five PPP projects, but implementation at the federal level faltered
Improve customs effectiveness	• Government simplified exports procedures and clearing • The expected outcome of reducing release times achieved
Reduce transport costs on the federal road networks	• The remaining nontrunk roads of the federal network were transferred to state management and the government stepped up efforts to rehabilitate roads • Transport costs in roads fell and road conditions improved • By 2007 some 37 percent of the federal road network was under output-based maintenance contracts (surpassing the 30 percent target), about 50 percent of the federal road network was considered to be in good condition, and road transport cost had decreased by about 11 percent, relative to 2003
Foster multimodal transport	• The government restructured railways concessions and advanced in the regulation of railways, but did not make operational the Inter-Ministerial Committee for the Integration of Transport Policies • The productivity of railroad operations increased, but the expected 10 percent increase in the share of nonroad transportation was not attained
Reduce port costs and delays	• A plan for ports defining policies and guidelines was approved • Ports improved their operational performance; port handling times reduced: the average port and terminal handling time fell from 13.8 to 4 days for imports and from 8.4 to 3 days for exports

SOURCE: IEG 2009b.
NOTE: ICR = Implementation Completion and Results Report.

framework for PPP and a follow-up of progress before release of the second tranche was an explicit feature of the operation. In Minas Gerais, the SWAp had agreements on the number of PPPs to be contracted, particularly in transport. For example, a minimum percentage of state highways had to have maintenance contracts to be renovated with clear targets.

Sector Investment Operations

The GDPL series and other DPL and SWAp operations were complemented by sector-specific investment and technical assistance activities. The major sectors were transport and energy, discussed below.

More than half of the infrastructure lending was directed to transport. The $3.25 billion for that sector accounted for the largest share of the Bank's total lending during the period evaluated. The assistance focused on roads and highways and on urban transport and mass transit systems. (Appendix G provides additional information on the Bank's support for infrastructure.)

The Bank made a major contribution in roads and highways through continuous dialogue across federal and state agencies and the complementarity between lending and knowledge sharing. The projects approved earlier but still active during the period, such as the Federal Highways Decentralization Project, started several institutional practices that were maintained and replicated by subsequent federal and subnational operations. These innovations included output-based management and improved sector planning, as well as outsourcing of routine maintenance and rehabilitation. Technical assistance components and extensive AAA supported institutional reforms in appraisal frameworks, the use of toll roads, and PPP arrangements. Major analytical work also was done on how to decrease freight logistics costs.

Private participation in roads was facilitated by IFC involvement in selected projects that set new requirements for performance standards for road concessions. The federal government and the state of São Paulo used the standards in bidding for concessions. With its advisory work for another transport project in FY08, IFC introduced the Equator Principles and social standards for expropriation and resettlement rules for road concession projects. This project was also the first concession of a metropolitan road network with urban tolling. As a natural extension in improving trade logistics, IFC led mobilization of financial support to the port of Santos. It provided financing of nearly $100 million and helped mobilize about $600 million from other lenders.

Yet a number of issues remain, including the planning and management of investments. Financial sustainability remains as a critical challenge, and so do the incentives needed to mobilize private participation—some of the latest concessions have reportedly not materialized. In addition, as the demand for high-quality infrastructure continues to grow, particularly in states and municipalities, and the IBRD lending capacity is not without a limit, assistance in the sector will have to rely increasingly on knowledge support rather than large investment operations.

The largest operations in urban transport and mass transit during the period were those in São Paulo and Rio de Janeiro, which totaled about $1.8 billion in commitments.[2] These projects built on earlier operations in these cities and focused on metro and urban rail systems aimed at improving the quality of urban transport, particularly benefitting the lower-income populations, who are the main users, and reducing the environmental impact of motorized vehicle use. The projects supported multimodal integration, decentralization of the federal CBTU (Brazilian urban train company) to states and municipalities, and private sector participation in the operation and management of the systems (many with large operating subsidies), as well as introducing appropriate cost recovery, tariff, and subsidy policies. Given the magnitude of urbanization challenge in Brazil, there was a strong rational for the Bank to engage in sustained dialogue on urban transport in these cities.

These operations generally have had positive results. In São Paulo, the completed Metro Line 4 project and private concession arrangements have been widely recognized as particularly innovative.[3] Demand projections were exceeded in the first year of operation and the share of metro trips increased despite rapid growth in motorization. In addition, financial sustainability has been enhanced and accessibility has been improved for the low-income population in the periphery of the metro region. The ongoing operation in Rio de Janeiro has contributed to further improvements in strategic planning and tariff setting, regulatory, and subsidy policies.

The Bank has also supported gender-related improvements, such as enhancing the security of women, who did not feel safe in the overcrowded trains and degraded system. In both São Paulo and Rio de Janeiro, counterparts stressed that, in addition to the advice provided and the transfer of knowledge, the use of Bank financing and procurement procedures helped improve the quality and lower the cost of the procured equipment.

The significant lending commitments for the urban and mass transit projects, and in the transport sector in general, also pose an important question about selectivity in the allocation of IBRD lending capacity. The issue is particularly acute for the metro and suburban train systems in São Paulo and Rio de Janeiro. The project objectives supported by these loans were achieved. However, the question is whether the large amounts of Bank financing for these projects were critical or whether some of the financing could have been mobilized from the financial markets, given the two cities' high levels of income, creditworthiness, and financial sophistication, as well as the cost recovery possibilities in these projects. An important question for the future program is how the Bank can ensure the largest catalytic effect per dollar loaned to address the critical challenge in infrastructure bottlenecks.

In energy, the Bank historically has been a major partner and lender, financing power infrastructure in the 1970s and 1980s. Even though lending volumes declined in the 1990s, the Bank remained engaged in policy dialogue when sector reforms were initiated to enhance the reliability and efficiency of the sector and attract private investors.

The severe energy supply crisis in 2001 encouraged the federal government to consolidate the regulatory and institutional framework for the sector and introduce an auction-based wholesale market. The Bank resumed lending in the sector with a fast-disbursing, single-tranche operation (energy sector reform loan, $455 million in 2002) to address the immediate regulatory problems underlying the crisis. The operation was accompanied by technical assistance activities to support regulatory reforms and the establishment of mandatory energy auctions to introduce competition.[4] The Energy Sector Technical Assistance Loan provided long-term support and addressed key areas, including development of the electricity market and regulation, access and affordability for the poor, environmental licensing, long-term expansion planning, and institutional strengthening and coordination.[5]

Because the project was motivated by a major crisis, it also built in flexibility and a mechanism to permit high-level exchange of views between the Brazilian authorities and the Bank on the implementation of the sector reform program (De Gouvello 2009). Although the loan had considerable implementation challenges, the project came to be broadly recognized as being highly relevant to a wide range of sector reform issues. It also contributed to large savings (estimated at $12 billion) by helping the government shift from noncompetitive negotiated contracts to competitive international bidding in connection with the two Rio Madeira hydropower plants (Santo Antonio and Jirau). Its success led to the broader adoption of a competitive auction strategy for hydroelectric generation.[6]

The only Bank operation approved during the FY04–11 period was the Eletrobras Distribution Rehabilitation Project (FY10, $495 million). This project focused on improving the quality of electricity service by six poorly performing state distribution companies in the north and northeast that had been transferred to Eletrobras in 1996 because they had not been picked up in the privatization of the more profitable distribution companies. These companies supply electricity to more than 3 million people in some of the poorest regions in Brazil and face significant challenges, including service interruptions and losses and poor collection rates.

A cross-cutting issue emerging from the experiences in sector investment operations is with regard to the capacity of the public sector to plan and execute infrastructure investments.

Several stakeholders expressed concerns during this evaluation about limited project cost-benefit analysis and sectoral planning as well as shortcomings in project implementation caused by budgetary rigidities and capacity limitations. This issue received attention in 2005 when Brazil decided to participate in the pilot program on fiscal space, whereby the International Monetary Fund relaxed its fiscal targets to accommodate increased public investment. The Bank participated in this pilot, and a key finding of the joint missions was the remarkable weaknesses in Brazil's public investment management and the need to install adequate capacities for managing PPP operations. An Institutional Development Fund grant helped improve the quality of public spending and appears to have had some positive impact in one of the core ministries, but the need to enhance capacity to appraise, execute, monitor, and evaluate public sector investment projects remained.

Regulatory Constraints to Private Sector Participation in Infrastructure

The report *How to Revitalize Infrastructure Investments in Brazil: Public Policies for Better Private Participation* (World Bank 2007) was based on the experience of technical assistance activities. The report, which discusses factors constraining private participation in infrastructure in a comprehensive framework, was carried out by a large number of sectoral experts and suggests several policy directions to address the problem.

The report points to a need to reduce regulatory risks and enhance the autonomy of regulators to revitalize infrastructure investments. An important component of that risk is the frequency of concessions renegotiation that often stems from the lack of independent regulators, the fact that the regulatory framework is embedded in the contract rather than in a sector law, the use of price cap as a tariff policy, and the use of the lowest tariff as the criterion for awarding a concession. The PPP law provides assurances for compliance with the financial obligations established in a PPP contract, but not against regulatory risk. In fact, a 2005 survey of 21 regulatory agencies in Brazil found that most of the elements for good governance transferable by law were in place; the main challenges are how to develop more detailed attributes that cannot be covered by law and how to ensure enforcement. The report also provides several examples of how independence and transparency of regulator decisions is compromised in practice and the problems of enforcement.

The report also suggests policy steps to strengthen the fundamentals for infrastructure concessions in specific sectors. In the water sector, addressing uncertainty about who has the power to award concessions for metropolitan regions and defining an overall regulatory framework are key. In ports, the policy steps involve clarifying the role of regulators and advancing the decentralization process, the latter being true for nontrunk federal roads as well. In the energy sector, policy steps include the approval of a new sector law for the natural gas sector. This report proved useful for discussions with the Ministry of Finance, Planning, the Civil Cabinet, the *Tribunal de Contas de União*, and sectoral agencies.

However, that work did not lead to further dialogue or broader engagement during the second CAS period. In light of the increasing urgency of the topic, the report offers an excellent analytical platform to build on in the future country program. The ongoing effort to assess the status of PPP practices in Brazil is a timely development in this context.

IMPROVING THE BUSINESS CLIMATE AND THE ENVIRONMENT FOR COMPETITION

The FY04–07 CAS is based on a premise that improving the business climate is both most urgent for the development of Brazil and one of the areas where the Bank Group has a clear comparative advantage. That advantage lies in its capability to draw on lessons from the variety of experiences in Brazil and other countries. The Bank Group's strategy in this area was to assist both the federal and state governments, combining lending, technical assistance, and analytical work. It did this through two main vehicles: DPLs, specifically the GDPL series, and activities to document the cost of doing business as well as to provide relevant technical assistance.

Specific objectives included in the GDPL series were to support application of the new antitrust law and reduce the time to register a business through unified registries across the country. According to IEG's ICR Review of the two GDPL series loans, only modest progress had been made in this area by 2009, three years after the second loan was approved (Table 4.2). One problem noted in the ICR Review (IEG 2009b) is the lack of a baseline at the state level against which progress could have been assessed systematically over time.

A pilot exercise was undertaken in 2006 at the request of the Ministry of Finance to investigate selected indicators of the cost of doing business in 12 states and a federal district of different income levels (Figure 4.1). The study found that generally the higher the income of the state or municipality, the easier it was to do business. But there is significant variability in specific indicators, indicating that low-income states can outperform better-off states when they introduce specific reforms. Maranhão—with the lowest per capita income of the group—has introduced digitalized registries (*cartorios*) that reduced the time to register property to 27 days, less time than any of the other states surveyed. Starting a business takes 47 days, compared with 152 days in São Paulo and 68 days in Rio de Janeiro.

The pilot was a very useful exercise, but its value could be further increased if it were replicated over time. It would allow examination of the variability across Brazil and the factors behind such variability, which could lead to learning and further replication. It was an important first step and provided a baseline for further work and follow-up by the Bank and IFC.

TABLE 4.2 Establishing a Successful Climate and Environment for Competition: Progress of Reforms Supported by the Programmatic Growth Loan Series (FY04–07)

Objectives	Achievements
Enhance the competitiveness environment and strengthen the corporate insolvency framework	• Congress approved the Bankruptcy and Insolvency Law and amendments to the Tax Code in 2005, aligning bankruptcy legislation with international practice. The Law reduced the time of the bankruptcy process and increased recovery rates • Antitrust law amendments had not been approved by Congress at the time of ICR Review
Simplify entry and business operations	• In 2006 Congress passed a new law for SMEs combining federal with state and municipal taxes • Doing Business did not detect a difference in the time needed to comply with paying taxes between 2006 and 2009 • The simplification of export norms and procedures to register companies in some cities was supported by the loan; no information on the extent of simplification of export norms at the time of ICR Review • No progress had been made in simplifying conditions to start a business at the time of ICR Review • The number of days necessary to open a business varies by state but there is no data at the state level to assess improvements over time

SOURCE: IEG 2009b.
NOTE: ICR = Implementation Completion and Results Report; SME = small and medium-size enterprise.

The FY08–11 CPS also acknowledged that starting a business, registering property, and paying taxes were more time consuming and costly in Brazil than the average for Latin America. It also recognized that some states had already started to simplify procedures for registering a business, including "one-stop shops," but in most cases the process remained costly and lengthy. The CPS committed itself to do more in this area.

The main vehicles to address the cost of doing business in states were components of subnational DPLs and SWAps in Minas Gerais, Ceará, Rio State, and Rio municipality. The main goal for all was to reduce the cost of opening and registering a new firm. Table 4.3 shows the specific reforms each operation addressed. IEG's ICR Review of the first Minas Gerais operation (IEG 2008) judged the achievement of these objectives to have been substantial, and self-evaluations by regional staff regarding the other operations also show improvements.

FIGURE 4.1 Number of Days Needed to Start a Business

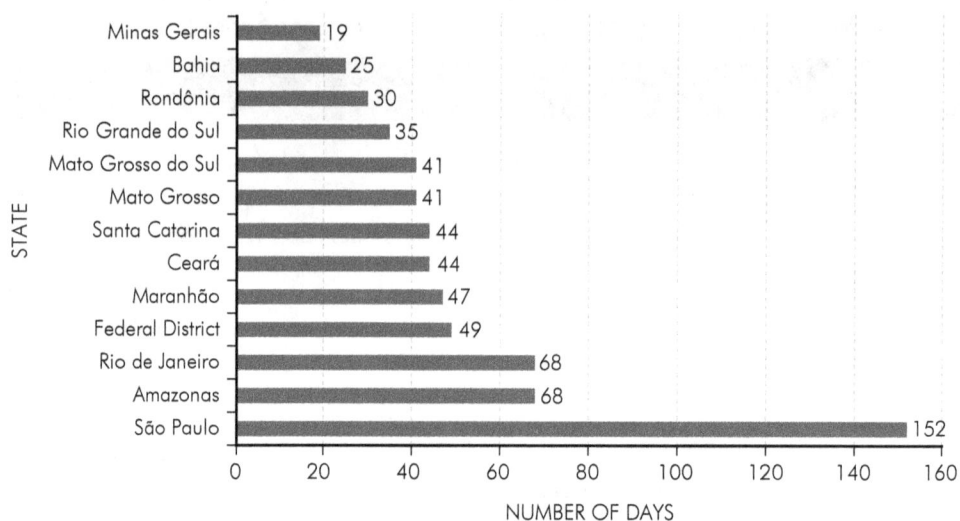

SOURCE: IFC 2006.

TABLE 4.3 Business Climate Reform Components in Subnational DPLs and SWAps

Operation	Business Climate Reform Components
Minas Gerais DPL, FY 2006	Administrative simplification, one-stop shop for registering new firms, simplified tax system for small firms. Create a specialized PPP unit. Integrating a taxpayer registration with supplier's registry. Designing a mechanism of state guarantees for PPPs.
Minas Gerais SWAp, FY 2008	Reduce time to start a business through a one-stop shop. Implement *Minas Facil* in the entire state. Achieve a target number of PPPs contracted.
Ceará SWAp, FY09	Urban populations in municipal centers with access to public broadband internet service. Business registration in the Secretary of Finance General registry completed within 72 hours.
Rio State DPL, FY 2010	Streamline business registration with SEFAZ and implement Integrated Service Centers consolidating registration and permits in one location.
Rio Municipality DPL, FY 2011	Reduce the number of days needed to start a business through the Alvara Ja Project. It will simplify registration and issuance of business licenses for activities of low sanitary risks or environmental impact. Rio will be joining the Brazil Integrated Registration System.

SOURCE: IEG, based on project documents.
NOTE: DPL = development policy loan; PPP = public-private partnership; SEFAZ = Secretaria de Estadoda Fazenda; SWAp = sector-wide approach.

IFC also has had relevant initiatives in municipalities. In 2006, it offered 10 municipalities in northeast Brazil[7] technical assistance under its advisory service program for regulatory reforms; the goals were to reduce the time to open a business and obtain construction permits and to create municipal scorecards. Cooperation agreements were signed with two municipalities, Fortaleza and Teresina. In Teresina, there has been some progress in reducing the time for issuing operation licenses. However, both IFC and IEG judged the development effectiveness of this initiative as unsuccessful. It will be important to draw lessons from this experience in the design of future Bank Group operations to reduce the cost of doing business at the local level.

Given the wide variability of indicators across states and the various reform efforts states have made in recent years, it is critical to monitor these indicators over time in a comparable manner. Thus, the ongoing initiative to develop a comprehensive Doing Business report for Brazil, covering all states and the federal district, is timely. This exercise, undertaken in partnership with the Brazilian authorities, would provide considerably richer perspectives of the cost of doing business in Brazil than the global Doing Business report, in which Brazil is represented by São Paulo as the largest business center. The urgency of this exercise is that, despite some progress, Brazil still lags behind such comparator countries as Argentina, Chile, China, India, Japan, and Mexico (World Bank 2013) in the time it takes to open a business (119 days relative to 7–38 days for comparators), time to deal with construction permits (469 days versus 81–365 for comparators), and paying taxes (2,600 hours versus 254–415 for comparators).

Finally, in spite of the importance attached to competition and productivity of an open trade regime in the FY04–07 CAS, no AAA was envisaged during the overall evaluation period to investigate the degree of openness of the Brazilian trade regime. A recent study by the Bank calls attention to the low level of trade openness in Brazil, particularly in relation to other BRICS countries (Brazil, China, India, the Russian Federation, and South Africa), and the way it may affect overall productivity growth (Canuto, Cavallari, and Reis 2013). Earlier analytical work to understand the factors behind this low level of trade openness—for example, the degree of import protection being potentially a reason—might have been highly useful in addressing this key area to enhance Brazil's competitiveness.

ENHANCING COMPETITION IN THE FINANCIAL SECTOR

The objectives of the FY04–07 CAS in this area were broad. They included policy steps, such as supporting the new bankruptcy law and antitrust regulation of the financial sector, and reducing the interest rates by enhancing competition in the financial sector. But they also included highly ambitious objectives, given the instruments available to the Bank Group, such as to increase private sector intermediation and long-term investment financing and to expand microcredit and nonbank financial services. The main vehicles the Bank deployed were the GDPL series, a series of technical assistance loans, and AAA that examined the sources of high interest rates in Brazil. The provision of credit through financial intermediaries was a major IFC activity.

Policy-Based Operations, Technical Assistance, and AAA

Many of the reform steps supported by the GDPL series were carried out, and some of the impacts on financial intermediation were positive (Table 4.4). However, the effect of these measures on the level of interest rates and the cost of credit, particularly to SMEs, depended on many variables unaffected by the projects. Some of those variables are related to the overall dominance of government players, which influences the cost of borrowing for other sectors. This was recognized by the CASCR for the period.

TABLE 4.4 Financial Sector: Results in the Reforms Supported by the Programmatic Growth Series (FY04–07)

Objectives	Achievements
Increase financial competition	• A draft law extending the application of the antitrust law to banking submitted to Congress; no clear way to measure medium-term effects
Improve efficient access to financial services including to the poor and SMEs	• A law to expand financial access to banks and regulations authorizing voluntary payroll deductions to civil servants, and pensioners of the government's Executive Branch established; payroll deduction loans, the number of bank accounts, and overall bank credit increased significantly from December 2005 to August 2008 • Whether access to credit for the poor and to SMEs improved could not be confirmed due to lack of relevant information
Mobilize long-term resources in the insurance sector	• The monopoly of reinsurance held by the state-owned Reinsurance Institute of Brazil eliminated, allowing new entrants into the system • The private insurance supervisor registered 41 reinsurance companies since then and about 15 percent of the market premiums in reinsurance were underwritten by the private sector in 2008, compared to zero in 2006

SOURCE: IEG 2009b.
NOTE: SME = small and medium-size enterprise.

The FY08–11 CPS proposed a more limited set of activities. First, implementation of the Financial Sector Technical Assistance Loan approved in 2001 continued with a focus on studies, technical advice, and training on regulation and supervision of the banking system as well as on surveillance and investor protection in the capital markets. According to the IEG ICR Review of the loan (IEG 2009a), which rated the outcome as moderately satisfactory, the objectives of the project were partly achieved, several studies were cancelled, and the achievements of some subcomponent objectives were rated as modest. Nonlending technical assistance focusing the Brazilian capital markets was being prepared in 2008, but it did not materialize.

Second, analytical work was undertaken to understand the factors behind the high cost of borrowing in Brazil, in particular the extent it was influenced by macroeconomic factors or by structural features of the financial sectors, such as publicly directed credit crowding out private credit, and whether directed credit was reaching smaller enterprises. This work consisted of several studies, the most recent being *The Real Paradox: Untangling Credit Markets Outcomes in Brazil* (World Bank 2012) and the report based on the work of a joint IMF-World Bank Financial Sector Assessment Program mission to Brazil in 2012 (IMF 2012). These studies have provided a good platform for dialogue with the authorities.

Given the limited scale of activities during FY08–11, the overall contribution by the Bank is judged modest. This is in contrast with the clearly positive assessment reported by the CASCR. It argues that the expansion of credit that occurred during this period took place in the context of a strong regulatory framework to which the Bank has contributed through several technical assistance operations such as the financial sector technical assistance loan.

IFC Financial Intermediation Activities

Financial intermediation was an important component of IFC activities in Brazil. It consisted of short-term trade financing under the Global Trade Financing Program (GTFP) and longer-term financing using second-tier, mid-sized banks as intermediaries (Table 4.5).

Short-term trade financing became the predominant IFC financial product for its financial markets operations in Brazil during the evaluation period, growing from 50 percent of the total in the mid-2000s to almost 90 percent in FY12. The sharpest increase took place as a response to the global financial crisis in 2008–09. IFC played an important role in finding international corresponding banks willing to work with mid-sized banks when international credit was drying up. The commitment volume of trade credit remained high rather than to restore the pre-crisis proportion of longer-term lending. This is puzzling because as the

TABLE 4.5 IFC Net Commitments for Financial Markets Operations in Brazil

Fiscal Year	Trade Finance	%	Financial Market	%	Total ($ 000s)
2004	n.a.	0.0	–36,000	100.0	–36,000
2005	n.a.	0.0	173,252	100.0	173,252
2006	44,976	37.7	74,177	62.3	119,152
2007	122,539	50.6	119,693	49.4	242,232
2008	248,965	41.5	350,525	58.5	599,490
2009	478,700	86.5	74,851	13.5	553,551
2010	788,137	89.2	95,460	10.8	883,597
2011	755,163	84.0	143,432	16.0	898,595
2012	768,016	87.4	111,107	12.6	879,123
Total	3,206,495	74.3	1,106,498	25.7	4,312,993

SOURCE: IFC data.
NOTE: The trade finance program in Brazil started in FY06. n.a. = not applicable.

immediate impact of the crisis subsided, the additionality of IFC for trade credit should have declined relative to that for long-term financing.

One reason IFC increasingly focused on mid-sized banks was that they tend to serve more SMEs than larger banks. The Bank studies mentioned earlier also showed that public-directed credit had not yet significantly benefited SMEs. The question is how IFC could ensure that these banks maintained and possibly increased their lending to SMEs. A preliminary effort was made in this evaluation to examine the process by which IFC objectives regarding SMEs are set and monitored by reviewing IFC project documents and loan agreements for 23 operations to banking institutions in Brazil and undertaking more detailed analysis of 9 of those. This analysis showed that the conditions regarding the banks' lending to SMEs are not as stringent as the developmental objectives presented in the project documents. In addition, the monitoring of compliance of those conditions may not have been as systematic or thorough over the period evaluated.[8]

More specifically, the definitions of "eligible sub-borrower" in all nine loan agreements examined in detail leave room to include enterprises that are far larger than those typically considered SMEs. The purpose of these loans as stated in project documents includes providing liquidity to support the borrowing bank increase its share of loans to SME sub-borrowers. However, the "eligible sub-borrower" is defined in the legal documents as one that has annual average net sales of less than either R$300 million or R$150 million.

These figures are considerably higher than the definitions of SMEs in similar circumstances. For example, IDB defined SMEs in a series of its programs in Brazil as having 20–499 employees and gross annual sales of $400,000–$20 million. The European Union defines medium-sized firms as sales below €50 million (IFC 2010). As the IFC's working definition of SMEs for monitoring uses loan size at origination—$2 million in advanced countries like Brazil—as a proxy,[9] this evaluation could not confirm whether systematic analysis of the increase in the share of loans to SMEs as typically defined are being undertaken within IFC.[10]

Measuring the extent of GTFP's reach to SMEs faces a similar challenge. For the GTFP, IFC uses the proxy measure of transactions of less than $1 million to indicate whether the trade financing is reaching SMEs. Using this measure, $452 million (18.6 percent of the GTFP commitment) and 1,316 transactions (65.4 percent of the GTFP transactions) have been estimated to support SMEs between FY06 and FY11. However, a recent IEG evaluation on the GTFP (IEG 2013) concluded that additional study is needed to determine whether this definition is a good proxy for the SME status of the emerging market party of a trade transaction.

HELPING DEVELOP A MORE MODERN INNOVATION POLICY

This objective was included only in the first CAS. Some of the related subobjectives were specific and near term, such as supporting the passage and funding of the innovation law and reducing the time to register a patent and the authorization of a technology transfer. Other subobjectives were broader and more ambitious, such as increasing the percentage of secondary students continuing to university education and encouraging overall levels of investment lending in science and technology. Achieving these subobjectives requires many factors beyond the Bank Group influence unless major catalytic effects emanating from Bank assistance are assumed. The main vehicles to achieve the latter subobjectives were to be AAA on innovation, World Bank Institute innovation system assistance, and IFC activities in support of higher education. The CAS does not specify how the Bank could influence a countrywide increase in higher education enrollments or the share of public and private investment going to science and technology.

The CASCR for the FY04–07 CAS states that the Bank has done a major and well-received report on barriers to innovation in Brazil and that the report is being "drilled down" in the states of Minas Gerais and Acre. IFC made several investments in the education sector in Brazil, as discussed in Chapter 3. No mention is made in the CASCR of how the Bank contributed to higher education enrollment or a higher share of investment lending to science and technology.

RATING OF THE "MORE COMPETITIVE BRAZIL" PILLAR

Growth and competitiveness depend on many factors, some of which can be influenced by policies, whereas others depend on exogenous factors as developments in the world economy and in world capital markets. The Bank Group can assist and influence only a small part of this picture; hence, it is critical to have a sense of perspective in judging the contribution of the Bank Group and the realism of its objectives. This is particularly pertinent in Brazil, given the large size and complexity of its economy.

Brazil grew modestly compared to other major emerging economies during the period, and research suggests that growth was probably below its potential. Infrastructure bottlenecks in key sectors, particularly those associated with trade logistics, private investment affected by *Custo Brasil* and high interest rates, and low factor productivity growth due to modest pressures for competition may be factors constraining the achievement of that growth potential.

The Bank Group program addressed elements of those constraints. The issue is whether the Bank Group could have focused more on knowledge sharing and technical assistance that would have facilitated federal and subnational policies to identify more options in these areas. The Bank Group tried to achieve catalytic effects, particularly during the FY04–07 CAS, by supporting country-level regulatory reforms through broad policy operations, support to improve the quality of public investment, a major study on constraints to private sector participation in infrastructure investment, and a pilot study on the cost of doing business across states. The direct channel for countrywide catalytic effect was weakened during the second period, when the Bank shifted its focus from federal to subnational entities. A considerable amount of financing was provided for large urban and mass transit infrastructure in southeastern states. Although they were successful as projects, they had less obvious effects on relieving the key constraints to Brazil's competitiveness. This is also an area where private sector financing might have been able to play a stronger role. These projects increased the level of Bank exposure in Brazil, possibly at the expense of other activities with more potential to reduce infrastructure bottlenecks and mobilize private sector resources.

The shift toward multisector operations at the subnational level contributed to increasing private investment in infrastructure and reducing the cost of doing business in such places as the state of Minas Gerais and Rio de Janeiro Municipality. Some private participation in roads was facilitated by the Bank and IFC involvement in selected projects that set output-based management system and new performance standards requirements for road concessions. Important analytical work on how to reduce freight logistics costs was undertaken.

However, substantial gaps remain in financing of infrastructure, particularly in trade logistics. The progress in reducing the cost of doing business varies across states, and there was no follow-up to the countrywide regulatory study of 2007. The capacity of the public sector to plan and execute infrastructure investment is key to relieving the infrastructure bottleneck, but it remains a challenge. Overall, the Bank Group was not particularly effective in advancing the dialogue on regulatory reforms to reduce the *Custo Brasil,* the use of PPP in infrastructure, and the improvement in public investment quality.

The Bank undertook a number of important analytical works to examine factors behind the high interest rates and how the dual credit market influenced by directed credit may have affected the cost of credit to firms, particularly SMEs. However, given the limited scale of activities, the Bank's contributions in this area were likely modest. IFC's financial markets operation was dominated by short-term trade finance credits, even after the global crisis period. The effect of IFC's financial intermediation activities to support SMEs with longer-term credit is difficult to assess because of the issues in the definition of SMEs, design of legal documents, and monitoring that can better ensure that SMEs as typically defined are being reached.

Finally, the Bank has made few efforts to document the level of import protection in Brazil and how this may have reduced the pressures for competition and productivity improvement. Many areas under the competitive pillar were those where the interest on the side of the counterparts to involve the Bank Group in a collaborative effort is limited. Nevertheless, based on these assessments, this evaluation rates the performance of the Bank Group in this area as moderately unsatisfactory.

Sound Macroeconomic and Public Sector Management

Fiscal sustainability, anchored in strong institutions, reduces the vulnerability of the economy to shocks and helps achieve a smooth growth process. It also provides important signals to investors in a world of fluid capital mobility. Both are highly complementary to the objectives set in the Bank Group assistance strategy for Brazil. At a microeconomic and structural level, improved public expenditure management capable of selecting appropriate expenditure priorities and effectively monitoring expenditures can help address growth bottlenecks and increase the productivity of government resources. Because of the critical role of subnational governments in Brazil, these objectives are particularly relevant for those governments and in their relations with the federal government.

Bank assistance in macroeconomic and public sector management focused on areas where it is considered to have a comparative advantage. Strengthening fiscal sustainability, achieving more efficient public expenditure management, and enhancing results-based public sector management were at the heart of the Bank assistance in this area. These objectives were to be pursued at the federal and state levels. More than with any other objective discussed so far, the Bank had to adapt to changing external conditions and the evolution of the fiscal intragovernmental relations in Brazil. Thus, the assistance had to be highly adaptable.

CONTRIBUTING TO FISCAL SUSTAINABILITY

The FY04–07 CAS was conceived amid a strong macroeconomic program by the incoming administration based on three elements: a commitment to a primary surplus target of about 4 percent of GDP and consistent with a gradual reduction in the public debt-to-GDP ratio; an inflation targeting scheme to gradually reduce inflation; and a flexible exchange rate regime to help adjust to shocks while maintaining competitiveness.

Key to the consistency and success of this troika of policies was a strong fiscal program that could be sustained. It was also consistent with the goal of restoring growth and financing critical social spending. Thus, fiscal resources were at a premium, particularly during the first years of the period, and were a key concern in the design of the Bank assistance program. Hence, the financing strategy envisaged a high share of adjustment lending to the federal government—about 50 percent of total lending—with a strong degree of front loading. The strategy was based on the presumption of continuing progress in reduction of the public debt-to-GDP ratio, strengthening of fiscal rules and institutions, implementation of the Fiscal Responsibility Law, reduction in the level of earmarking, and implementation of social security reform.

The actual pattern of assistance matched the one outlined in the CAS. Total adjustment lending to the federal government amounted to about 55 percent of the $5 billion lending program during the CAS period. Front loading of adjustment lending was extensive, and the loans were extended in the years when financing was most needed. Brazil's macroeconomic achievement also broadly met expectations: inflation was reduced from

8.5 to 3.6 percent between 2002 and 2007, the public debt-to-GDP ratio was reduced by almost 10 percentage points, and foreign exchange indexed debt was basically eliminated. This macroeconomic resilience served Brazil well in confronting the 2008–09 global crises.

The major Bank activity in support of specific structural components of fiscal reform was assistance for pension reform. Imbalances in the pension system had emerged as a major threat to fiscal sustainability; the deficit of the total system as a share of GDP almost doubled over 1994–2004, from 3 to 5.6 percent of GDP. A constitutional amendment introduced in December 2003 addressed major areas requiring reforms, such as stricter rules for retirement in the public sector, adjustment to more sustainable benefit and indexation formulas, more realistic survivor pensions, the possibility for imposing an overall benefit ceiling subject to the creation of a complementary pension fund, and imposition of a tax on public sector workers. The reforms also implied a partial harmonization for the pay-as-you-go systems for the private and public sectors. The purpose of the reform package was to stabilize and, if possible, reduce pension expenditures and deficits and to move toward the harmonization of national and civil service pension schemes. The package also aimed to improve labor mobility between the private and public sectors and to allow provision of adequate pension benefits for the population on a sustainable basis.

The Bank operations consisted of closely coordinated lending, analytical work, and technical assistance. A DPL was approved in 2006 to support specific reform steps for both the public and private sector schemes. Significant background analytical and technical work was undertaken to simulate alternative scenarios and share lessons from other reform experience that could serve as inputs to the Brazilian authorities. At the local level the process was helped by three technical assistance loans for the preparation and implementation of the DPL. The technical assistance loans continued supporting the states and municipalities beyond the lifetime of the DPL, focusing on difficult but critical institutional steps of the pension reforms. They focused on assisting states in a cadastre upgrading program to eliminate unwarranted beneficiary payments. About 17 states are participating, somewhat below the original target of 24 states. Policy dialogue also remained active thereafter, taking advantage of the extensive analytical work undertaken.

In this area most indicators show a useful contribution by the Bank. Brazilian counterparts value highly the knowledge sharing, technical dialogue, and support at the local level. IEG's ICR Review considers the DPL and associated technical assistance activities an example of good design and relevance.

CONTRIBUTING TO A MORE EFFECTIVE BUDGET AND EXPENDITURE MANAGEMENT

Progress in the macroeconomic front and a favorable external environment during the mid-2000s helped improve the external and foreign exchange position of the federal government and reduced the need for budgetary support operations. The authorities increasingly gave attention to the quality of public spending given that the tax burden was already reaching levels of about 35 percent of GDP.

Activities at the Federal Level

At the federal level the Bank undertook some limited but important analytical activities that were useful in generating dialogue with the authorities. In 2005, a pilot program to achieve fiscal space for public investment was launched with the assistance of the International Monetary Fund to identify projects with a potential for high rates of return. The Bank participated in the project from its inception through an Institutional Development Fund grant as well as economic and sector work. In these efforts, the Bank focused on weaknesses in the public investment process that prevented Brazil from taking full advantage of the pilot program. The government subsequently announced its Growth Acceleration Program.

An important analytic activity examined several aspects of the trend and structure of public expenditures and identified possible reforms with potential to increase the contribution of that spending to growth (Weisman and Blanco 2007). The report suggests reducing earmarking to achieve greater flexibility to reallocate budget, reducing subsidies through public financial institutions, and enhancing participation of the private sector in infrastructure to complement the low levels of public investment. The Bank also did some informal analytical work on fiscal federalism and the challenges it presents in taxation, transfers, and subnational indebtedness and identified technical options to address some of these challenges.

Evolution toward Assisting Subnational Governments

The Fiscal Responsibility Law, approved in 2000, was starting to be implemented during the beginning of the evaluation period, providing the framework and rules for fiscal sustainability and borrowing to state government (Box 4.1). It also provided state governments with incentives to rationalize and reallocate expenditures. Given these considerations, the authorities requested the Bank to enhance support to state government in these areas. The result was a sharp shift toward operations providing budget support to states and municipalities (DPLs and SWAps) complying with the Fiscal Responsibility Law. These operations covered a wide range of cross-sectoral issues. States had to identify their policy and expenditure priorities consistent with budget constraints and the borrowing guidelines

BOX 4.1 Fiscal Responsibility Law

The Fiscal Responsibility Law established three types of fiscal rules:

• *General targets and limits* for selected fiscal indicators

• *Corrective institutional mechanisms* in case of noncompliance

• *Fiscal and penal sanctions* for noncompliance.

Targets are established on key indicators, aiming at ensuring fiscal sustainability through:

• *Fiscal austerity,* by conditioning that new recurrent expenditures be matched with new permanent revenue, by budgeting tax expenditures, by limiting personnel expenditures and credit operations, by not allowing rollover of unfunded expenditures to the next government period, by not allowing credit operations between federation entities to finance current expenditures or refinance standing debt (thereby eliminating hazard incentives to subnational governments), and by not allowing public financial institutions lending to their main shareholders

• *Fiscal consistency* over time, that is, between debt limits and primary surpluses

• *Integration of the budget preparation process* on a medium-term perspective

• *Transparency* by the periodic submission and publication of the "Relatório Resumido da Execução Orçamentária" and "Relatório de Gestão Fiscal," and enforcing a comprehensive monitoring of fiscal accounts.

In case of noncompliance with the targets established for the fiscal indicators, the Fiscal Responsibility Law provides correction mechanisms that the federation entities are obliged to adopt to recoup a sustainable path. For instance, if by the end of the fiscal period the personnel expenditure is found to be above the legal limit, the Fiscal Responsibility Law (art. 23) provides the rules that the entity has to follow in the next two four-month periods to adjust its fiscal stance. Noncompliance may imply severe sanctions (fiscal penalties), which can range from withholding federal transfers to denial of sovereign guarantees to credit or outright banning new borrowing by the faulty entity.

SOURCE: IEG.

of the law. To facilitate implementation, technical assistance accompanied these operations. These types of operations increased from less than $0.5 billion (8 percent of the lending program) to about $3.4 billion (30 percent of the lending program) between the two strategy periods, FY04–07 and FY08–11.

The state DPL and SWAp operations supported a wide range of policy and institutional reforms that state authorities considered priorities. Many of the sectoral reform components of these operations have been discussed earlier under sectoral sections. Because of their multisectoral nature, these operations were ideal vehicles to address major institutional reforms on the fiscal side that cut across sectors, particularly those requiring difficult steps and a consensus across agencies and different stakeholders. Many were necessary to comply with the Fiscal Responsibility Law and other reforms that were taken at the federal level, such as pension reform. In some cases, these operations allowed restructuring of the subnational debt. Reducing the cost of servicing that debt and extending maturities provided short-term fiscal space that facilitated such reforms.

Specific areas supported by these state-level operations include tax administration reforms to reduce tax evasion and provide better incentives for tax collectors, as well as pension reforms covering indexation, ceilings, and improvement of the registry of beneficiaries. Civil service census, certification of positions, and audits of state payrolls were also important actions taken to reduce current expenditures. Improvements in procurement procedures were emphasized in several operations. Results agreements with the different agencies and secretariats, including tracking of performance, together with efforts at implementing medium-term expenditure frameworks, were also prominent in some cases (Table 4.6).

Four of these operations have gone through review by IEG. In three of them—Rio Grande do Sul, the first Minas Gerais operation, and the first Rio State DPL—the fiscal and public sector management component of the operation was judged successful. This was not the case for the first Ceará operation, where the success of that component was judged as modest.

The officials in selected states interviewed by the evaluation team noted that the process of preparing these operations was highly useful as the Bank team had to harmonize project objectives with the government's priorities. It also encouraged state teams to interact with each other and face common trade-offs and budgetary constraints. The associated technical support activities were judged to have been critical to the success of the operations. Other knowledge-sharing activities, including sharing of experience on the operations between states, generated important externalities beyond the operation: officials judged seminars and workshops, training programs and courses, and visits within Brazil and abroad to have created important long-term benefits.

IEG interviews also revealed several areas that may need attention in future operations. The officials pointed out the need to avoid a proliferation of indicators and asserted that all indicators should be simple, well-defined, and focused on the essential goals of the program.

TABLE 4.6 Fiscal and Budget Management Measures Supported by State DPLs and SWAps

Project	Year Approved (Commitment)	Description
Alagoas Fiscal and Public Management Reform (DPL)	FY10 ($195.45 million)	Implement integrated data system to identify tax evasion and incentives schemes for collectors. Reforms of the procurement system. Complete civil service census and audit of state payroll, including pensioners. Implement gradual transition to a fully funded pension system combined with the previous system. Adopt federal legislation regarding benefit calculations and ceilings.
Ceará Multisector Social Inclusion Development (SWAp)	FY06 ($149.80 million)	Maintain debt/net current revenue not higher than 1.5. Improve external audit compliance with legal deadlines. Annual results-based management reports by secretariats validated by the State Secretary of Planning and output-based results for priority multiyear programs. Implementation of procurement reforms. Crossing state pension cadastres with federal database to identify irregularities.
Ceará Inclusive Growth SWAp (II)	FY09 ($240 million)	
Minas Gerais Partnership for Development (DPL)	FY06 ($170 million)	Target primary surplus and personal expenditure ratios as specified in the PAF. Reducing floating debt and increase computerization of tax systems. Improvement in procurement process and implementation of results agreements across agencies. Track performance in six state secretariats as specified in the results agreements. Certification of public sector positions.
Second Minas Gerais Development Partnership (SWAp)	FY08 ($976 million)	
(AF) Second Minas Gerais Development Partnership (SWAp)	FY10 ($461 million)	
Rio de Janeiro DPL	FY10 ($495 million)	Capitalization of pension system with oil-based revenues, electronic invoices to improve tax compliance and oversight, reorganization of the budget process including financial programming, and budgetary execution, introducing public timetable for tax invoice payments.

continued on page 82

Project	Year Approved (Commitment)	Description
Rio de Janeiro Municipality Fiscal Consolidation DPL	FY11 ($1,045 million)	Submit legislation consistent with the constitutional amendment regarding pension benefits, ceilings, and indexation. Reduce actuarial deficits resulting from recapitalization measures. Approval of results-based agreements with agencies and entities. Initiate implementation of medium-term expenditure framework.
RG do Sul Fiscal Sustainability DPL	FY09 ($1,100 million)	Increase primary surplus and reduce operating expenditures according to the PAF. Adoption of the tax substitution regime for the value-added tax and reduction of tax expenditures. Reforms of procurement systems. Reductions of debt-to-revenues ratios according to PAF. Submission of law creating complementary pension fund for new civil servants. Committee to control state-owned enterprise.

SOURCE: World Bank project documents.
NOTE: AF: additional financing; DPL = development policy loan; PAF = annual borrowing plan; SWAp = sectorwide approach.

They also suggested that cross-sectoral issue indicators should have precedence and that focus should be on realistic indicators and targets that are under the control of the executive authorities. Engagement of the relevant sectoral secretariat from the outset in defining the results indicators and technical assistance needs would likely increase their ownership of the program. Overall, it is important to seek a balance in implementation results between short-term policies (fiscal adjustment, debt restructuring) and structural reforms (state social security, civil service reform, public sector management, poverty reduction) and to boost implementation technical support to the latter. More information on the findings is available in Appendix H.

RATING THE MACROECONOMIC AND PUBLIC SECTOR MANAGEMENT

The objective of this pillar is very broad, and in a large country like Brazil, the outcomes are influenced by many factors that can predominate over the instruments that the Bank can deploy. Thus, the contribution of the Bank could only be catalytic either through engaging in sustained dialogue over a long period or fostering replication and dissemination of good practices. The Bank's technical work on pension reform is an example of knowledge sharing and dialogue over a sustained period. The work on local government finances and fiscal reforms for growth represented a good example of informal analytical work that encouraged a candid exchange of views in some critical areas.

The impact of the work with selected subnational government on institutional reforms to improve their fiscal systems and make them consistent with the Fiscal Responsibility Law could be expanded, if active knowledge sharing among subnational governments takes place. But replication and demonstration across states are not automatic and will take time. Progress so far has been positive, and the possibilities of replication may be significant (see Chapter 5). Based on these assessments, the contribution of the Bank in this area is judged to have been satisfactory.

Endnotes

[1] An earlier project that closed in 2002 and focused on railway restructuring achieved some success in reducing freight transport costs by restructuring and concessioning of operations to private operators.

[2] They followed earlier projects in those and several other metropolitan areas (Recife, Belo Horizonte, Salvador, and Fortaleza).

[3] São Paulo Metro Line 4 project is also included in the KPMG's 100 most innovative projects.

[4] The activities were funded by the PPIAF.

[5] The Energy Sector Technical Assistance Loan project also supported studies on the mineral sector.

[6] The Bank continues to engage in dialogue on sector policy and institutional issues through a technical assistance operation approved in FY12.

[7] Project ID 550527: Improving the Regulatory Environment in Brazil.

[8] More emphasis on monitoring has been placed in the second half of the assessment period when the Development Outcome Tracking System was put in place.

[9] IFC officially defines a small enterprise as one that qualifies for two of three indicators: (i) the number of employees of 10 or more and less than 50; (ii) total assets of $100,000 or more and less than $3 million; and (iii) total annual sales of $100,000 or more and less than $3 million. A medium enterprise is one that qualifies for two of three indicators: (i) the number of employees of 50 or more and less than 300; (ii) total assets of $3 million or more and less than $15 million; and (iii) total annual sales of $3 million or more and less than $15 million.

[10] IFC notes that the sub-borrower eligibility was established based on the company size classification used by local institutions such as BNDES and the Central Bank. According to the information provided by IFC, BNDES classifies companies up to R$300 million in sales as SMEs. The BNDES website indicates that it classifies companies with annual or annualized gross operating income higher than or equal to R$90 million and lower than or equal to R$300 million as medium-large companies, distinguishing them from medium-sized and smaller companies. Medium-sized companies are those with annual or annualized gross operating income higher than R$16 million and lower than or equal to R$90 million, which is more consistent with the definition of medium-sized companies as typically defined. IFC also indicated that the Central Bank classifies companies up to R$360 million in sales as SMEs.

References

Canuto, Otaviano, Matheus Cavallari, and José Guilherme Reis. 2013. "The Brazilian Competitiveness Cliff." *Economic Premise* 105.

De Gouvello, Christophe. 2009. *Brazil—Brazil's Energy Services Technical Assistance Loan (ESTAL): Lessons Learned: How Can We Improve the Effectiveness of Technical Assistance Loans?* Washington, DC: World Bank.

IEG (Independent Evaluation Group). 2004. *Brazil: Forging a Strategic Partnership for Results: An OED Evaluation of World Bank Assistance.* Washington, DC: World Bank.

——. 2008. "Implementation Completion Report Review—*Minas Gerais* Partnership for Development." World Bank, Washington, DC.

——. 2009a. "Implementation Completion Report Review—Financial Sector Technical Assistance Loan." World Bank, Washington, DC.

——. 2009b. "Implementation Completion Report Review—Second Programmatic Sustainable and Equitable Growth Loan." World Bank, Washington, DC.

——. 2013. *Evaluation of the International Finance Corporation's Global Trade Finance Program, 2006–12.* Washington, DC: World Bank.

IFC (International Finance Corporation). 2006. *Doing Business in Brazil.* Washington, DC: World Bank.

——. 2010. *Scaling Up SME Access to Financial Services in the Development World.* Washington, DC: World Bank.

IMF (International Monetary Fund). 2012. "Brazil: Financial System Stability Assessment." IMF, Washington, DC.

Rebelo, Jorge. 2012. "How to Decrease Freight Logistics Costs in Brazil." Transport Paper, World Bank, Washington, DC.

Weisman, Ethan, and Fernando Blanco. 2007. "Brazil—Improving Fiscal Circumstances for Growth." *En breve* 104.

World Bank. 2007. *How to Revitalize Infrastructure Investments in Brazil (Public Policies for Better Private Participation).* FPSI/LAC Report #36624BR, World Bank, Washington, DC.

——. 2008. *International Bank for Reconstruction and Development and International Finance Corporation Country Partnership Strategy for the Federative Republic of Brazil for the Period FY2008–2011.* Washington, DC: World Bank.

——. 2011. *International Bank for Reconstruction and Development and International Finance Corporation Country Partnership Strategy for the Federative Republic of Brazil for the Period FY2012–2015.* Washington, DC: World Bank.

——. 2012. *The Real Paradox: Untangling Credit Market Outcomes in Brazil.* Washington, DC: World Bank.

——. 2013. *Doing Business 2013: Smarter Regulations for Small and Medium-Size Enterprises.* Washington, DC: World Bank.

5 Emerging Messages and Recommendations

Overall, the outcome of the Bank Group assistance to Brazil was moderately satisfactory, although with some important synergies and variability across pillars. For example, the multisectoral SWAp model generated synergies across pillars and made significant contributions to the development of the Program-for-Results lending instrument—one of the Bank's key corporate-level efforts to improve its operational effectiveness. As for variability across pillars, assistance for equitable Brazil was judged satisfactory, while assistance on competitiveness was judged less than satisfactory. Outcomes also varied within pillars, which provides valuable information from which to draw lessons and recommendations (see Appendix I for the summary assessment by pillars).

One question that emerges regarding the overall strategy was whether the use of a few very large operations (metro and urban rail projects and the sustainable economic management DPL totaling $3 billion) with high opportunity cost relative to the IBRD exposure limit was appropriate. The metro and urban rail projects had clear benefits, but alternative sources of financing might have been available; the SEM DPL was not the proper instrument, given the objectives at hand.

Emerging Messages

The Bank Group had significant impact in Brazil when it served as a trusted partner to think through evolving policy issues that Brazilian counterparts were tackling. In its support for *Bolsa Familia*, improving learning outcomes in education, pension reforms, and reducing the pace of deforestation, the Bank provided timely analytical inputs and technical assistance to address urgent needs. In Minas Gerais, the Bank worked with the state government to operationalize the results management system. IFC's advisory support for structuring PPP projects in partnership with BNDES effectively delivered global expertise in project financing. The sharing of specific global experiences relevant to Brazil was particularly valued by the Brazilian authorities as a unique contribution of the Bank Group.

The Bank Group has also made important contributions by creating a platform where diverse stakeholders can examine issues that cut across organizational and sectoral boundaries. This is particularly important when facing trade-offs that involve collective action and resolution. The Bank was instrumental in convening various stakeholders to discuss a standardized approach to water resource management at the federal and regional level. Arguably the largest contribution of the successful series of multisector SWAps in Ceará was the regular intersectoral meetings to discuss expenditure priorities, monitor progress of activities in various parts of the government, creating synergies, and raising awareness of dependencies among sectoral departments.

Typically these interventions generated long-lasting benefits as their effects evolved and matured beyond the lifetime of the intervention. The benefits can also be replicated across states and municipalities. Assistance to *Bolsa Familia*, pension reforms, and water systems had long-term and countrywide impact, and multisectoral SWAps had important effects at the state level. The pilot work on classroom dynamics, though taking place in a few localities, may over time generate critical knowledge of high relevance at the national level.

SUBNATIONAL FOCUS

The focus on subnational clients will continue, given the strong demand for Bank financial and knowledge support among states and municipalities, limited needs for financing at the federal level, and the federal authorities' strong support for subnational lending by the Bank. During the period evaluated, the Bank supported the priorities defined in the dialogue involving the highest level of the subnational authorities—in some cases those priorities emerged through a longstanding relationship that spanned many years, as in Ceará. The Bank coordinated with the federal authorities to ensure that its support was consistent with the framework governing the relationship between the federal and subnational governments, most importantly the Fiscal Responsibility Law. Based on these considerations, as well as the assessments of the commitment for and capacity to implement the agreed activity, the Bank developed its subnational portfolio.

This shift to subnational support has been a success for the Bank. It enabled the Bank to provide customized support to a wide variety of state and municipality challenges. It also helped the Bank remain relevant in Brazil by establishing a mechanism to respond to strong demand for Bank financing and knowledge among subnational governments. The Bank and IFC, with support from the federal authorities, have also been working to direct their operational focus on the north and northeast regions during this period. Progress has been made, although the largest share of Bank lending commitments went to the richer southeast region because of the size of the economies there and sustained dialogue with the Bank over years. The constraint in institutional capacity is particularly relevant in these regions. For IFC, identifying the right investment opportunities was challenging during the period evaluated.

The continuing focus on subnational clients may require identifying specific measures to encourage replication. Eventually, the accumulation of subnational experience may be able to influence countrywide development. The Bank Group has successfully induced such a catalytic process, but the strategy can be further refined. In particular, the Bank Group has yet to identify specific vehicles to facilitate and encourage the replication of positive results achieved in one subnational entity to others.

COMPETITIVENESS

There are also several areas with significant potential for catalytic impact but where the Bank Group has not been particularly effective. Most of these areas are in the competitiveness pillar: addressing bottlenecks in infrastructure, particularly in logistics, and the cost of doing business—areas that represent a major constraint to growth and an increasing preoccupation of the authorities. Several Bank documents have also identified a weak environment for competition as a major challenge.

Given the already high tax burden and competing demands for public spending, an improved public investment process and a modern regulatory framework that provides incentives for private sector investment in infrastructure are priorities for Brazil. Although the Bank Group has achieved some success through IFC support for structuring PPP projects in collaboration with BNDES and in selected state DPL and SWAp operations, significant challenges remain. The Bank and IFC have accumulated experience in different aspects of private participation in infrastructure investment; opportunities for synergies through knowledge exchange may exist in this area. Apart from a few successful cases in the water sector, very little else was done to explore this possibility during the period evaluated. Demonstrating the value of Bank Group collaboration in Brazil remains a challenge for the future.

The country strategies and a body of literature on Brazil's economic growth also recognize the need to address the high cost of doing business. Although some analytical efforts and advisory services have been made, for example, in documenting the variability of this cost across states, the Bank Group has been unable to make a noticeable difference. Similarly, the importance of keeping an open trade regime and its impact on the competitive environment has been raised in the country strategies. So far, little analytical work has been done to document the extent of import protection (and its variance) in Brazil. A common thread in these areas seems to be a limited interest on the side of the counterparts to involve the Bank Group in a collaborative effort.

A challenge for the Brazil country strategy is to maintain flexibility in responding to evolving client demand while ensuring a level of specificity that makes it a meaningful guide for operations. Achieving flexibility by defining very wide objectives over many areas—a "just-in-case approach," in which the Bank Group puts on the table all development issues—could serve both the Brazilian authorities and the Bank Group well in a rapidly changing environment. However, an excessively flexible framework could result in pursuing only the outcomes that receive traction from the main counterpart, leaving out other areas even if their importance for overall development is recognized. (Appendix J identifies some instances where CAS outcome indicators were modified midway in the progress report without a clear justification for the changes.) It also risks weakening the Bank Group's credibility because it could be perceived to have too many institutional objectives and to need better understanding of country challenges. The challenge is to find a balance between flexibility and a strategic vision based on realistic assumptions. For this, a strong and candid consultation with the authorities during the CAS design process is critical.

The country strategies examined in this evaluation included numerous objectives that covered a very wide range of development issues in Brazil. These objectives were often set high in the results chain, far removed from the Bank Group points of intervention. Setting high-level objectives clarifies the strategic direction of the program and helps align individual efforts toward results that can only be achieved through leveraging the linkages between interventions. However, achieving those objectives depends on many factors outside the control of the Bank Group; hence, specifying how Bank Group activities could lead to the intended outcomes requires strong assumptions about catalytic effects and external factors. This is particularly relevant when the size of Bank Group operations is small relative to the size of the economy, as in Brazil. The critical issue with the absence of a clear results chain is that it hampers ex post evaluation and thus learning from experience.

Self-evaluation has the potential to provide useful learning, but significant variability exists in the analyses presented in the CASCRs reviewed for this evaluation. The CASCRs of the FY00–03 and FY04–08 periods are candid in recognizing both successes and shortcomings, providing critical perspectives of program results. In the FY08–11 CASCR, there is less elaboration of problems encountered. Increasing candor in self-evaluation is important for learning from experience.

MIDDLE-INCOME COUNTRIES

Some of the findings of this evaluation may be relevant to the Bank Group work in middle-income countries generally. Many middle-income countries have good access to the international financial markets and well-established fiscal or quasifiscal tools to finance their development activities. They also have advanced institutions and a high level of human capital. In these countries, Bank Group financial contributions are marginal and its knowledge services add value only when they bring perspectives that are not available in the country. The Bank Group is mostly a catalyst that triggers replication and synergies to generate impacts larger than a single intervention. From the experience in Brazil, the IBRD and IFC have a comparative advantage in sharing lessons from cross-country experiences in areas of interest to the authorities.

Focusing on geographical areas that are less developed would also be relevant. Many middle-income countries have significant regional differences in the level of poverty and strength of institutions. The need for financial and technical assistance is greatest in the areas that are falling behind in various aspects of development. The value of Bank Group support that embodies practical know-how would be high, although the challenges in achieving results would also be greater than in well-off regions.

The "just-in-case" approach noted earlier epitomizes a challenge in working with middle-income countries. Country programs need to combine the flexibility that allows for responding to demands as they emerge and the medium-term strategy that encompasses issues with limited traction from the client in the short-term. This is a difficult balance, but it can be struck through strong, candid dialogue with the relevant authorities as well as candor in self-evaluation.

The nature of engagement also depends on the administrative links between the local and central government. Hence, the lessons in Brazil need to be interpreted in a particular context of countries with a federal system. For Bank Group engagement in federal states, the experience with multisectoral operations—SWAps and DPLs—at the subnational level can be particularly relevant. These operations can contribute to intersectoral dialogue and help resolve trade-offs of a cross-sectoral nature through involving the highest authorities at the regional level and fostering subnational government ownership. Strong institutional capacity for coordination and results monitoring is essential for success in these operations—requirements often fulfilled in advanced middle-income countries. In Brazil, the Fiscal Responsibility Law provided an effective incentive framework for reform.

Finally, middle-income countries have more access to international capital flows, but the flip side is that they can also face unexpected reversal in such flows. It would be prudent for the Bank Group to maintain some lending space to respond to unanticipated shocks, particularly to support the sectors and population groups that are most vulnerable to those shocks.

Recommendations

These issues are particularly relevant as the demand for Bank Group operations remains strong, particularly with regard to subnational entities. A single borrower limit for Bank lending may also become binding in the near future. Cautious management of Brazil's exposure level would suggest keeping some room to maneuver in case domestic or external shocks call for a rapid countercyclical increase in Bank lending. Thus, leveraging results from lending is more important than ever. The crucial criteria for lending should be interventions that are highly catalytic per dollar loaned. Priorities should be based on their externalities, knowledge sharing, and prospects for demonstration effects and replicability. Synergies among lending, AAA, technical assistance, and Bank Group–wide collaborations need to be explored and maximized. Proliferation of activities should be avoided. The need for leveraging is further pronounced for IFC and MIGA, given the smaller size of their portfolios in Brazil.

The Bank Group program should focus on areas where it has comparative advantage—mainly its ability to examine and discuss issues and trade-offs across sectors and themes. The Bank Group has also been effective in facilitating the dialogue among stakeholders to discuss trade-offs and identify solutions. Hence, areas where there are an important element of public good and calls for collective action are particularly suitable. Given the size of Brazil, these activities are more manageable in the context of assisting subnational governments—a point recognized by both the authorities and the Bank.

There are also activities that fit the above criteria less than others. For the Bank, very large projects relative to total exposure, producing services with an important element of cost recovery, and sponsored by agencies or states that are perceived as creditworthy are less obvious activities to finance. Sometimes the Bank's financial involvement brings with it knowledge sharing and technical assistance activities, which would lead to broad-based institutional strengthening. In such a case, the financing and knowledge component could be unbundled—with the Bank focusing mostly on the latter.

The Bank estimates that Brazil's GDP grew by 0.9 percent in 2012, and its latest forecast for growth in 2013 is 2.9 percent (World Bank 2013)—both numbers substantially below the average growth rate of 4.25 percent achieved between 2004 and 2011. As Brazil faces the possibility of lower growth and less favorable global economic conditions, the importance of ensuring the effectiveness of Bank Group operations is growing. Moreover, increased quality of public services and expenditures will remain priorities in coming years. For the Bank Group to remain a valuable partner in addressing these challenges, this evaluation makes the following recommendations.

1. Use the potential for wider catalytic effects as one of the main criteria for selecting the sectors and subnational entities with which to engage. In selecting programs and projects to support in future strategies, the Bank Group should focus on areas where it has comparative advantage and can expect to generate benefits beyond the individual intervention. To identify the combination of Bank Group instruments that can enhance catalytic effects, the results chain must be identified that links individual interventions and objectives, and the intermediate goals need to be specified. This could also help avoid proliferation of objectives and increase selectivity.

Within the FY12–15 CPS, several areas seem to fit these criteria. For example, the continued emphasis on northeast Brazil provides operational focus. Of particular importance is assisting the efforts to develop the capacity to screen, select, and appraise public sector projects, reduce *Custo Brasil,* and strengthen the institutional and regulatory framework for PPP, particularly in infrastructure. Many of these interventions could have a subnational focus that could be followed up with efforts to encourage replication.

The Bank has developed a comparative advantage in several areas that are also of interest to the Brazilian authorities. Assistance in the design and implementation of *Brasil sem Miseria* and further strengthening *Bolsa Familia*—particularly in monitoring and impact evaluation—is a case in point. Potential for catalytic effects could be high in supporting pilot projects in ECD and disseminating the knowledge developed about how classroom dynamics influence students' learning outcomes.

One of the most important contributions of the Bank program was the development of a multisectoral model, as most successfully demonstrated in Ceará and Minas Gerais. Even when operations are not multisectoral by design, the Bank's convening role has proved effective where aspects of multiple sectors intersect, for example, in water resource management. Given the promising results, the Bank should continue pursuing opportunities for such an engagement, incorporating lessons from experience. Some of these lessons are that coordination across sector departments within the government is crucial for success and that the capacity of the counterpart authorities to promote collaboration across sectoral boundaries is key. In addition, the success in multisectoral operations depends much on the degree of ownership of the program by these authorities. More important, the activities that cut across sectors sometimes involve difficult trade-offs and political decisions; thus, involvement of the leadership at the highest level is important.

Given the strong demand for Bank Group support in states and municipalities, the Brazil country program will continue to focus on supporting subnational clients. To further enhance the leverage and catalytic effect of subnational operations, the Bank Group should identify ways to encourage the replication and demonstration effects of positive results achieved in one subnational entity or regions in others.

2. Enhance lending and nonlending support for improvement in the quality of public investment and the enabling environment for private sector investment. This could be done through a combination of financial support as well as knowledge and advisory services. Because the room for expansion in public spending is limited, it is important to continue undertaking various analytical work to identify the constraints to private participation in infrastructure investments and reduce the cost of doing business. Equally important would be new avenues through which the Bank could work with the federal and subnational governments to strengthen their capacity for public investment planning and project selection.

Given that both the IBRD and IFC have accumulated knowledge on private participation in infrastructure, this is an area where synergies from Bank Group collaboration can be usefully explored. For example, IBRD could help improve regulatory frameworks at the state and federal level, with IFC inputs based on its experience in structuring specific projects, which could then be followed up by an expansion of PPP transactions with IFC support. If necessary, this could be done by focusing on states that are particularly interested in attracting private investment—ideally to be replicated later in other states. The ongoing and future analytical work on private participation in infrastructure investments could provide impetus to this work. Similarly, IFC's diagnostic work and advisory services on business environment could provide inputs into the Bank's work on ways to address the cost of doing business. MIGA could also offer guarantees that would facilitate private sector participation in infrastructure investments. For that, MIGA needs to strengthen its business development capacity.

3. Continue to promote sustainable rural development, taking advantage of the opportunities presented by the new Forest Code. Brazil's recently adopted Forest Code provides a new framework for strengthening the harmonization of conservation, development, and poverty reduction. Brazil will face economic and institutional challenges in implementing the Code's provisions. These include completing a universal rural environmental cadastre in the near term and finding productive, cost-effective, and environmentally beneficial ways for private landholders to comply with forest reserve obligations under the Code. Building on past and ongoing work, the Bank and IFC should be prepared to offer technical and financial assistance, as required, to help meet

the challenges of implementing the new Forest Code in a way that is cost-effective, poverty-reducing, and environmentally sound.

4. Enhance dialogue with authorities and think tanks to identify policy issues where the Bank Group could provide timely knowledge and advisory support. **Knowledge** activities are areas where the Bank Group can have important positive externalities and catalytic effects per dollar loaned and per dollar of Bank budget resources. The Bank's managerial focus, staff incentives, and internal resource allocation need to ensure sufficient budgetary resource allocation to enable high-quality knowledge activities with potential for catalytic impact.

This, however, should not mean undermining the role of lending. Experience shows that value often comes from a combination of lending and knowledge support: several counterpart officials have pointed to the significance of learning that takes place during project implementation. The Bank Group was effective when it sustained close interactions during implementation, as in the case of its support for *Bolsa Familia* and multisectoral programs in Ceará and Minas Gerais. IFC's advisory support for PPP project structuring is also associated with providing "how-to" advice on during implementation. The effort is rather in search of an optimal mix of lending and knowledge support, acknowledging that the emphasis on knowledge may have to intensify, given the constraints in lending.

The findings of this evaluation show that the Bank Group can provide unique perspectives on issues that the authorities need to tackle in the short run, particularly if provided in a timely basis. The ability to engage and have a candid dialogue at both the federal and subnational levels will be important for identifying the issues of immediate interest for the relevant authorities. Strengthening of regular dialogue with various think tanks, such as the Institute of Applied Economic Research, would likely bring in further insights in this respect.

5. Continue analytical work on selected topics with important long-term implications, even though traction with the authorities may be limited in the short term. The focus on issues that have short-term value should be balanced with continued work on issues of significance to Brazil over the medium term. This would help avoid the risk of adopting an excessively flexible strategy that could result in pursuing only the outcomes that receive strong traction from the main counterparts, leaving out areas recognized as important for overall long-term development. The authorities may consider the longer-term matters less urgent either because they are not needed for inputs to policymaking or because

they involve difficult political trade-offs. Even so, the Bank Group would be advised to continuously undertake some minimum analytical work in these areas to balance the flexibility in operational response with the stability in the strategic directions of the program.

In this evaluation, several such issues have been identified, particularly in competitiveness, where sustained analytical efforts are especially relevant. For example, a review of Brazil's experiences with concessions in different sectors to extract lessons would benefit the Bank and IFC support to PPPs. An assessment of institutional and regulatory constraints affecting public agencies in the planning, selection, and execution of public sector investment projects could help improve the quality of public investments. Analyses of the experience with direct credit and the implications of the open trade regime could shed light on medium-term efforts to enhance competitive environment.

In this context, continued strengthening of networks with Brazilian think tanks and institutions would be beneficial. It would also be useful to broaden knowledge exchange among development partners in Brazil, given that the need to seek catalytic effects is common across these organizations. It would also allow the Bank Group to keep updated on critical long-term development issues, balancing the operational focus on practical policy applications in the short term.

6a. Expand IFC's work on PPPs. IFC has added significant value in its support for PPP project structuring, and demand remains high for innovative projects that can be replicated and scaled up elsewhere in Brazil. Thus, the PPP collaboration with BNDES could be expanded further. The expansion of PPP projects in Brazil depends critically on the enabling regulatory environment and its predictability. This link provides an area for close collaboration between the IFC and the Bank as noted earlier.

IFC should also pursue further expansion of direct investment in infrastructure projects and project sponsors. IFC's direct investments in infrastructure and public service delivery have the potential to transfer nonrecourse and limited-recourse project financing as well as its environment and social standards—the skill that is highly needed in Brazil to broaden private participation in infrastructure investment. As its work in the water sector has shown, involving Bank sector experts for technical advice, particularly in areas where IFC is entering with limited past experience, would be useful.

6b. Enhance the design and targeting of IFC's activities to expand SMEs' access to long-term financing. IFC has pursued its strategic objective of supporting SMEs through financial intermediation via second-tier banks. To make this program more effective, IEG suggests several courses of action. First, the high levels of short-term trade finance guarantees triggered by the global financial crisis in 2008–09 should now be rebalanced by shifting the emphasis toward the expansion of long-term loan and equity financing, where the SMEs face a strong constraint. Second, the present definition of sub-borrowers includes enterprises that are far larger than those typically considered as SMEs. This needs to be modified to increase precision in targeting SMEs.

Reference

World Bank. 2013. *Global Economic Prospects. Volume 7, June 2013*. Washington, DC: World Bank.

Appendix A
World Bank Group Strategies: 1995–2003

The World Bank Group strategy during 1995 and 2003 had to take into account a major development—the Bank Group was rapidly becoming a less important source of finance for Brazil—a decline from 12.4 percent of total debt financing in 1990–94 to 4.5 percent at the end of the decade, including the International Finance Corporation (IFC) (IEG 2004).[1] Assistance focused on areas where a maximum impact on poverty could be expected—the social sectors and social protection—and on the poorest states, including northeast Brazil. Lending directly to these states and municipalities was also a way to complement the 1988 Constitution, which gave regional governments a mandate to provide key public services.

The Bank expanded its lending to Brazil between 1995 and 2003 with a noticeable shift toward adjustment lending. The success in stabilization led to improvement in the quality of the portfolio and a stronger rationale for increased lending. The government became progressively more engaged in the elaboration of the assistance strategy, and the decentralization of the Country Management Unit to Brasilia in 1997 facilitated policy dialogue. Since 1997, the country strategy has been prepared jointly by the International Bank for Reconstruction and Development (IBRD) (the World Bank) and IFC.

The significant expansion of Bank investment lending in this period was led by efforts to deal with rural poverty through community-driven approaches, mainly in the northeastern states. The Bank also supported projects in poor regions that aimed to improve school management and quality and improve delivery of health care. In infrastructure, the Bank assisted the federal government in the development of regulatory frameworks and agencies in the energy and water sectors; the lending was largest in the transportation sector. IFC started investing in infrastructure, primarily in ports and roads. The Multilateral Investment Guarantee Agency (MIGA), which started operations in Brazil in 1994, provided guarantees on foreign investments mostly in infrastructure. The Bank also started to provide support for the stabilization effort, particularly in addressing fiscal imbalances at the federal and state levels. The Bank initiated policy dialogue with several states and provided four loans that supported the privatization of banks and several infrastructure enterprises owned by the states.

After the 1997 Asian crisis and the 1998 Russian crisis, Bank Group strategies in Brazil stressed the need to avoid economic stagnation and rising poverty. The government's commitment for critical reforms and the increased difficulty in ensuring counterpart funds for investment lending due to fiscal tightening led to a significant shift to adjustment lending.[2] The support to infrastructure was scaled down to make room for adjustment lending and to maintain support to the social sectors.

The Independent Evaluation Group (IEG) previously evaluated World Bank assistance in Brazil between 1990 and 2002 (IEG 2004). That evaluation rated the program satisfactory. IEG found that Bank support for poverty alleviation produced satisfactory results, in particular through important contributions to education and health. The effort to help stimulate private investment efficiency and growth produced mixed results: the Bank strategy was reasonable, but it did not succeed in increasing savings and investment or in removing key bottlenecks. The strategy for ensuring environment sustainability was initially rigid but improved later and made a satisfactory contribution. Finally, adjustment lending had an effect in reforming on public finances.

In this evaluation, IEG concluded that the macroeconomic stability and minimum political stability that allows the government to articulate a minimum program of reforms is critical for Bank Group assistance. It stressed the importance of the social security system in maintaining fiscal stability and creating fiscal space for much needed investments. Continuing support to education was considered important, particularly for the quality of teaching in poorer states and for monitoring student learning. Early childhood development and nutrition were identified as priorities, and maternal mortality remained a challenge. As public finance management at the subnational level remained weak, the evaluation recommended that the Bank identify ways to assist in these areas. The report also suggested that the Bank strengthen support to private sector development—the judiciary was found to be a major bottleneck and assistance to the regulatory agencies at the state level could help improve the environment for private investment.

The Bank's self-assessment of the FY00 Country Assistance Strategy (CAS Completion Report) covered operations through the end of FY03 and provided additional insight. The assessment found that the Bank assistance was in line with government goals and its role was satisfactory. The main success area was poverty reduction through interventions in health and education; social protection had less success, although the Bank did produce some important analytical and advisory activities (AAA) in that area. The use of sectorwide approaches

(SWAps) in health also seems to have been successful. The major area where outcomes were below expectations was growth. The report explicitly acknowledged that the Bank program had failed to mobilize growth. It states that the authorities and the Bank expected private investment would meet infrastructure need, which did not happen.

Endnotes

[1] The figure includes IBRD, IFC own account, and IFC B-loans.

[2] The shift was also a response to a government complaint that the Bank had been inconsistent—advocating fiscal adjustment at the macroeconomic level while pressing for project lending at the sectoral and state levels.

Reference

IEG (Independent Evaluation Group). 2004. *Brazil: Forging a Strategic Partnership for Results: An OED Evaluation of World Bank Assistance*. Washington, DC: World Bank.

Appendix B
Guide to IEG's Country Program Evaluation Methodology

This methodological note describes the key elements of IEG's Country Program evaluation (CPE) methodology.[1]

▶ CPEs rate the outcomes of World Bank Group assistance programs, not the country's overall development progress.

A World Bank Group assistance program needs to be assessed on how well it met its particular objectives, which are typically a subset of the country's development objectives. If a Bank Group assistance program is large in relation to the country's total development effort, the program outcome should be similar to the country's overall development progress. However, most Bank Group assistance programs provide only a fraction of the total resources devoted to a country's development by development partners, stakeholders, and the government itself. In CPEs, IEG rates only the outcome of the Bank Group's program, not the country's overall development outcome, although the latter is clearly relevant for judging the program's outcome.

The experience gained in CPEs confirms that Bank Group program outcomes sometimes diverge significantly from the country's overall development progress. CPEs have identified Bank Group assistance programs that had:

• Satisfactory outcomes matched by good country development

• Unsatisfactory outcomes in countries which achieved good overall development results, notwithstanding the weak Bank Group program

• Satisfactory outcomes in countries which did not achieve satisfactory overall results during the period of program implementation.

▶ Assessments of assistance program outcome and Bank Group performance are not the same.

By the same token, an unsatisfactory Bank Group assistance program outcome does not always mean that Bank Group performance was also unsatisfactory, and vice versa. This becomes clearer in considering that the Bank Group's contribution to the outcome of its assistance program is only part of the story. The assistance program's outcome is determined by the *joint* impact of four agents: (i) the country; (ii) the Bank Group; (iii) partners and other stakeholders; and (iv) exogenous forces (for example, events of nature, international economic shocks, and so forth). Under the right circumstances, a negative contribution from any one agent might overwhelm the positive contributions from the other three and lead to an unsatisfactory outcome.

IEG measures Bank Group performance primarily on the basis of contributory actions the Bank Group directly controlled. Judgments regarding Bank Group performance typically consider the relevance and implementation of the strategy, the design and supervision of the Bank Group's lending and financial support interventions, the scope, quality and follow-up of diagnostic work and other AAA, the consistency of the Bank Group's lending and financial support with its nonlending work and with its safeguard policies, and the Bank Group's partnership activities.

Rating Assistance Program Outcome

In rating the outcome (expected development impact) of an assistance program, IEG gauges the extent to which major strategic objectives were relevant and achieved, without any shortcomings. In other words, did the Bank Group do the right thing, and did it do it right? Programs typically express their goals in terms of higher-order objectives, such as poverty reduction. The Country Assistance Strategy (CAS) may also establish intermediate goals, such as improved targeting of social services or promotion of integrated rural development, and specify how they are expected to contribute toward achieving the higher-order objective. IEG's task is then to validate whether the intermediate objectives were the right ones and whether they produced satisfactory net benefits, as well as whether the results chain specified in the CAS was valid. Where causal linkages were not fully specified in the CAS, it is the evaluator's task to reconstruct this causal chain from the available evidence and assess relevance, efficacy, and outcome with reference to the intermediate and higher-order objectives.

For each of the main objectives, the CPE evaluates the relevance of the objective; the relevance of the Bank Group's strategy toward meeting the objective, including the balance between lending and nonlending instruments; the efficacy with which the strategy was implemented; and the results achieved. This is done in two steps. The first is a top-down review of whether the Bank Group's program achieved a particular Bank Group objective or planned outcome and had a substantive impact on the country's development. The second step is a bottom-up review of the Bank Group's products and services (lending, AAA, and aid coordination) used to achieve the objective. Together these two steps test the consistency of findings from the products and services and the development impact dimensions. Subsequently, IEG makes an assessment of the relative contribution to the results achieved by the Bank Group, other development partners, the government and exogenous factors.

Evaluators also assess the degree of country ownership of international development priorities, such as the Millennium Development Goals, and Bank Group corporate advocacy priorities, such as safeguards. Ideally, any differences on dealing with these issues would be identified and resolved by the CAS, enabling the evaluator to focus on whether the trade-offs adopted were appropriate. However, in other instances, the strategy may be found to have glossed over certain conflicts, or avoided addressing key country development constraints. In either case, the consequences could include a diminution of program relevance, a loss of country ownership, and/or unwelcome side-effects, such as safeguard violations, all of which must be taken into account in judging program outcome.

Ratings Scale

IEG utilizes six rating categories for **outcome,** ranging from highly satisfactory to highly unsatisfactory:

Highly satisfactory:	The assistance program achieved at least acceptable progress toward all major relevant objectives, and had best practice development impact on one or more of them. No major shortcomings were identified.
Satisfactory:	The assistance program achieved acceptable progress toward all major relevant objectives. No best practice achievements or major shortcomings were identified.
Moderately satisfactory:	The assistance program achieved acceptable progress toward most of its major relevant objectives. No major shortcomings were identified.
Moderately unsatisfactory:	The assistance program did not make acceptable progress toward most of its major relevant objectives, or made acceptable progress on all of them, but either (i) did not take into adequate account a key development constraint or (ii) produced a major shortcoming, such as a safeguard violation.

Unsatisfactory:	The assistance program did not make acceptable progress toward most of its major relevant objectives, and either (i) did not take into adequate account a key development constraint or (ii) produced a major shortcoming, such as a safeguard violation.
Highly unsatisfactory:	The assistance program did not make acceptable progress toward any of its major relevant objectives and did not take into adequate account a key development constraint, while also producing at least one major shortcoming, such as a safeguard violation.

The **institutional development impact** can be rated at the project level as *high, substantial, modest,* or *negligible.* This measures the extent to which the program bolstered the country's ability to make more efficient, equitable and sustainable use of its human, financial, and natural resources. Examples of areas included in judging the institutional development impact of the program are:

• The soundness of economic management

• The structure of the public sector, and, in particular, the civil service

• The institutional soundness of the financial sector

• The soundness of legal, regulatory, and judicial systems

• The extent of monitoring and evaluation systems

• The effectiveness of aid coordination

• The degree of financial accountability

• The extent of building capacity in nongovernmental organizations

• The level of social and environmental capital.

However, IEG increasingly factors institutional development impact ratings into program outcome ratings, rather than rating them separately.

Sustainability can be rated at the project level as *highly likely, likely, unlikely, highly unlikely,* or, if available information is insufficient, *nonevaluable.* Sustainability measures the resilience to risk of the development benefits of the country program over time, taking into account eight factors:

• Technical resilience

• Financial resilience (including policies on cost recovery)

- Economic resilience

- Social support (including conditions subject to safeguard policies)

- Environmental resilience

- Ownership by governments and other key stakeholders

- Institutional support (including a supportive legal/regulatory framework, and organizational and management effectiveness)

- Resilience to exogenous effects, such as international economic shocks or changes in the political and security environments.

At the program level, IEG is increasingly factoring sustainability into program outcome ratings, rather than rating them separately.

Risk to development outcome. According to the 2006 harmonized guidelines, sustainability has been replaced with a "risk to development outcome," defined as the risk, at the time of evaluation, that development outcomes (or expected outcomes) of a project or program will not be maintained (or realized). The risk to development outcome can be rated at the project level as *high, significant, moderate, negligible to low,* and *nonevaluable.*

Endnote

[1] In this context, *assistance program* refers to products and services generated in support of the economic development of a country over a specified period.

Appendix C
Reference Tables

TABLE C.1 Brazil at a Glance

4/2/12

	Brazil	Latin America & Carib	Upper Middle Income
Key Development Indicators (2010)			
Population, mid-year (millions)	194.9	583	2,452
Surface area (thousand sq km)	8,515	20,394	59,328
Population growth (%)	0.9	1.1	0.7
Urban population (% of total population)	87	79	57
GNI (Atlas method, $ billions)	1,830.4	4,505	14,429
GNI per capita (Atlas method, $)	9,390	7,733	5,884
GNI per capita (PPP, international $)	11,000	10,926	9,970
GDP growth (%)	7.5	6.2	7.8
GDP per capita growth (%)	6.6	5.0	7.1
(most recent estimate, 2004–10)			
Poverty headcount ratio at $1.25 a day (PPP, %)	6	6	—
Poverty headcount ratio at $2.00 a day (PPP, %)	11	12	—
Life expectancy at birth (years)	73	74	73
Infant mortality (per 1,000 live births)	17	18	17
Child malnutrition (% of children under 5)	2	3	3
Adult literacy, male (% of ages 15 and older)	90	92	96
Adult literacy, female (% of ages 15 and older)	90	90	91
Gross primary enrollment, male (% of age group)	132	119	111
Gross primary enrollment, female (% of age group)	123	115	111
Access to an improved water source (% of population)	98	94	93
Access to improved sanitation facilities (% of population)	79	79	73

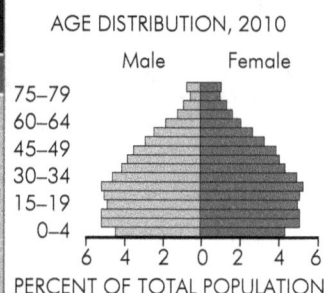

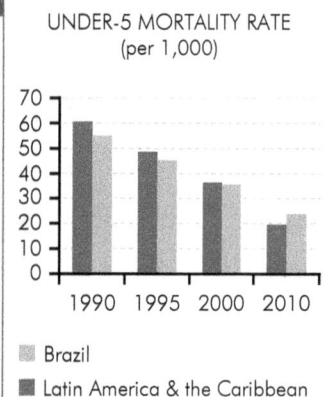

AGE DISTRIBUTION, 2010

Male   Female

75–79
60–64
45–49
30–34
15–19
0–4

6 4 2 0 2 4 6
PERCENT OF TOTAL POPULATION

UNDER-5 MORTALITY RATE
(per 1,000)

1990 1995 2000 2010

Brazil
Latin America & the Caribbean

	1980	1990	2000	2010
Net Aid Flows ($ millions)				
Net ODA and official aid	85	151	231	664
Top 3 donors (in 2010):				
Germany	48	31	49	247
Norway	0	1	2	245
France	9	19	24	47
Aid (% of GNI)	0.0	0.0	0.0	0.0
Aid per capita ($)	1	1	1	3
Long-Term Economic Trends				
Consumer prices (annual % change)	95.6	1,621.0	6.0	5.3
GDP implicit deflator (annual % change)	87.3	2,735.5	6.2	7.3
Exchange rate (annual average, local per $)	0.0	0.0	1.8	1.8
Terms of trade index (2000 = 100)	147	164	100	124

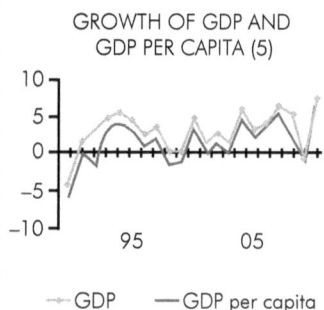

GROWTH OF GDP AND
GDP PER CAPITA (5)

95   05

GDP   GDP per capita

	1980	1990	2000	2010	1980–90	1990–2000	2000–10
Long-Term Economic Trends					*(average annual growth %)*		
Population, mid-year (millions)	121.7	149.7	174.4	194.9	2.1	1.5	1.1
GDP ($ millions)	235,025	461,952	644,702	2,087,890	2.7	2.7	3.7
(% of GDP)							
Agriculture	11.0	8.1	5.6	5.8	2.8	3.6	3.6
Industry	43.8	38.7	27.7	26.8	2.0	2.4	2.8
Manufacturing	33.5	25.3	17.2	15.8	—	2.0	2.5
Services	45.2	53.2	66.7	67.4	3.3	3.8	3.9
Household final consumption expenditure	69.7	59.3	64.3	60.6	1.2	3.7	4.0
General gov't final consumption expenditure	9.2	19.3	19.2	21.2	7.3	1.0	3.3
Gross capital formation	23.3	20.2	18.3	19.2	3.3	4.2	4.7
Exports of goods and services	9.1	8.2	10.0	11.2	7.5	5.9	6.4
Imports of goods and services	11.3	7.0	11.7	12.1	0.5	11.6	8.5
Gross savings	17.8	18.9	13.9	16.6			

	2000	2010
Balance of Payments and Trade *($ millions)*		
Total merchandise exports (fob)	54,187	230,377
Total merchandise imports (cif)	55,783	198,192
Net trade in goods and services	–7,860	–10,586
Current account balance as a % of GDP	–24,225	–47,365
	–3.8	–2.3
Workers' remittances and compensation of employees (receipts)	1,649	4,000
Reserves, including gold	33,011	297,571
Central Government Finance *(% of GDP)*		
Current revenue (including grants)	16.5	25.0
Tax revenue	14.7	19.2
Current expenditure	18.7	20.4
Overall surplus/deficit	–2.1	–2.2
Highest marginal tax rate (%)		
Individual	—	28
Corporate	37	34
External Debt and Resource Flows *($ millions)*		
Total debt outstanding and disbursed	241,550	346,978
Total debt service	64,843	45,806
Debt relief (HIPC, MDRI)	n.a.	n.a.
Total debt (% of GDP)	37.5	16.6
Total debt service (% of exports)	89.7	16.4
Foreign direct investment (net inflows)	32,779	48,438
Portfolio equity (net inflows)	3,076	37,684

COMPOSITION OF TOTAL EXTERNAL DEBT, 2010

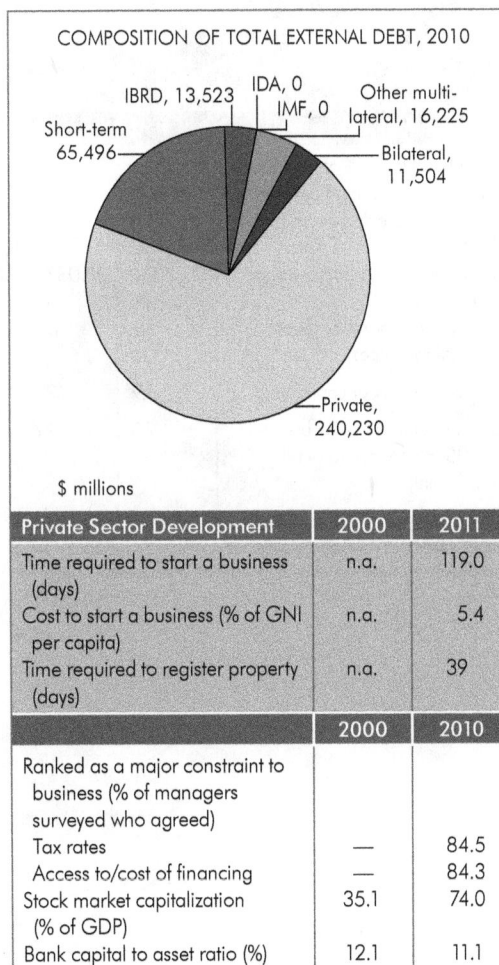

IBRD, 13,523
IDA, 0
IMF, 0
Other multi-lateral, 16,225
Short-term 65,496
Bilateral, 11,504
Private, 240,230

$ millions

Private Sector Development	2000	2011
Time required to start a business (days)	n.a.	119.0
Cost to start a business (% of GNI per capita)	n.a.	5.4
Time required to register property (days)	n.a.	39

	2000	2010
Ranked as a major constraint to business (% of managers surveyed who agreed)		
Tax rates	—	84.5
Access to/cost of financing	—	84.3
Stock market capitalization (% of GDP)	35.1	74.0
Bank capital to asset ratio (%)	12.1	11.1

continued on page 110

GOVERNANCE INDICATORS, 2000 AND 2010

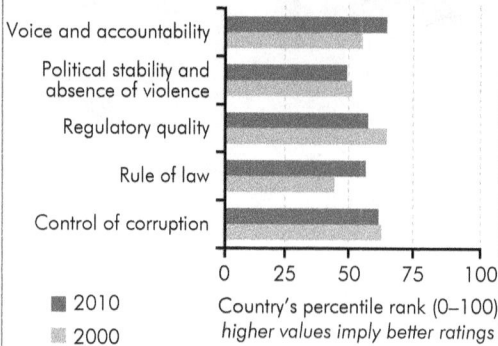

- ■ 2010
- ▨ 2000

Country's percentile rank (0–100)
higher values imply better ratings

SOURCE: Worldwide Governance Indicators
(http://www.govindicators.org).

Technology and Infrastructure	2000	2010
Paved roads (% of total)	5.5	—
Fixed line and mobile phone subscribers (per 100 people)	31	126
High technology exports (% of manufactured exports)	18.7	11.2
Environment		
Agricultural land (% of land area)	31	*31*
Forest area (% of land area)	64.5	61.4
Terrestrial protected areas (% of land area)	16.9	26.3
Freshwater resources per capita (cu meters)	*30,219*	28,037
Freshwater withdrawal (% of internal resources)	1.1	0.7
CO_2 emissions per capita (mt)	1.9	2.1
GDP per unit of energy use (2005 PPP $ per kg of oil equivalent)	7.3	7.6
Energy use per capita (kg of oil equivalent)	1,084	*1,243*

World Bank Group portfolio ($ millions)	2000	2010
IBRD		
Total debt outstanding and disbursed	7,377	13,523
Disbursements	1,692	4,472
Principal repayments	887	960
Interest payments	464	180
IDA		
Total debt outstanding and disbursed	0	0
Disbursements	0	0
Total debt service	0	0
IFC *(fiscal year)*		
Total disbursed and outstanding portfolio	2,146	3,133
of which IFC own account	1,157	2,141
Disbursements for IFC own account	160	261
Portfolio sales, prepayments and repayments for IFC own account	111	356
MIGA		
Gross exposure	706	193
New guarantees	315	33

4/2/12

Millennium Development Goals

With selected targets to achieve between 1990 and 2015
(estimate closest to date shown, +/– 2 years)

	Brazil			
	1990	1995	2000	2010
Goal 1: halve the rates for extreme poverty and malnutrition				
Poverty headcount ratio at $1.25 a day (PPP, % of population)	17.2	12.3	11.8	6.1
Poverty headcount ratio at national poverty line (% of population)	41.9	35.2	35.2	21.4
Share of income or consumption to the poorest quintile (%)	2.2	2.2	2.1	2.9
Prevalence of malnutrition (% of children under 5)	—	4.5	—	2.2
Goal 2: ensure that children are able to complete primary schooling				
Primary school enrollment (net, %)	—	—	92	94
Primary completion rate (% of relevant age group)	93	90	10	106
Secondary school enrollment (gross, %)	—	—	104	101
Youth literacy rate (% of people ages 15–24)	—	—	94	98
Goal 3: eliminate gender disparity in education and empower women				
Ratio of girls to boys in primary and secondary education (%)	—	—	103	102
Women employed in the nonagricultural sector (% of nonagricultural employment)	35	39	40	42
Proportion of seats held by women in national parliament (%)	5	7	6	9
Goal 4: reduce under-5 mortality by two-thirds				
Under-5 mortality rate (per 1,000)	59	48	36	19
Infant mortality rate (per 1,000 live births)	50	41	31	17
Measles immunization (proportion of one-year olds immunized, %)	78	87	99	99
Goal 5: reduce maternal mortality by three-fourths				
Maternal mortality ratio (modeled estimate, per 100,000 live births)	120	98	79	58
Births attended by skilled health staff (% of total)	70	88	96	97
Contraceptive prevalence (% of women ages 15–49)	59	77	—	81
Goal 6: halt and begin to reverse the spread of HIV/AIDS and other major diseases				
Prevalence of HIV (% of population ages 15–49)	—	—	—	—
Incidence of tuberculosis (per 100,000 people)	84	71	60	43
Tuberculosis case detection rate (%, all forms)	60	79	74	88
Goal 7: halve the proportion of people without sustainable access to basic needs				
Access to an improved water source (% of population)	89	91	94	98
Access to improved sanitation facilities (% of population)	68	71	74	79
Forest area (% of total land area)	68	—	64.5	61.4
Terrestrial protected areas (% of land area)	9.0	11.1	16.9	26.3
CO_2 emissions (metric tons per capita)	1.4	1.7	1.9	2.1
GDP per unit of energy use (constant 2005 PPP $ per kg of oil equivalent)	7.7	7.8	7.3	7.6
Goal 8: develop a global partnership for development				
Telephone mainlines (per 100 people)	6.3	8.2	17.7	21.6
Mobile phone subscribers (per 100 people)	0.0	0.8	13.3	104.1
Internet users (per 100 people)	0.0	0.1	2.9	40.7
Computer users (per 100 people)	—	—	—	44.1

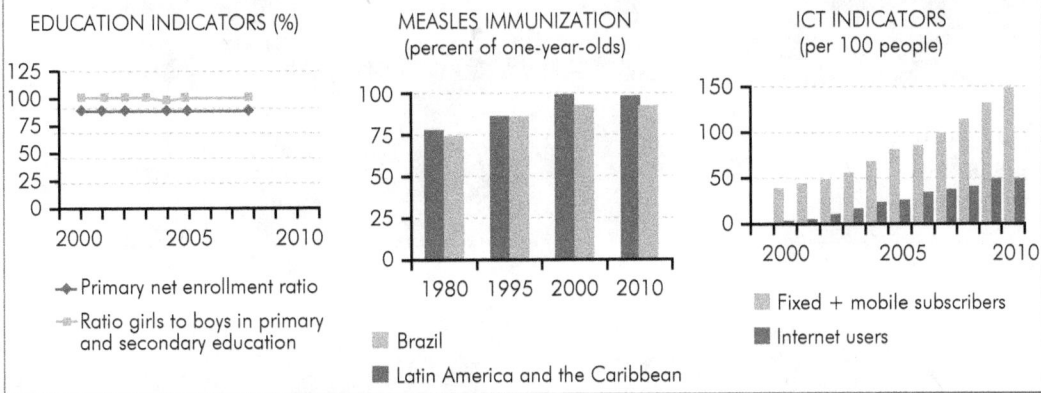

EDUCATION INDICATORS (%)

- ◆ Primary net enrollment ratio
- ■ Ratio girls to boys in primary and secondary education

MEASLES IMMUNIZATION
(percent of one-year-olds)

- Brazil
- Latin America and the Caribbean

ICT INDICATORS
(per 100 people)

- Fixed + mobile subscribers
- Internet users

SOURCE: Development Economics, Development Data Group.

NOTE: Figures in italics are for years other than those specified. cif = cost, insurance, and freight; fob = free on board; GDP = gross domestic product; HIPC = Heavily Indebted Poor Country Initiative; ICT = information and communication technology; MDRI = Multilateral Debt Relief Initiative; ODA = official development assistance; PPP = public-private partnership. n.a. indicates observation is not applicable. — indicates data are not available as of April 2013.

TABLE C.2 Brazil Economic and Social Indicators, 2004–11

Series Name	2004	2005	2006	2007	2008	2009	2010	2011
Growth and Inflation								
GDP growth (annual %)	5.7	3.2	4.0	6.1	5.2	(0.3)	7.5	2.7
GDP per capita growth (annual %)	4.4	2.0	2.9	5.1	4.2	(1.2)	6.6	1.8
GNI per capita, Atlas method (current $)	3,310	3,960	4,800	6,110	7,490	8,150	9,540	10,720
GNI per capita, PPP (current international $)	7,830	8,270	8,810	9,570	10,160	10,180	11,000	11,500
Inflation, consumer prices (annual %)	6.6	6.9	4.2	3.6	5.7	4.9	5.0	6.6
Composition of GDP								
Agriculture, value added (% of GDP)	6.9	5.7	5.5	5.6	5.9	5.6	5.3	5.5
Industry, value added (% of GDP)	30.1	29.3	28.8	27.8	27.9	26.8	28.1	27.5
Services, etc, value added (% of GDP)	63.0	65.0	65.8	66.6	66.2	67.5	66.6	67.0
External Accounts								
Exports of goods and services (% of GDP)	16.4	15.1	14.4	13.4	13.7	11.0	10.9	11.9

Series Name	2004	2005	2006	2007	2008	2009	2010	2011
Imports of goods and services (% of GDP)	12.5	11.5	11.5	11.8	13.5	11.1	11.9	12.6
Current account balance (% of GDP)	1.8	1.6	1.3	0.1	(1.7)	(1.5)	(2.2)	(2.1)
Present value of external debt (% of GNI)	—	—	—	—	—	—	18.8	—
Total debt service (% of GNI)	8.3	7.3	5.9	4.1	3.5	2.8	2.2	—
Other Macroeconomic Indicators								
Gross fixed capital formation (% of GDP)	16.1	15.9	16.4	17.4	19.1	18.1	19.5	19.3
Gross fixed capital formation, private sector (% of GDP)	—	—	—	13.4	16.8	15.3	16.5	16.4
Gross domestic savings (% of GDP)	21.0	19.8	19.7	19.8	20.9	17.7	19.2	19.0
Gross savings (% of GDP)	18.5	17.3	17.6	18.1	18.8	15.9	17.5	17.2
Fiscal Accounts								
Revenue, excluding grants (% of GDP)	21.5	22.7	22.9	23.2	23.6	23.1	—	—

continued on page 114

Series Name	2004	2005	2006	2007	2008	2009	2010	2011
General government final consumption exp (% of GDP)	19.2	19.9	20.0	20.3	20.2	21.2	21.1	20.7
Gross national expenditure (% of GDP)	96.1	96.4	97.1	98.5	99.8	100.2	101.0	100.7
Cash surplus/deficit (% of GDP)	(1.9)	(3.6)	(2.9)	(1.9)	(1.2)	(3.5)	—	—
Social Indicators								
Life expectancy at birth, total (years)	71.3	71.5	71.8	72.1	72.4	72.8	73.1	—
Immunization, DPT (% of children ages 12–23 months)	96.0	96.0	97.0	97.0	98.0	98.0	98.0	—
Mortality rate, infant (per 1,000 live births)	24.8	23.3	22.0	20.8	19.6	18.4	17.3	—
Out-of-pocket health exp (% of private exp on health)	62.6	63.0	61.8	58.5	56.0	57.2	57.8	—
Health expenditure, public (% of GDP)	3.4	3.3	3.5	3.5	3.7	4.1	—	—
School enrollment, primary (% gross)	141.0	136.7	—	—	—	—	—	—
School enrollment, secondary (% gross)	106.0	105.8	—	—	—	—	—	—

Series Name	2004	2005	2006	2007	2008	2009	2010	2011
School enrollment, tertiary (% gross)	23.8	25.6	—	—	—	—	—	—
Telephone lines (per 100 people)	21.5	21.4	20.6	20.8	21.5	21.5	21.6	—
Unemployment, total (% of total labor force)	8.9	9.3	8.4	8.1	7.1	8.3	—	—
Poverty headcount ratio at nat'l poverty line (% of pop)	33.7	30.8	26.8	24.2	22.6	21.4	—	—
Improved water source (% of pop with access)	95.0	96.0	96.0	97.0	97.0	97.0	98.0	—
Improved sanitation facilities (% of pop with access)	76.0	76.0	78.0	78.0	78.0	78.0	79.0	—
School enrollment, preprimary (% gross)	64.0	69.2	—	—	—	—	—	—
Population growth (annual %)	1.2	1.1	1.1	1.0	0.9	0.9	0.9	0.9
Population, female (% of total)	50.7	50.7	50.7	50.7	50.7	50.8	50.8	50.8
Population, male (% of total)	49.3	49.3	49.3	49.3	49.3	49.2	49.2	49.2
Population, total (million)	183.9	186.0	188.0	189.8	191.5	193.2	194.9	196.7

SOURCE: World Bank database.
NOTE: DPT = diphtheria, pertussis, and tetanus; GDP = gross domestic product; GNI = gross national income; PPP = public-private partnership; — = not available.

TABLE C.3 Brazil and Comparators: Economic and Social Indicators, Average 2003–11

Series name	Brazil	LAC	MIC	Russia
Growth and Inflation				
GDP growth (annual %)	3.9	4.1	6.6	4.8
GDP per capita growth (annual %)	2.8	2.9	5.4	5.1
GNI per capita, Atlas method (current $)	6,336.7	5,991.2	2,683.6	7,016.7
GNI per capita, PPP (current international $)	9,400.0	9,729.6	5,469.1	15,421.1
Inflation, consumer prices (annual %)	6.5			10.8
Composition of GDP				
Agriculture, value added (% of GDP)	5.9	6.2	10.0	4.9
Industry, value added (% of GDP)	28.2	32.6	36.4	35.9
Services, value added (% of GDP)	65.8	61.2	53.7	59.2
External Accounts				
Exports of goods and services (% of GDP)	13.5	24.4	30.4	31.7
Imports of goods and services (% of GDP)	12.1	23.6	28.7	21.7
Current account balance (% of GDP)	(0.2)			7.2
Present value of external debt (% of GNI)	18.8			24.7

	India	China	Argentina	Chile	Colombia	Mexico
	8.1	10.7	7.8	4.4	4.7	2.4
	6.5	10.1	6.8	3.3	3.2	1.1
	943.3	2,765.6	6,231.1	8,233.3	4,083.3	8,378.9
	2,666.7	5,585.6	12,613.3	12,948.9	7,964.4	13,133.3
	7.2	3.0	9.1	2.4	5.0	4.3
	18.4	11.2	9.4	4.1	7.8	3.8
	27.7	46.6	33.0	39.3	33.4	34.5
	53.9	42.2	57.6	56.7	58.8	61.7
	20.5	33.2	23.9	39.7	17.1	28.0
	24.0	28.1	18.6	32.6	19.1	29.5
	(1.1)	6.3	2.6	1.6	(2.1)	(0.8)
	17.7	10.1	37.5	47.7	37.5	18.0

continued on page 118

Series name	Brazil	LAC	MIC	Russia
Total debt service (% of GNI)	5.6	5.2	4.1	4.4
Other Macroeconomic Indicators				
Gross fixed capital formation (% of GDP)	17.5	19.4	30.5	20.4
Gross fixed capital formation, private sector (% of GDP)	15.7	15.6	21.3	17.4
Gross domestic savings (% of GDP)	19.5	21.8	33.7	32.1
Gross savings (% of GDP)	17.4	21.3	29.8	28.8
Fiscal Accounts				
Revenue, excluding grants (% of GDP)	22.6	20.2	19.2	28.8
General government final consumption exp (% of GDP)	20.2	14.6	13.9	18.0
Gross national expenditure (% of GDP)	98.5			90.0
Cash surplus/deficit (% of GDP)	(2.8)	(2.6)	(2.0)	3.9
Social Indicators				
Life expectancy at birth, total (years)	72.0	73.3	68.1	66.9
Immunization, DPT (% of children ages 12–23 months)	97.3	92.6	80.3	97.8
Mortality rate, infant (per 1,000 live births)	21.6	21.1	41.7	12.0

	India	China	Argentina	Chile	Colombia	Mexico
	2.4	1.2	6.3	9.3	5.7	4.1
	30.2	41.8	21.5	21.2	20.7	20.5
	22.5	19.6	17.7	—	—	16.2
	30.8	49.3	26.8	29.5	19.5	23.3
	33.3	50.2	23.5	22.9	18.0	24.1
	12.3	11.1	17.7	23.5	18.9	
	11.1	13.7	11.9	11.3	15.2	11.2
	103.6	94.9	94.8	92.9	102.0	101.5
	(3.3)	(2.2)	(1.6)	2.8	(4.2)	
	63.9	72.5	75.0	78.4	72.6	75.9
	68.0	92.6	92.6	93.9	91.5	97.0
	52.9	19.5	14.0	7.9	18.7	17.2

continued on page 120

Series name	Brazil	LAC	MIC	Russia
Out-of-pocket health exp (% of private expense on health)	59.9	73.8	78.5	81.9
Health expenditure, public (% of GDP)	3.5	3.4	2.6	3.3
School enrollment, preprimary (% gross)	66.8	66.1	44.5	87.6
School enrollment, primary (% gross)	140.0	116.5	107.1	101.3
School enrollment, secondary (% gross)	104.7	88.1	66.9	86.1
School enrollment, tertiary (% gross)	23.9	34.4	22.2	72.2
Telephone lines (per 100 people)	21.3	17.8	14.1	29.6
Unemployment, total (% of total labor force)	8.5	8.0	6.1	7.3
Poverty headcount ratio at nat'l poverty line (% of population)	27.9			13.6
Improved water source (% of population with access)	96.4	93.0	87.5	96.5
Improved sanitation facilities (% of pop with access)	77.4	77.9	56.7	70.9
Population growth (annual %)	1.0	1.2	1.1	(0.3)
Population, female (% of total)	50.7	50.6	49.3	53.7
Population, male (% of total)	49.3	49.4	50.7	46.3
Population, total (million)	189.5	569.0	4,803.7	142.7

SOURCE: World Bank database.
NOTE: DPT = diphtheria, pertussis, and tetanus; GDP = gross domestic product; GNI = gross national income; LAC = Latin America and the Caribbean Region; MIC = middle-income country; PPP = public-private partnership; — = not available.

India	China	Argentina	Chile	Colombia	Mexico
88.2	83.0	62.8	64.7	64.7	93.5
1.2	1.9	4.9	3.1	5.3	2.7
44.3	44.2	67.9	54.0	44.8	99.0
111.3	111.4	114.8	104.2	119.3	112.0
56.2	76.0	85.8	89.6	88.2	84.4
13.3	21.0	66.8	49.5	32.4	25.4
3.5	24.7	24.0	20.7	17.5	17.7
4.4	4.2	10.6	8.2	11.8	3.9
33.5	2.8		15.8	43.3	47.2
88.3	87.8	96.2	95.9	91.9	93.9
31.0	57.9	90.0	95.8	75.6	81.5
1.5	0.5	0.9	1.0	1.5	1.2
48.3	48.1	51.1	50.5	50.8	50.7
51.7	51.9	48.9	49.5	49.2	49.3
1,173.8	1,317.2	39.4	16.6	44.3	109.3

TABLE C.4 List of IBRD Lending Operations, FY04–11

FY	Project ID	Project Name	Product Line	Project Status
2004	P080830	BR Maranhao Integrated: Rural Dev	IBRD	Closed
2004	P080827	BR Loan for Sust and Equitable Growth	IBRD	Closed
2004	P083013	BR Disease Surveillance & Control APL 2	IBRD	Closed
2004	P087713	BR Bolsa Familia 1st APL	IBRD	Closed
2004	P060573	BR Tocantins Sustainable Regional Dev	IBRD	Closed
2005	P096300	BR Capac Building for Mgmt of Publ Infr	IDF	Closed
2005	P069934	BR-Pernambuco Integ Dev: Educ Qual Impr	IBRD	Closed
2005	P066536	BR Bonito/Rio Mimosa Wtrshd	GEF Med Size	Closed
2005	P068730	Science and Technology Subprogram Phase 2	Rainforest	Closed
2005	P075379	BR GEF-RJ Sust IEM in Prod Landscapes	GEF	Closed
2005	P076924	BR-Amapa Sustainable Communities	IBRD	Closed
2005	P077047	Mata Atlantica Subprogram (FAO)	Rainforest	Closed
2005	P080829	BR 1st PRL for Environmental Sustainability	IBRD	Closed
2005	P082328	BR-Integ / Munic Proj-Betim Municipality	IBRD	Closed
2005	P088009	BR GEF-São Paulo Riparian Forests	GEF	Closed

Lending Instrument	Sector Board	IBRD Commitment Amt	Grant Amt	IBRD + Grant Amt
Specific Investment Ln	ARD	30.0	0	30.0
Prog Struct ADJ Ln	Financial & Private Sector Dev (I)	505.1	0	505.1
Adaptable Program Ln	HNP	100.0	0	100.0
Adaptable Program Ln	Social Protection	572.2	0	572.2
Sector Invest/Maint Ln	Transport	60.0	0	60.0
Not assigned	Economic Policy	n.a.	0	0
Specific Investment Ln	Education	31.5	0	31.5
Trust Fund	Environment	n.a.	0.7	0.7
Not assigned	Environment	n.a.	0.7	0.7
Specific Investment Ln	Environment	n.a.	6.7	6.7
Specific Investment Ln	Environment	4.8	0	4.8
Not assigned	Environment	n.a.	0.8	0.8
Structural ADJ Ln	Environment	502.5	0	502.5
Specific Investment Ln	Environment	24.1	0	24.1
Specific Investment Ln	Environment	n.a.	7.8	7.8

continued on page 124

FY	Project ID	Project Name	Product Line	Project Status
2005	P093594	Support to Atlantic Forest NGO Network	Rainforest	Closed
2005	P069672	Support to Sust Business Practices	Rainforest	Closed
2005	P083533	BR TA-Sustain & Equit Growth	IBRD	Closed
2005	P090313	BR Building Capacity for M&E in Tourism	IDF	Closed
2005	P086525	BR 1st Prog Fiscal Ref—Soc Sec Reform	IBRD	Closed
2005	P078716	BR(CRL1)Prog Growth for Housing	IBRD	Closed
2005	P087711	BR Espirito Santo Wtr & Coastal Pollu	IBRD	Closed
2006	P093787	BR Bahia State Integ Proj Rural Pov	IBRD	Active
2006	P052256	BR-MG Rural Poverty Reduction	IBRD	Closed
2006	P100791	BR Ceará Rural Pov Add'l Financing	IBRD	Closed
2006	P088543	BR MG Partnership for Development	IBRD	Closed
2006	P082523	BR HD Technical Assistance Loan	IBRD	Closed
2006	P079182	BR Nova Gerar Landfill Rio de Janeiro	Carbon Offset	Active
2006	P081023	BR-Sugar Bagasse Cogeneration Project	Carbon Offset	Active
2006	P066535	BR GEF Amazon Aquatic Res—AquaBio	GEF	Closed
2006	P066537	BR SC Tabuleiro St Par	GEF Med Size	Closed
2006	P089440	BR-Brasilia Environmentally Sustainable	IBRD	Closed

Lending Instrument	Sector Board	IBRD Commitment Amt	Grant Amt	IBRD + Grant Amt
Trust Fund	Environment	n.a.	0.9	0.9
Trust Fund	Financial & Private Sector Dev (I)	n.a.	1.2	1.2
Adaptable Program Ln	Financial & Private Sector Dev (I)	12.1	0	12.1
Not assigned	Social Development	n.a.	0	0
Development Policy	Social Protection	658.3	0	658.3
Development Policy	Urban Development	502.5	0	502.5
Specific Investment Ln	Water	36.0	0	36.0
Specific Investment Ln	ARD	54.4	0	54.4
Specific Investment Ln	ARD	35.0	0	35.0
Specific Investment Ln	ARD	37.5	0	37.5
Structural ADJ Ln	Economic Policy	170.0	0	170.0
Technical Assistance Ln	Education	8.0	0	8.0
Specific Investment Ln	Environment	n.a.	8.5	8.5
Specific Investment Ln	Environment	n.a.	0.6	0.6
Specific Investment Ln	Environment	n.a.	7.2	7.2
Not assigned	Environment	n.a.	0.7	0.7
Specific Investment Ln	Environment	57.6	0	57.6

continued on page 126

FY	Project ID	Project Name	Product Line	Project Status
2006	P090041	BR Environmental Sust Agenda TAL	IBRD	Closed
2006	P096740	Social Participation in BR-163 Highway	Rainforest	Closed
2006	P097327	Support to Pilot Program Coordination	Rainforest	Closed
2006	P095675	BR-2nd Prog Sust & Equit Growth	IBRD	Closed
2006	P069671	PPG7 Coordination	Rainforest	Closed
2006	P082142	BR-Ceara Multisector Social Inclusion Dev	IBRD	Closed
2006	P100816	BR Youth IDF	IDF	Closed
2006	P092990	BR-Road Transport Project	IBRD	Active
2006	P081436	BR-Bahia Poor Urban Areas Integrated Dev	IBRD	Active
2006	P050761	BR-Housing Sector TAL	IBRD	Closed
2007	P101359	BR-Piauí Rural Pov Add'l Financing	IBRD	Closed
2007	P101879	BR Pernambuco Rural Pov Add'l Financing	IBRD	Closed
2007	P104346	BR Strengthen Amazon Initiative Consort	IDF	Closed
2007	P070867	BR GEF Caatinga Conserv and Sust Mgmt	GEF	Active
2007	P082651	BR APL 1 Para Integrated Rural Dev	IBRD	Active
2007	P091407	BR Lages Woodwaste Cogeneration	Carbon Offset	Active

Lending Instrument	Sector Board	IBRD Commitment Amt	Grant Amt	IBRD + Grant Amt
Technical Assistance Ln	Environment	8.0	0	8.0
Not assigned	Environment	n.a.	0.5	0.5
Not assigned	Environment	n.a.	0.9	0.9
Development Policy	Financial & Private Sector Dev (I)	601.5	0	601.5
Not assigned	Public Sector Governance	n.a.	1.0	1.0
Adaptable Program Ln	Public Sector Governance	149.8	0	149.8
Not assigned	Social Development	n.a.	0	0
Sector Inv/Maint Ln	Transport	501.3	0	501.3
Specific Investment Ln	Urban Development	49.3	0	49.3
Specific Investment Ln	Urban Development	4.0	0	4.0
Specific Investment Ln	ARD	22.5	0	22.5
Specific Investment Ln	ARD	30.0	0	30.0
Not assigned	ARD	n.a.	0	0
Specific Investment Ln	Environment	n.a.	10.0	10.0
Adaptable Program Ln	Environment	60.0	0	60.0
Specific Investment Ln	Environment	n.a.	7.5	7.5

continued on page 128

FY	Project ID	Project Name	Product Line	Project Status
2007	P104639	BR GTA Institutional Development	Rainforest	Closed
2007	P104640	BR COIAB Institutional Development	Rainforest	Closed
2007	P104374	BR-Improving Public Procurement Systems	IDF	Closed
2007	P089793	BR State Pension Reform TAL II	IBRD	Closed
2007	P104398	BR Strengthening Monitoring & Evaluation	IDF	Closed
2007	P095460	BR-Bahia Integr Hwy Mgmt	IBRD	Active
2007	P089011	BR Municipal APL1: Uberaba	IBRD	Active
2007	P100154	BR Fed Wtr Res Mgmt Add'l Financ	IBRD	Closed
2008	P101507	BR (AF)RGN Rural Pov Reduction	IBRD	Closed
2008	P094715	BR GEF National Biod Mainstreaming	GEF	Active
2008	P097322	Amazon Cartographic Base	Rainforest	Closed
2008	P109826	BR (IDF) Enhanc Op Capacity of Controller	IDF	Closed
2008	P083997	BR (MST) AltoSolimoes Bsc Srvcs and Sust	IBRD	Active
2008	P095626	BR (APL2) Family Health Extension 2nd APL	IBRD	Active
2008	P101324	BR-Second Minas Gerais Dev Partnership	IBRD	Active
2008	P109751	BR (IDF) Capacity Buildg for M&E at PMSP	IDF	Active
2008	P106038	BR São Paulo Trains and Signaling	IBRD	Active

Lending Instrument	Sector Board	IBRD Commitment Amt	Grant Amt	IBRD + Grant Amt
Not assigned	Environment	n.a.	0.5	0.5
Not assigned	Environment	n.a.	0.3	0.3
Not assigned	Procurement	n.a.	0	0
Technical Assistance Ln	Public Sector Governance	5.0	0	5.0
Not assigned	Public Sector Governance	n.a.	0	0
Sector Inv/Maint Ln	Transport	100.0	0	100.0
Adaptable Program Ln	Water	17.3	0	17.3
Specific Investment Ln	Water	50.0	0	50.0
Specific Investment Ln	ARD	22.5	0	22.5
Specific Investment Ln	Environment	n.a.	22.0	22.0
Not assigned	Environment	n.a.	4.5	4.5
Not assigned	Financial Management	n.a.	0	0
Adaptable Program Ln	HNP	24.3	0	24.3
Adaptable Program Ln	HNP	83.5	0	83.5
Specific Investment Ln	Public Sector Governance	976.0	0	976.0
Not assigned	Public Sector Governance	n.a.	0	0
Specific Investment Ln	Transport	550.0	0	550.0

continued on page 130

FY	Project ID	Project Name	Product Line	Project Status
2008	P105959	BR (AF-C)SP Metro Line 4 (Add'l Fin)	IBRD	Closed
2008	P106427	BR (AF-C)RJ Mass Transit	IBRD	Closed
2008	P089013	BR Municipal APL: Recife	IBRD	Active
2008	P094199	BR-(APL) RS (Pelotas) Integr Mun Dev	IBRD	Active
2008	P088966	BR Municipal APL3: Teresina	IBRD	Active
2008	P089929	BR RGN State Integrated Water Res Mgmt	IBRD	Active
2009	P104752	BR Paraiba 2nd Rural Pov Reduction	IBRD	Active
2009	P107146	BR Acre Social Economic Inclusion Sust D	IBRD	Active
2009	P110614	BR: Sergipe State Int Proj: Rural Pov	IBRD	Closed
2009	P106208	BR Pernambuco Educ Results & Accountability	IBRD	Active
2009	P094233	BR GEF Espirito Santo Biodiversity	GEF	Active
2009	P095205	BR 1st Prog DPL for Sust Env Mgmt	IBRD	Closed
2009	P111940	RMA Capacity Building and Institutional	Rainforest	Closed
2009	P115180	Strengthening Brazil Subnational Audit	IDF	Active
2009	P088716	BR Health Network Formation & Quality Im	IBRD	Active
2009	P107843	BR Fed District Multisector Mgmt Project	IBRD	Active

Lending Instrument	Sector Board	IBRD Commitment Amt	Grant Amt	IBRD + Grant Amt
Specific Investment Ln	Transport	95.0	0	95.0
Specific Investment Ln	Transport	44.0	0	44.0
Adaptable Program Ln	Urban Development	32.8	0	32.8
Adaptable Program Ln	Urban Development	18.9	0	18.9
Adaptable Program Ln	Water	31.1	0	31.1
Specific Investment Ln	Water	35.9	0	35.9
Specific Investment Ln	ARD	20.9	0	20.9
Specific Investment Ln	ARD	120.0	0	120.0
Specific Investment Ln	ARD	20.8	0	20.8
Specific Investment Ln	Education	154.0	0	154.0
Specific Investment Ln	Environment	n.a.	4.0	4.0
Development Policy	Environment	1,300.0	0	1,300.0
Not assigned	Environment	n.a.	0.3	0.3
Not assigned	Financial Management	n.a.	0	0
Adaptable Program Ln	HNP	235.0	0	235.0
Specific Investment Ln	HNP	130.0	0	130.0

continued on page 132

FY	Project ID	Project Name	Product Line	Project Status
2009	P115262	BR Ministerio Publico in Minas Gerais	IDF	Active
2009	P106765	BR Ceara Inclusive Growth (SWAp II)	IBRD	Closed
2009	P106767	BR RGS Fiscal Sustainability DPL	IBRD	Closed
2009	P099369	BR Ceara Regional Development	IBRD	Active
2009	P105389	BR Nova Gerar CDM SWM Project 2	Carbon Offset	Active
2009	P111511	BR (APL2) RS Bage Integr Munic Dev	IBRD	Active
2009	P111513	BR (APL2) RS Santa Maria Integ Munic Dev	IBRD	Active
2009	P111514	BR (APL2) RS Uruguaiana Int Mun Dev	IBRD	Active
2009	P094315	BR Municipal APL4: São Luis	IBRD	Active
2009	P102818	BR (AF-C) Espirito Santo Wtr & Coastal Pollution	IBRD	Closed
2009	P110487	BR (AF) Ceara Integ Wtr Res Mgmt	IBRD	Closed
2010	P101508	BR-RJ Sustainable Rural Development	IBRD	Active
2010	P108443	BR SP Sust Rural Dev & Access to Markets	IBRD	Active
2010	P110617	BR (AF) Bahia State Integ Pr Rural	IBRD	Active
2010	P103770	BR Alagoas Fiscal & Public Mgmt Reform	IBRD	Closed
2010	P117244	BR Rio State DPL	IBRD	Closed

Lending Instrument	Sector Board	IBRD Commitment Amt	Grant Amt	IBRD + Grant Amt
Not assigned	Public Sector Governance	n.a.	0	0
Adaptable Program Ln	Public Sector Governance	240.0	0	240.0
Development Policy	Public Sector Governance	1,100.0	0	1,100.0
Specific Investment Ln	Urban Development	46.0	0	46.0
Not assigned	Urban Development	n.a.	10.0	10.0
Adaptable Program Ln	Urban Development	6.6	0	6.6
Adaptable Program Ln	Urban Development	14.0	0	14.0
Adaptable Program Ln	Urban Development	6.8	0	6.8
Specific Investment Ln	Water	35.6	0	35.6
Specific Investment Ln	Water	71.5	0	71.5
Specific Investment Ln	Water	103.0	0	103.0
Specific Investment Ln	ARD	39.5	0	39.5
Specific Investment Ln	ARD	78.0	0	78.0
Specific Investment Ln	ARD	30.0	0	30.0
Development Policy	Economic Policy	195.5	0	195.5
Development Policy	Education	485.0	0	485.0

continued on page 134

FY	Project ID	Project Name	Product Line	Project Status
2010	P114204	Eletrobras Distribution Rehabilitation	IBRD	Active
2010	P086341	BR GEF Rio Grande do Sul Biodiversity	GEF	Active
2010	P091827	BR GEF Sust Cerrado Initiative	GEF	Active
2010	P099469	BR (APL2) 2nd National Environmental	IBRD	Active
2010	P121671	BR (APL2) GEF Cerrado Init: Goias & ICMBio	GEF	Active
2010	P119215	BR (AF) 2nd MG Dev Partnership SWAp	IBRD	Active
2010	P120377	BR Strengthening TCU Financial Audit	IDF	Active
2010	P113540	BR AIDS-SUS	IBRD	Active
2010	P121738	BR-Procurement Reform in Alagoas	IDF	Active
2010	P106390	BR SP Metro Line 4 (Phase 2)	IBRD	Active
2010	P106663	BR São Paulo Feeder Roads Project	IBRD	Active
2010	P111996	BR RJ Mass Transit II	IBRD	Active
2010	P114010	BR GEF Sustainable Transport & Air Quality	GEF	Active
2010	P116170	BR São Paulo Metro Line 5	IBRD	Active
2010	P118410	BR Mato Grosso do Sul Road	IBRD	Active
2010	P104995	BR Municipal APL5: Santos	IBRD	Active
2010	P111512	BR (APL2) RS Rio Grande Integrated Municipal Development	IBRD	Active

Lending Instrument	Sector Board	IBRD Commitment Amt	Grant Amt	IBRD + Grant Amt
Specific Investment Ln	Energy and Mining	495.0	0	495.0
Specific Investment Ln	Environment	n.a.	5.0	5.0
Specific Investment Ln	Environment	n.a.	7.0	7.0
Adaptable Program Ln	Environment	24.3	0	24.3
Adaptable Program Ln	Environment	n.a.	6.0	6.0
Specific Investment Ln	Financial & Private Sector Dev (I)	461.0	0	461.0
Not assigned	Financial Management	n.a.	0	0
Specific Investment Ln	HNP	67.0	0	67.0
Not assigned	Procurement	n.a.	0	0
Specific Investment Ln	Transport	130.0	0	130.0
Sector Inv/Maint Ln	Transport	166.7	0	166.7
Specific Investment Ln	Transport	211.7	0	211.7
Adaptable Program Ln	Transport	n.a.	8.5	8.5
Specific Investment Ln	Transport	650.4	0	650.4
Specific Investment Ln	Transport	300.0	0	300.0
Adaptable Program Ln	Urban Development	44.0	0	44.0
Adaptable Program Ln	Urban Development	8.1	0	8.1

continued on page 136

FY	Project ID	Project Name	Product Line	Project Status
2010	P006553	BR SP APL Integrated Water Mgmt	IBRD	Active
2010	P106703	BR SP Water Reagua	IBRD	Active
2010	P108654	BR Pernambuco Sustainable Water	IBRD	Active
2011	P118540	BR Santa Catarina Rural Competitiveness	IBRD	Active
2011	P111665	BR-RJ Municipal Fiscal Consolidation DPL	IBRD	Closed
2011	P096337	BR AES-Tiete Reservoirs Riparian Forests	Carbon Offset	Active
2011	P125006	BR N_2O Emission Reduction Project	Carbon Offset	Active
2011	P120490	BR Degraded Areas in the Amazon	Rainforest	Closed
2011	P120523	BR Rural Environmental Cadastre	Rainforest	Closed
2011	P095171	BR (MST) Bahia Health and Wtr Mgmt (SWAp)	IBRD	Active
2011	P120391	BR-Federal Univ Hospitals Modernization	IBRD	Closed
2011	P106768	BR Rio de Janeiro PSM/Fiscal MST	IBRD	Active
2011	P101504	BR Bolsa Familia 2nd APL	IBRD	Active
2011	P117122	BR (AF) SP Trains and Signaling	IBRD	Active
2011	P118077	BR (AF) SP Feeder Roads	IBRD	Active
2011	P106702	BR Integrated Solid Waste & Carbon Finance	IBRD	Active
2011	P122391	BR-Rio de Janeiro Urban and Housing DPL	IBRD	Closed

SOURCE: World Bank.

NOTE: ARD = Agriculture and Rural Development Sector; GEF = Global Environment Facility; HNP = Health, Nutrition, and Population Sector; n.a. = not applicable.

Lending Instrument	Sector Board	IBRD Commitment Amt	Grant Amt	IBRD + Grant Amt
Adaptable Program Ln	Water	104.0	0	104.0
Specific Investment Ln	Water	64.5	0	64.5
Specific Investment Ln	Water	190.0	0	190.0
Specific Investment Ln	ARD	90.0	0	90.0
Development Policy	Economic Policy	1,045	0	1,045
Not assigned	Environment	n.a.	4.9	4.9
Not assigned	Environment	n.a.	40.0	40.0
Not assigned	Environment	n.a.	0.7	0.7
Not assigned	Environment	n.a.	3.5	3.5
Specific Investment Ln	HNP	60.0	0	60.0
Specific Investment Ln	HNP	150.0	0	150.0
Technical Assistance Ln	Public Sector Governance	18.7	0	18.7
Adaptable Program Ln	Social Protection	200.0	0	200.0
Specific Investment Ln	Transport	112.9	0	112.9
Specific Investment Ln	Transport	326.8	0	326.8
Finan Intermediary Ln	Urban Development	50.0	0	50.0
Development Policy	Urban Development	485.0	0	485.0

TABLE C.5 IBRD Analytical and Advisory Work, FY04–11

Fiscal Year	Project ID (AAA)	Project Name	Sector Board
	Economic and Sector Work		
FY04	P082748	BR Fiscal Policy for Investment Grade	Economic Policy
FY04	P087444	Brazil—Insolvency ROSC	Financial and Private Sector Dev (I)
FY04	P074672	BR-Access to Financial Services	Financial and Private Sector Dev (I)
FY04	P085234	BR-Rede-NOS (Locked 7/07)	Poverty Reduction
FY04	P085739	BR-Conversion of OPR Into CPAR	Procurement
FY04	P074794	BR Judicial Performance and & PS Impacts	Public Sector Governance
FY04	P082760	BR Pernambuco PPA/Integration	Public Sector Governance
FY04	P074839	BR-Social Exclusion Study	Social Development
FY04	P078828	BR-Social Protection Phase 1	Social Protection
FY05	P077039	BR IRRIG Social Externalities in BR NE	ARD
FY05	P078817	BR Local Economic Development	Financial and Private Sector Dev (I)
FY05	P081498	BR: Investment Climate Assessment	Financial and Private Sector Dev (I)
FY05	P093557	CCGPP: Brazil 3 Country Assessment	Financial and Private Sector Dev (I)
FY05	P092501	Brazil A&A ROSC	Financial Management
FY05	P078797	BR-Hospital Finance Performance Phase 1	HNP
FY05	P078826	BR-Noncommunicable Diseases, Health	HNP
FY05	P078909	BR Social Security Reform Update	Public Sector Governance

Fiscal Year	Project ID (AAA)	Project Name	Sector Board
FY05	P084763	BR Judicial Reform	Public Sector Governance
FY05	P085164	BR-Youth at Risk	Social Protection
FY05	P087688	BR-Social Protection Phase 2	Social Protection
FY05	P089567	Brazil Land Markets TUDUR	Urban Development
FY06	P084714	BR Spatial Approach to Poverty Reduction	Environment
FY06	P094556	BR Crime and Violence in Brazil	Public Sector Governance
FY06	P082761	BR Federal Public Expenditures	Public Sector Governance
FY06	P089792	BR Prog State Integration I & Governance	Public Sector Governance
FY06	P100225	BR Governance in Brazil's Unified Health	Public Sector Governance
FY06	P078837	BR Poverty Measurement	Sector Board not Applicable (I)
FY06	P089995	BR-Social Protection Phase 3	Social Protection
FY07	P101323	BR State Strategy	Economic Policy
FY07	P103854	BR Strengthening Macro Monitoring	Economic Policy
FY07	P100197	BR- Human Capital Programmatic AAA	Education
FY07	P095907	BR Land Administration Study	Environment
FY07	P074676	BR Regulation for Infras PSP	Financial and Private Sector Dev (I)
FY07	P106584	BR (FSE) Industry Struct of Banking Serv	Financial and Private Sector Dev (I)
FY07	P089791	BR Interest Rates	Financial and Private Sector Dev (I)
FY07	P095728	Brazil PFM Policy Note	Financial Management
FY07	P106246	BR-Hospital Performance Phase II	HNP
FY07	P099988	BR-Towards a Sustainable & Fair Pension	Public Sector Governance

continued on page 140

Fiscal Year	Project ID (AAA)	Project Name	Sector Board
FY07	P095802	BR Porto Alegre Participatory Budgeting	Social Development
FY07	P101554	BR Labor Markets and Jobs	Social Protection
FY07	P089842	BR Urban Policy Strategy	Urban Development
FY07	P091061	BR (CRL2) São Paulo Study	Urban Development
FY08	P101562	BR Quality of Education Spending	Education
FY08	P100976	BR Biodiesel Study	Energy and Mining
FY08	P101407	BR (Joint) Energy Security	Energy and Mining
FY08	P099985	BR Environmental Licensing Study	Environment
FY08	P101329	BR Directed Credit aka 2nd prg ESW	Financial and Private Sector Dev (I)
FY08	P108653	BR (SCL) Aviation	Transport
FY09	P116619	BR Public Debt Management	Economic Policy
FY09	P101436	BR Fiscal Federalism	Public Sector Governance
FY09	P106727	BR (SCL) Countercyclical Fiscal Policy	Social Protection
FY09	P106612	BR Labor Programmatic AAA Phase 2	Social Protection
FY09	P101433	BR Freight Logistics	Transport
FY10	P105702	BR CCH Low Carbon Country Case Study	Energy and Mining
FY10	P101889	BR Amazon Regional Programmatic	Environment
FY10	P115228	BR-Evaluating and Improving Efficiency	HNP
FY11	P102871	BR Land Management and Governance	ARD
FY11	P118307	BR Climate Change	ARD
FY11	P116844	BR Achieving World Class Education	Education

Fiscal Year	Project ID (AAA)	Project Name	Sector Board
FY11	P117588	BR Early Childhood	Education
FY11	P103070	BR Equality of Opportunity	Poverty Reduction
FY11	P123070	BR Inequality Recent Trends & Perspective	Poverty Reduction
FY11	P120916	Brazil Procurement	Procurement
FY11	P112026	BR Involuntary Resettlement: Review of P	Social Development
FY11	P116659	BR Building Evidence for C&V Reduction	Social Development
FY11	P116850	BR Aging Country Study	Social Protection
FY11	P117463	BR MST Job Quality	Social Protection
FY11	P118238	BR-Green City Development	Urban Development
Non-Lending Technical Assistance			
FY04	P078859	FSE-Brazil FSAP Follow Up	Financial and Private Sector Dev (I)
FY04	P079224	FSE-Access to Finance	Financial and Private Sector Dev (I)
FY04	P085497	FSE: BR Bankruptcy & Collateralized Credit	Financial and Private Sector Dev (I)
FY04	P085503	FSE: Credit Co-ops & Acc to Fin Services	Financial and Private Sector Dev (I)
FY05	P084713	Amazon Strategy	Environment
FY05	P092573	BR-BR 163 Environmental Mitigation	Environment
FY05	P092725	BR São Francisco River TA	Environment
FY05	P078433	CA: São Paulo (Brazil) "Bairro Legal"	Urban Development
FY05	P086517	CA: Brazil-Housing & Urban Dev Policy	Urban Development
FY06	P090042	BR Environmental Safeguards	Environment

continued on page 142

Fiscal Year	Project ID (AAA)	Project Name	Sector Board
FY06	P097331	BR Strength Plann Capacity in São Paulo	Public Sector Governance
FY06	P094567	BR-BRAVA Program Phase 1	Social Protection
FY06	P074058	CA: Salvador, Bahia (Brazil) upgrading	Urban Development
FY07	P101574	BR Governance (Programmatic)	Public Sector Governance
FY07	P100493	BR-BRAVA Program Phase 2	Social Protection
FY07	P094134	CA: Brazil-National Urban Dev Strategy	Urban Development
FY08	P103271	BR PROESCO Implementation Support	Energy and Mining
FY08	P103811	BR Energy Efficiency Strategy	Energy and Mining
FY08	P104071	BR Energy Development	Energy and Mining
FY08	P101812	BR Financial Sector NLTA	Financial and Private Sector Dev (I)
FY08	P106749	BR-BRAVA Program Phase 3	Public Sector Governance
FY08	P107528	BR(EFO) Good Governance Program AAA 2	Public Sector Governance
FY08	P101424	BR City Econ Growth and Competitiveness	Urban Development
FY09	P115569	BR Early Childhood Development Conferencce	Education
FY09	P115985	BR Skills Innovation Assessment	Education
FY09	P108338	BR (FBS) Concession Pub Irrig Perimeters	Environment
FY09	P110003	BR (FBS) Baixio do Irece II	Environment
FY09	P110164	Governance Capacity in the Health Sector	HNP
FY09	P114330	BR Good Governance Prog	Public Sector Governance

SOURCE: World Bank.

NOTE: AAA = analytic and advisory activity; ARD = Agriculture and Rural Development Sector; HNP = Health, Nutrition, and Population Sector.

Fiscal Year	Project ID (AAA)	Project Name	Sector Board
FY09	P109362	BR Nat'l Housing Plan-Policy (Cities Alliance)	Urban Development
FY10	P106688	BR Education Quality PAR	Education
FY10	P115550	BR SNTA Nova Eletrobras	Energy and Mining
FY10	P109761	BR (CCH) Amazon dieback analysis	Environment
FY10	P117727	BR Housing Sector TA	Financial and Private Sector Dev (I)
FY10	P114306	BR BRAVA Program	Public Sector Governance
FY10	P116385	BR PEFA-plus (Federal)	Public Sector Governance
FY10	P101417	BR-Improve quality of road investments	Transport
FY10	P112056	BR Proposed High-Speed Train Project	Transport
FY11	P105104	BR BM&F carbon market strengthening	Environment
FY11	P117619	CA-Brazil TA & Gdnce on National Housing Plan	Financial and Private Sector Dev (I)
FY11	P124405	GCMSM: BR Gemloc TA	Financial and Private Sector Dev (I)
FY11	P123754	BR Financial Literacy Seminar	Financial Inclusion Practice
FY11	P117946	BR Public Sector NLTA	Public Sector Governance
FY11	P123221	BR Public Investment Efficiency	Public Sector Governance
FY11	P109281	Conservation/Tourism for São Luis	Urban Development
FY11	P122718	Brazil Housing Sector NLTA Phase II	Urban Development

TABLE C.6 Brazil and Comparators IBRD Portfolio Status Indicators FY04–11

Country		Fiscal Year							
		2004	2005	2006	2007	2008	2009	2010	2011
Brazil	# Proj	48	49	48	46	46	49	53	49
	Net Comm Amt	4,075	4,948	4,429	4,316	4,992	7,978	9,953	9,468
	# Prob Proj	9	9	3	7	8	5	7	9
	# Pot Proj	0	0	0	0	1	2	1	0
	# Proj At Risk	9	9	3	7	9	7	8	9
	Comm At Risk	686	627	63	1,221	277	201	1,817	920
	% Commit at Risk	17	13	1	28	6	3	18	10
Argentina	# Proj	31	29	25	26	26	31	33	35
	Net Comm Amt	5,169	4,569	3,438	3,867	3,941	5,725	5,841	7,218
	# Prob Proj	10	9	8	1	7	1	4	3
	# Pot Proj	2	5	5	10	9	6	4	3
	# Proj At Risk	12	14	13	11	16	7	8	6
	Comm At Risk	1,600	1,714	1,312	832	2,391	1,480	1,720	850
	% Commit at Risk	31	38	38	22	61	26	29	12

Country		Fiscal Year							
		2004	2005	2006	2007	2008	2009	2010	2011
Chile	# Proj	6	5	7	7	8	7	6	5
	Net Comm Amt	290	185	215	208	233	194	135	105
	# Prob Proj	0	0	0	1	1	1	2	0
	# Pot Proj	0	0	0	0	1	0	0	0
	# Proj At Risk	0	0	0	1	2	1	2	0
	Comm At Risk	0	0	0	50	35	5	42	0
	% Commit at Risk	0	0	0	24	15	2	31	0
Colombia	# Proj	16	18	17	17	20	15	18	18
	Net Comm Amt	1,147	1,351	1,323	1,900	2,866	1,857	2,489	1,940
	# Prob Proj	0	2	0	0	2	1	2	3
	# Pot Proj	0	0	0	0	0	1	0	0
	# Proj At Risk	0	2	0	0	2	2	2	3
	Comm At Risk	0	48	0	0	170	130	120	148
	% Commit at Risk	0	4	0	0	6	7	5	8

continued on page 146

Country		Fiscal Year							
		2004	2005	2006	2007	2008	2009	2010	2011
Mexico	# Proj	18	16	18	16	15	16	20	18
	Net Comm Amt	3,527	2,767	2,630	2,178	2,057	3,795	6,775	7,507
	# Prob Proj	2	1	2	2	2	4	3	3
	# Pot Proj	0	0	0	0	0	0	0	2
	# Proj At Risk	2	1	2	2	2	4	3	5
	Comm At Risk	750	350	371	270	129	324	558	262
	% Commit at Risk	21	13	14	12	6	9	8	3
China	# Proj	83	80	71	66	65	69	70	71
	Net Comm Amt	12,298	11,201	9,954	9,109	8,954	9,641	9,599	9,820
	# Prob Proj	3	2	1	3	3	3	9	8
	# Pot Proj	0	0	0	0	1	1	2	3
	# Proj At Risk	3	2	1	3	4	4	11	11
	Comm At Risk	350	425	199	388	522	502	1,413	1,800
	% Commit at Risk	3	4	2	4	6	5	15	18

Country		Fiscal Year							
		2004	2005	2006	2007	2008	2009	2010	2011
India	# Proj	60	61	53	65	57	58	70	76
	Net Comm Amt	11,911	12,639	11,129	14,123	13,564	14,755	21,156	25,068
	# Prob Proj	9	9	5	7	13	9	7	7
	# Pot Proj	1	0	1	1	1	0	1	1
	# Proj At Risk	10	9	6	8	14	9	8	8
	Comm At Risk	2,621	1,102	1,736	2,555	3,174	2,153	2,522	3,150
	% Commit at Risk	22	9	16	18	23	15	12	13
Russia	# Proj	23	22	22	20	18	14	12	10
	Net Comm Amt	1,985	1,977	1,951	1,771	1,676	1,297	1,136	987
	# Prob Proj	4	3	1	0	1	5	2	3
	# Pot Proj	0	1	1	0	0	0	0	0
	# Proj At Risk	4	4	2	0	1	5	2	3
	Comm At Risk	364	380	250	0	80	310	100	110
	% Commit at Risk	18	19	13	0	5	24	9	11

TABLE C.7 IBRD Project Ratings for Brazil and Comparators, FY04–11

Country/Region	Total Evaluated		Outcome % Moderately Satisfactory or Better		RDO % Moderate or Lower		Institutional Development Impact, % Substantial		Sustainability % Likely	
	($ millions)	%	($)	%	($)	%	($)	%	($)	%
Brazil	9,714.7	78	92.1	86.8	90.7	79.2	65	82.6	89.9	95.5
Argentina	5,027.4	35	97.6	88.6	91.2	88.0	36	30.0	93.8	87.5
Chile	534.5	12	100.0	90.9	46.7	66.7	100	100.0	100.0	100.0
China	14,024.0	106	94.6	95.3	95.2	97.1	87	84.2	99.9	97.3
Colombia	4,779.0	39	95.4	84.2	96.8	87.5	73	71.4	83.1	84.6
India	14,629.8	74	84.4	82.4	77.7	71.1	59	64.3	83.5	88.5
Mexico	7,797.3	44	88.3	75.6	71.7	70.0	93	75.0	98.9	91.7
Russia	1,990.1	31	79.0	77.4	65.9	72.2	48	46.2	75.5	75.0
LAC	37,276.8	458	90.6	78.4	84.3	72.2	66	55.4	88.5	82.1
Overall result	95,774	877	91.3	84.4	80.0	78.2	69.7	67.7	90.3	89.1

SOURCE: World Bank database as of June 18, 2013, for Projects at Exit for the FY04–11 period.
NOTE: LAC = Latin America and the Caribbean Region; RDO = risk to development outcome.

TABLE C.8 IBRD Net Disbursement and Net Transfer, FY04–11 ($ thousands)

Period	Disb Amt	Repay Amt	Net Amt	Charges	Fees	Net Transfer
Jul 2003–Jun 2004	1,397,716	1,862,556	(464,840)	316,041	18,109	(798,990)
Jul 2004–Jun 2005	997,841	1,298,559	(300,718)	261,381	12,085	(574,185)
Jul 2005–Jun 2006	2,162,641	719,072	1,443,570	338,185	12,956	1,092,429
Jul 2006–Jun 2007	830,985	793,102	37,883	506,470	4,773	(473,360)
Jul 2007–Jun 2008	741,876	815,554	(73,678)	551,968	4,612	(630,259)
Jul 2008–Jun 2009	1,781,136	879,231	901,905	418,291	9,913	473,701
Jul 2009–Jun 2010	2,636,575	1,849,252	787,323	228,378	10,900	548,045
Jul 2010–Jun 2011	3,065,687	4,169,492	(1,103,805)	174,306	37,170	(1,315,281)
Total	18,132,982	16,821,157	1,311,825	3,342,621	141,784	(2,172,579)

SOURCE: World Bank database as of April 19, 2013.

TABLE C.9 IEG Rated Operations in Brazil, Exit FY04–11

Exit FY	Project ID	Project Name
2004	P006436	Ceara Urban Development & Water Resource
2004	P006554	BR-Health Sector Reform - Reforsus
2004	P006564	BR Belo H Mtsp
2004	P006571	Demonstration Projects
2004	P038882	BR Recife Mtsp
2004	P038947	BR-SC & Tech 3
2004	P039200	BR Energy Efficiency (Eletrobras)
2004	P043874	BR-Disease Surveillance - VIGISUS
2004	P044597	GEF BR-Biodiversity Fund (FUNBIO)
2004	P051701	BR Maranhao Rpoverty
2004	P070641	BR-Prgmfiscal Ref II
2004	P080827	BR Loan for Sust and Equitable Growth
2005	P006559	BR (BF-R)SPTSP
2005	P006562	Bahia Municipal Inf Dev and Mgmt
2005	P035728	BR Bahia Wtr Resources
2005	P057649	BR Bahia Rural Poverty Reduction Project

IEG Outcome Rating	IEG Risk to DO Rating	IEG Sustainability	IEG ID Impact	Net Commit ($ Millions)
MODERATELY SATISFACTORY	n.a.	LIKELY	MODEST	136.2
UNSATISFACTORY	n.a.	UNLIKELY	MODEST	252.4
MODERATELY SATISFACTORY	n.a.	LIKELY	SUBSTANTIAL	92.1
MODERATELY SATISFACTORY	n.a.	LIKELY	SUBSTANTIAL	0
MODERATELY SATISFACTORY	n.a.	LIKELY	SUBSTANTIAL	100.5
SATISFACTORY	n.a.	LIKELY	SUBSTANTIAL	66.2
NOT RATED	NONEVALUABLE	n.a.	n.a.	0.4
SATISFACTORY	n.a.	LIKELY	SUBSTANTIAL	54.1
SATISFACTORY	n.a.	LIKELY	HIGH	0
SATISFACTORY	n.a.	LIKELY	SUBSTANTIAL	80.0
SATISFACTORY	n.a.	LIKELY	SUBSTANTIAL	404.0
MODERATELY SATISFACTORY	MODERATE	n.a.	n.a.	516.2
HIGHLY SATISFACTORY	n.a.	HIGHLY LIKELY	SUBSTANTIAL	45.0
SATISFACTORY	n.a.	LIKELY	SUBSTANTIAL	100.0
MODERATELY SATISFACTORY	n.a.	LIKELY	SUBSTANTIAL	51.0
SATISFACTORY	n.a.	LIKELY	SUBSTANTIAL	54.4

continued on page 152

Exit FY	Project ID	Project Name
2005	P058129	BR Emer Fire Prevention (ERL)
2005	P062619	BR Inss Ref LIL
2005	P080829	BR 1st PRL for Environmental Sustainab
2006	P006210	GEF BR-Nat'l Biodiversity
2006	P006532	BR Fed Hwy Decentr
2006	P006567	Indigenous Lands
2006	P034578	BR RGS Highway Management
2006	P035741	BR Natl Env 2
2006	P037828	BR (PR) Poverty
2006	P042565	BR Paraiba Poverty
2006	P043868	BR RGS Land MGT/Poverty
2006	P043873	BR AG Tech Dev
2006	P047309	BR Energy Efficiency (GEF)
2006	P050763	BR-Fundescola 2
2006	P057910	BR Pension Reform LIL
2006	P074085	BR Sergipe Rural Poverty Reduction
2006	P078716	BR(CRL1)Prog Growth for Housing

IEG Outcome Rating	IEG Risk to DO Rating	IEG Sustainability	IEG ID Impact	Net Commit ($ Millions)
SATISFACTORY	n.a.	LIKELY	SUBSTANTIAL	8.9
SATISFACTORY	n.a.	LIKELY	MODEST	4.9
NOT RATED	n.a.	LIKELY	MODEST	502.5
SATISFACTORY	n.a.	LIKELY	SUBSTANTIAL	0
MODERATELY SATISFACTORY	n.a.	LIKELY	SUBSTANTIAL	249.0
SATISFACTORY	MODERATE	n.a.	n.a.	0
MODERATELY SATISFACTORY	n.a.	NON-EVALUABLE	SUBSTANTIAL	70.0
SATISFACTORY	MODERATE	n.a.	n.a.	8.1
MODERATELY SATISFACTORY	MODERATE	n.a.	n.a.	164.7
MODERATELY SATISFACTORY	MODERATE	n.a.	n.a.	60.0
SATISFACTORY	n.a.	LIKELY	SUBSTANTIAL	100.0
SATISFACTORY	MODERATE	n.a.	n.a.	60.0
MODERATELY SATISFACTORY	MODERATE	n.a.	n.a.	0
MODERATELY SATISFACTORY	n.a.	HIGHLY LIKELY	SUBSTANTIAL	191.2
SATISFACTORY	n.a.	HIGHLY LIKELY	HIGH	4.5
SATISFACTORY	NEGLIGIBLE TO LOW	n.a.	n.a.	20.8
MODERATELY SATISFACTORY	MODERATE	n.a.	n.a.	502.5

continued on page 154

Exit FY	Project ID	Project Name
2006	P086525	BR 1st Prog Fiscal Ref - Soc Sec Reform
2007	P050776	BR NE Microfinance Development
2007	P055954	BR Goias State Highway Management
2007	P057665	BR-Family Health Extension Project I
2007	P070827	BR-2nd APL Bahia Dev Education Project
2007	P088543	BR MG Partnership for Development
2008	P006474	BR Land Mgt 3 (São Paulo)
2008	P039199	BR Prosanear 2
2008	P048869	BR Salvador Urban Trans
2008	P057653	BR- Fundescola IIIA
2008	P059566	BR- Ceara Basic Education
2008	P073192	BR TA Financial Sector
2008	P080400	BR-AIDS & STD Control 3
2008	P082142	BR-Ceara Multisector Social Inclus Dev

IEG Outcome Rating	IEG Risk to DO Rating	IEG Sustainability	IEG ID Impact	Net Commit ($ Millions)
SATISFACTORY	NEGLIGIBLE TO LOW	n.a.	n.a.	658.3
SATISFACTORY	NEGLIGIBLE TO LOW	n.a.	n.a.	38.5
SATISFACTORY	MODERATE	n.a.	n.a.	64.4
SATISFACTORY	MODERATE	n.a.	n.a.	67.9
MODERATELY UNSATISFACTORY	HIGH	n.a.	n.a.	60.0
HIGHLY SATISFACTORY	MODERATE	n.a.	n.a.	170.0
MODERATELY SATISFACTORY	MODERATE	n.a.	n.a.	45.0
MODERATELY SATISFACTORY	MODERATE	n.a.	n.a.	16.7
MODERATELY SATISFACTORY	SIGNIFICANT	n.a.	n.a.	118.0
MODERATELY UNSATISFACTORY	NEGLIGIBLE TO LOW	n.a.	n.a.	233.6
MODERATELY UNSATISFACTORY	SIGNIFICANT	n.a.	n.a.	90.0
MODERATELY SATISFACTORY	MODERATE	n.a.	n.a.	6.8
MODERATELY SATISFACTORY	NEGLIGIBLE TO LOW	n.a.	n.a.	100.0
MODERATELY SATISFACTORY	NEGLIGIBLE TO LOW	n.a.	n.a.	149.8

continued on page 156

Exit FY	Project ID	Project Name
2008	P095675	BR-2nd Progr Sustn & Equit Growth
2009	P043420	BR WATER SMOD2
2009	P043421	BR RJ M Transit PRJ
2009	P043869	BR Santa Catarina Natural Resourc & Pov
2009	P050772	BR Land-Based Povrty Alleviation I (SIM)
2009	P050875	BR Ceara Rural Poverty Reduction Project
2009	P058503	BR GEF Amazon Region Prot Areas (ARPA)
2009	P070552	BR GEF Parana Biodiversity Project
2009	P073294	BR Fiscal & Fin Mgmt TAL
2009	P080830	BR MaranhaoIntegrated: Rural Dev
2009	P082328	BR-IntegMunicProj-Betim Municipality
2010	P038895	BR Fedwtr Mgt
2010	P050880	BR-Pernambuco Rural Poverty Reduction
2010	P050881	BR-Piaui Rural Poverty Reduction

IEG Outcome Rating	IEG Risk to DO Rating	IEG Sustainability	IEG ID Impact	Net Commit ($ Millions)
MODERATELY SATISFACTORY	MODERATE	n.a.	n.a.	150.0
SATISFACTORY	MODERATE	n.a.	n.a.	25.0
MODERATELY SATISFACTORY	MODERATE	n.a.	n.a.	230.0
SATISFACTORY	MODERATE	n.a.	n.a.	62.8
MODERATELY SATISFACTORY	SIGNIFICANT	n.a.	n.a.	193.3
MODERATELY SATISFACTORY	MODERATE	n.a.	n.a.	75.0
MODERATELY SATISFACTORY	MODERATE	n.a.	n.a.	0
MODERATELY SATISFACTORY	NONEVALUABLE	n.a.	n.a.	0
MODERATELY SATISFACTORY	MODERATE	n.a.	n.a.	8.0
UNSATISFACTORY	SIGNIFICANT	n.a.	n.a.	18.1
MODERATELY SATISFACTORY	SIGNIFICANT	n.a.	n.a.	24.0
MODERATELY SATISFACTORY	MODERATE	n.a.	n.a.	183.8
MODERATELY SATISFACTORY	MODERATE	n.a.	n.a.	56.9
MODERATELY SATISFACTORY	SIGNIFICANT	n.a.	n.a.	45.0

continued on page 158

Exit FY	Project ID	Project Name
2010	P052256	BR-MG Rural Poverty Reduction
2010	P054119	BR Bahia Dev (Health)
2010	P069934	BR-Pernambuco Integ Dev: Educ Qual Impr
2010	P074777	BR-Municipal Pension Reform TAL
2010	P082523	BR HD Technical Assistance Loan
2010	P083013	BR Disease Surveillance & Control APL 2
2010	P087713	BRBolsa Familia 1st APL
2010	P103770	BR-Alogoas Fiscal & Public Management Reform
2010	P117244	BR Rio State DPL
2011	P050761	BR-Housing Sector TAL
2011	P051696	BR São Paulo Metro Line 4 Project
2011	P060221	BR Fortaleza Metropolitan Transport Proj
2011	P066170	BR-RGN Rural Poverty Reduction

IEG Outcome Rating	IEG Risk to DO Rating	IEG Sustainability	IEG ID Impact	Net Commit ($ Millions)
MODERATELY SATISFACTORY	SIGNIFICANT	n.a.	n.a.	34.8
MODERATELY SATISFACTORY	NEGLIGIBLE TO LOW	n.a.	n.a.	30.0
MODERATELY UNSATISFACTORY	NEGLIGIBLE TO LOW	n.a.	n.a.	31.5
MODERATELY SATISFACTORY	MODERATE	n.a.	n.a.	3.4
MODERATELY SATISFACTORY	NEGLIGIBLE TO LOW	n.a.	n.a.	5.9
SATISFACTORY	NEGLIGIBLE TO LOW	n.a.	n.a.	83.6
SATISFACTORY	NEGLIGIBLE TO LOW	n.a.	n.a.	561.7
MODERATELY SATISFACTORY	MODERATE	n.a.	n.a.	195.5
SATISFACTORY	MODERATE	n.a.	n.a.	485.0
MODERATELY UNSATISFACTORY	MODERATE	n.a.	n.a.	1.1
MODERATELY SATISFACTORY	MODERATE	n.a.	n.a.	304.0
MODERATELY UNSATISFACTORY	SIGNIFICANT	n.a.	n.a.	34.8
MODERATELY SATISFACTORY	SIGNIFICANT	n.a.	n.a.	44.3

continued on page 160

Exit FY	Project ID	Project Name
2011	P066170	BR-Amapa Sustainable Communities
2011	P083533	BR TA-Sustain & Equit Growth
2011	P088009	BR GEF São Paulo Riparian Forests
2011	P106767	BR RGS Fiscal Sustainability DPL

SOURCE: World Bank database.
NOTE: IEG key ratings as of 06/17/2013. DO = development objective; ID = institutional development; n.a. = not applicable.

TABLE C.10 IFC Investments, FY04–11

Project ID	Project Short Name	Institution Legal Name	FY Commitment Date	Project Status
11686	Fleury II	Laboratorio Fleury	2004	Closed
20933	UBB SWAp Gte	Banco Itau Unibanco SA	2004	Closed
21887	TRG Expansion	Tecon Rio Grande SA	2004	Active
21668	QGP SWAp	Queiroz Galvao Oleo e Gas SA	2004	Closed
21460	Comgas	Companhia de Gas de São Paulo	2004	Closed
22561	Amaggi Expansion	Amaggi Exportacao e Importacao Limitada	2005	Closed

IEG Outcome Rating	IEG Risk to DO Rating	IEG Sustainability	IEG ID Impact	Net Commit ($ Millions)
HIGHLY UNSATISFACTORY	HIGH	n.a.	n.a.	2.5
MODERATELY SATISFACTORY	MODERATE	n.a.	n.a.	6.2
MODERATELY UNSATISFACTORY	MODERATE			0.0
MODERATELY SATISFACTORY	MODERATE	n.a.	n.a.	1,100.0

Project Size	Primary Sector	Industry Group Sector Level 1	Original Loan	Original Equity	Total Net Commitment
60,400	Health Care	Consumer & Social Services	20,000	0	(20,000)
20,000	Finance & Insurance	Financial Markets	20,000	0	(20,000)
16,200	Transportation and Warehousing	Infrastructure	8,100	0	7,538
1,200	Oil, Gas and Mining	Oil, Gas & Mining	600	0	(450)
90,000	Utilities	Oil, Gas & Mining	45,000	0	(20,000)
125,000	Agriculture and Forestry	Agribusiness & Forestry	30,000	0	30,000

continued on page 162

Project ID	Project Short Name	Institution Legal Name	FY Commitment Date	Project Status
22819	Cosan SAIC	Cosan SA Industria e Comercio	2005	Closed
23271	Aracruz Corp	Aracruz Celulose SA	2005	Closed
22376	LOJAS II	Lojas Americanas SA	2005	Closed
8175	Cibrasec	Companhia Brasileira de Securitizacao	2005	Active
21922	TriBanco Brazil	TriBanco Brazil	2005	Active
22257	ABN AMRO REAL	Banco Santander (Brasil) SA	2005	Closed
24203	Banco Real II	Banco Santander (Brasil) SA	2005	Active
10476	Dynamo Puma II	Dynamo Puma II International	2005	Closed
23747	GP Capital III	GP Capital Partners III, LP	2005	Active
22505	Embraer	Embraer—Empresa Brasileira de Aeronautica SA	2005	Closed
24393	Embraer B Ln Inc	Embraer—Empresa Brasileira de Aeronautica SA	2005	Closed
24391	Dixie Toga—Wrnt	Dixie Toga SA	2005	Closed
24190	NetServicos RI3	Net Servicos de Comunicacao S A	2005	Closed
24173	Itambe	Cooperativa Central dos Produtores Rurais de Minas Gerais Ltda	2006	Closed
24398	Education Fund	Fundo de Educacao para o Brasil	2006	Active

Project Size	Primary Sector	Industry Group Sector Level 1	Original Loan	Original Equity	Total Net Commitment
345,000	Agriculture and Forestry	Agribusiness & Forestry	70,000	0	70,000
50,000	Pulp & Paper	Agribusiness & Forestry	50,000	0	50,000
35,000	Wholesale and Retail Trade	Consumer & Social Services	35,000	0	35,000
7,500	Finance & Insurance	Financial Markets	0	3,099	3,099
10,000	Finance & Insurance	Financial Markets	10,000	0	10,000
50,000	Finance & Insurance	Financial Markets	27,000	0	27,000
108,000	Finance & Insurance	Financial Markets	98,000	0	97,386
20,000	Collective Investment Vehicles	Funds	0	20,000	20,000
15,000	Collective Investment Vehicles	Funds	0	15,000	15,000
135,000	Industrial & Consumer Products	Manufacturing	35,000	0	35,000
45,000	Industrial & Consumer Products	Manufacturing	0	0	0
350	Plastics & Rubber	Manufacturing	0	350	350
7,300	Information	Telecom & IT	0	7,368	7,368
131,000	Food & Beverages	Agribusiness & Forestry	15,000	0	(15,000)
12,000	Education Services	Consumer & Social Services	12,000	0	12,000

continued on page 164

Project ID	Project Short Name	Institution Legal Name	FY Commitment Date	Project Status
22570	RBSec	Rio Bravo Securitizadora	2006	Closed
24147	BBM	Banco BBM SA	2006	Active
24434	RBSec CLG	Rio Bravo Securitizadora	2006	Closed
24901	Tribanco SWAp	TriBanco Brazil	2006	Active
11600	Termofortaleza	Central Geradora Termeletrica de Fortaleza	2006	Active
24158	Rio do Fogo	ENERBRASIL Energias Renovaveis do Brasil Ltda	2006	Closed
24743	Endesa Brasil	Endesa Brasil SA	2006	Closed
11017	Suape ICT	Tecon Suape SA	2006	Closed
24384	TAM Airlines	Tam Linhas Aereas, SA	2006	Active
24407	MRS	MRS Logistica SA	2006	Active
24295	Ipiranga II	Ipiranga Petroquímica SA	2006	Closed
24420	Suzano Petroquim	Suzano Petroquimica SA	2006	Closed
24735	GTFP BIC Banco	Banco Industrial e Comercial SA	2006	Active
24736	GTFP BM Brazil	Banco Mercantil do Brasil SA	2006	Closed
25196	GTFP Indusval	Banco Indusval SA	2006	Active
23792	BERTIN LTDA	Bertin LTDA	2007	Closed

Project Size	Primary Sector	Industry Group Sector Level 1	Original Loan	Original Equity	Total Net Commitment
1,494	Finance & Insurance	Financial Markets	0	1,494	1,494
50,000	Finance & Insurance	Financial Markets	50,000	0	50,000
23,436	Finance & Insurance	Financial Markets	22,331	0	(31,477)
325	Finance & Insurance	Financial Markets	325	0	325
273,697	Electric Power	Infrastructure	62,500	0	62,500
5,500	Electric Power	Infrastructure	0	5,500	5,500
50,000	Electric Power	Infrastructure	0	50,000	50,000
51,440	Transportation and Warehousing	Infrastructure	6,000	0	6,000
50,000	Transportation and Warehousing	Infrastructure	50,000	0	8,680
100,000	Transportation and Warehousing	Infrastructure	50,000	0	50,000
194,500	Chemicals	Manufacturing	50,000	0	(50,000)
505,000	Chemicals	Manufacturing	60,000	0	60,000
50,000	Finance & Insurance	Trade Finance (TF)	512,641	0	512,641
—	Finance & Insurance	Trade Finance (TF)	13,374	0	13,374
15,000	Finance & Insurance	Trade Finance (TF)	358,239	0	358,239
425,000	Food & Beverages	Agribusiness & Forestry	90,000	0	30,000

continued on page 166

Project ID	Project Short Name	Institution Legal Name	FY Commitment Date	Project Status
25008	Vale do Parana	Vale do Paraná SA	2007	Active
25765	Bauducco I	Pandurata Alimentos Ltda	2007	Active
25114	BICBanco II	Banco Industrial e Comercial SA	2007	Active
25429	BBM II	Banco BBM SA	2007	Active
25507	Banco Fibra	Banco Fibra SA	2007	Active
24609	GOL	GOL Transporte Aereos SA	2007	Active
25862	AGC Preemptive 1	Andrade Gutierrez Concessoes SA	2007	Active
24833	Randon II	Randon SA Implementos e Participacoes	2007	Active
25195	GTFP BMC SA	BMC SA	2007	Closed
25462	GTFP Daycoval	Banco Daycoval SA	2007	Active
25939	GTFP NBC Brazil	NBC Bank Brasil SA Banco Multiplo	2007	Active
25900	SLC Agricola	SLC Agricola S/A	2008	Closed
26135	USJ	USJ Acucar e Alcool SA	2008	Active
26800	Cosan Rights	Cosan SA Industria e Comercio	2008	Closed

Project Size	Primary Sector	Industry Group Sector Level 1	Original Loan	Original Equity	Total Net Commitment
144,000	Food & Beverages	Agribusiness & Forestry	35,000	0	35,000
166,400	Food & Beverages	Agribusiness & Forestry	30,000	0	30,000
40,000	Finance & Insurance	Financial Markets	40,000	0	40,000
50,000	Finance & Insurance	Financial Markets	50,000	0	50,000
50,000	Finance & Insurance	Financial Markets	30,000	20,000	50,000
50,000	Transportation and Warehousing	Infrastructure	50,000	0	50,000
6,500	Utilities	Infrastructure	0	6,500	6,500
350,000	Industrial & Consumer Products	Manufacturing	35,000	0	35,000
—	Finance & Insurance	Trade Finance (TF)	14,970	0	14,970
60,000	Finance & Insurance	Trade Finance (TF)	455,694	0	455,694
7,500	Finance & Insurance	Trade Finance (TF)	122,380	0	122,380
234,000	Agriculture and Forestry	Agribusiness & Forestry	40,000	0	40,000
393,000	Agriculture and Forestry	Agribusiness & Forestry	40,000	0	40,000
959,000	Food & Beverages	Agribusiness & Forestry	0	3,452	3,452

continued on page 168

Project ID	Project Short Name	Institution Legal Name	FY Commitment Date	Project Status
25527	Real Student Fin	Banco Real Student Financing	2008	Closed
25344	Hosp São Luiz	Hospital São Luiz	2008	Closed
25200	Banco Brascan	Banco Brascan SA	2008	Active
25762	Unik	Unik SA	2008	Closed
26080	Daycoval II	Banco Daycoval SA	2008	Active
26200	New BR SCL	Banco Santander (Brasil) SA	2008	Active
26336	Banco Fibra II	Banco Fibra SA	2008	Active
26475	Sofisa	Banco Sofisa SA	2008	Active
26505	Unibanco SCL	Banco Itau Unibanco SA	2008	Active
27443	BBM B Loan	Banco BBM SA	2008	Active
26370	CEMAR Maranhao	Companhia Energética do Maranhão—Cemar	2008	Active
25977	TS (Expansion)	Tecon Salvador SA	2008	Active
26555	AGC Preemptive 2	Andrade Gutierrez Concessoes SA	2008	Active
26099	Sabo	Sabo Industria e Comercio de Autopecas Ltda	2008	Active
25956	Armco	Armco do Brasil SA	2008	Active
25781	QGOG Rigs	Eiffel Ridge Group CV	2008	Active
26314	Schahin Rigs	Black Gold Drilling LLC	2008	Active

Project Size	Primary Sector	Industry Group Sector Level 1	Original Loan	Original Equity	Total Net Commitment
28,233	Education Services	Consumer & Social Services	13,369	0	(12,340)
34,000	Health Care	Consumer & Social Services	17,000	0	17,000
30,000	Finance & Insurance	Financial Markets	30,000	0	30,000
3,740	Finance & Insurance	Financial Markets	2,996	1,403	(230)
115,000	Finance & Insurance	Financial Markets	30,000	0	30,000
200,000	Finance & Insurance	Financial Markets	200,000	0	200,000
200,000	Finance & Insurance	Financial Markets	40,000	0	40,000
200,000	Finance & Insurance	Financial Markets	30,000	0	30,000
200,000	Finance & Insurance	Financial Markets	75,000	0	9,000
160,000	Finance & Insurance	Financial Markets	0	0	0
307,000	Electric Power	Infrastructure	80,000	0	80,000
11,400	Transportation and Warehousing	Infrastructure	5,900	0	5,100
14,250	Utilities	Infrastructure	0	14,250	14,250
222,000	Industrial & Consumer Products	Manufacturing	40,000	0	30,000
25,000	Primary Metals	Manufacturing	25,000	0	25,000
1,050,600	Oil, Gas and Mining	Oil, Gas & Mining	50,000	0	49,070
1,013,000	Oil, Gas and Mining	Oil, Gas & Mining	50,000	0	50,000

continued on page 170

Project ID	Project Short Name	Institution Legal Name	FY Commitment Date	Project Status
26162	Andrade G SA II	Andrade Gutierrez SA	2008	Closed
26278	Ruralfone	Local Serviços de Telecomunicações LTDA	2008	Closed
26163	GTFP Banco Pine	Banco Pine SA	2008	Active
26471	GTFP BPN Brasil	BPN Brasil Banco Multiplo SA	2008	Closed
26772	GTFP Sofisa	Banco Sofisa SA	2008	Active
27783	Bauducco NE	Pandurata Alimentos Ltda	2009	Active
26733	Banco Pecunia	Banco Pecúnia SA	2009	Active
27080	Indusval II	Banco Indusval SA	2009	Closed
27374	Banco Fibra RI	Banco Fibra SA	2009	Active
27455	Fibra B Loan	Banco Fibra SA	2009	Active
27702	Indusval Euro B	Banco Indusval SA	2009	Closed
27805	Daycoval III	Banco Daycoval SA	2009	Active
26512	Estre Ambiental	Estre Ambiental SA	2009	Active
27031	Latapack	Latapack Ball Embalagens Ltda	2009	Active
24738	GTFP ABC Brasil	Banco ABC Brasil SA	2009	Active

Project Size	Primary Sector	Industry Group Sector Level 1	Original Loan	Original Equity	Total Net Commitment
50,000	Collective Investment Vehicles	Other Infra Sectors	50,000	0	0
4,600	Information	Telecom & IT	3,000	0	0
40,500	Finance & Insurance	Trade Finance (TF)	588,012	0	588,012
—	Finance & Insurance	Trade Finance (TF)	21,319	0	21,319
10,000	Finance & Insurance	Trade Finance (TF)	84,676	0	84,676
63,900	Food & Beverages	Agribusiness & Forestry	25,000	0	25,000
20,000	Finance & Insurance	Financial Markets	19,962	0	19,962
65,000	Finance & Insurance	Financial Markets	15,000	0	15,000
21,247	Finance & Insurance	Financial Markets	0	10,674	10,674
70,000	Finance & Insurance	Financial Markets	0	0	0
19,190	Finance & Insurance	Financial Markets	0	0	0
54,995	Finance & Insurance	Financial Markets	43,161	0	43,161
55,886	Utilities	Infrastructure	24,433	0	24,433
135,000	Industrial & Consumer Products	Manufacturing	25,000	0	25,000
45,000	Finance & Insurance	Trade Finance (TF)	255,150	0	255,150

continued on page 172

Project ID	Project Short Name	Institution Legal Name	FY Commitment Date	Project Status
27779	GTFP Banco Fibra	Banco Fibra SA	2009	Active
27843	GTFP Unibanco Br	Banco Itau Unibanco SA	2009	Closed
28537	Brookfield Resid	Brookfield Incorporacoes SA	2010	Active
22497	Ideal Invest	Ideal Invest SA	2010	Active
28097	Anhanguera Edu	Anhanguera Educacional Participacoes SA	2010	Active
28755	Mauricio Nassau	Ensino Superior Bureau Juridico SA	2010	Active
27475	Ceape—MA	Centro de Apoio aos Pequenos Empreendimentos do Estado do Maranhao	2010	Active
27488	Tribanco II	TriBanco Brazil	2010	Active
28449	Bic SME FIDC	Banco Industrial e Comercial SA	2010	Active
28626	Bic Banco H&E	Banco Industrial e Comercial SA	2010	Active
29443	Daycoval Mobiliz	Banco Daycoval SA	2010	Active
27787	Foz do Brasil	Foz do Brasil SA	2010	Active
28512	Constellation	CIPEF Constellation Coinvestment Fund LP	2010	Active
28956	GTFP BI Brazil	Banco Industrial do Brasil SA	2010	Active

Project Size	Primary Sector	Industry Group Sector Level 1	Original Loan	Original Equity	Total Net Commitment
30,000	Finance & Insurance	Trade Finance (TF)	627,746	0	627,746
—	Finance & Insurance	Trade Finance (TF)	50,000	0	50,000
47,000	Construction and Real Estate	Consumer & Social Services	30,000	17,000	47,000
47,705	Education Services	Consumer & Social Services	0	6,713	6,713
51,048	Education Services	Consumer & Social Services	28,694	0	28,694
35,000	Education Services	Consumer & Social Services	35,000	0	(35,000)
2,492	Finance & Insurance	Financial Markets	2,138	0	2,138
45,000	Finance & Insurance	Financial Markets	15,000	0	15,000
28,675	Finance & Insurance	Financial Markets	28,919	0	28,919
25,000	Finance & Insurance	Financial Markets	25,000	0	25,000
165,887	Finance & Insurance	Financial Markets	25,000	0	25,000
999,000	Utilities	Infrastructure	50,000	0	50,000
433,000	Collective Investment Vehicles	Other Infra Sectors	0	103,000	103,000
15,000	Finance & Insurance	Trade Finance (TF)	73,294	0	73,294

continued on page 174

Project ID	Project Short Name	Institution Legal Name	FY Commitment Date	Project Status
29055	GTFP WestLB	Banco WestLB do Brasil SA	2010	Closed
28565	Estacio	Estacio Participacoes SA	2011	Active
28144	Rede DOr	Hospital e Maternidade São Luiz SA	2011	Active
28710	UBF Seguros	UBF Seguros SA	2011	Active
29362	Tribanco Eq	TriBanco Brazil	2011	Active
29471	Fibra Mobiliz	Banco Fibra SA	2011	Active
29916	BIB B loan	Banco Industrial do Brasil SA	2011	Active
29920	Bic Mobilization	Banco Industrial e Comercial SA	2011	Active
30444	Fibra RI 2010	Banco Fibra SA	2011	Active
30605	Fibra Cap Incr	Banco Fibra SA	2011	Active
31180	Fibra RI 2011	Banco Fibra SA	2011	Active
29505	BTP Santos	Brasil Terminal Portuario SA	2011	Active
27233	CASAN — Loan	Companhia Catarinense de Aguas e Saneamento	2011	Active
29016	DESO BRL Loan	Companhia de Saneamento de Sergipe—DESO	2011	Active
29628	Latapack Growth	Latapack Ball Embalagens Ltda	2011	Active
29428	Softwell	Softwell Solutions em Informatica SA	2011	Active

NOTE: — = not available.

Project Size	Primary Sector	Industry Group Sector Level 1	Original Loan	Original Equity	Total Net Commitment
—	Finance & Insurance	Trade Finance (TF)	29,000	0	29,000
259,200	Education Services	Consumer & Social Services	30,000	0	30,000
99,594	Health Care	Consumer & Social Services	50,000	0	50,000
10,512	Finance & Insurance	Financial Markets	0	10,512	10,512
23,517	Finance & Insurance	Financial Markets	0	23,517	23,517
135,576	Finance & Insurance	Financial Markets	15,000	0	15,000
73,024	Finance & Insurance	Financial Markets	15,000	0	15,000
50,000	Finance & Insurance	Financial Markets	25,000	0	25,000
4,646	Finance & Insurance	Financial Markets	0	4,646	4,646
194,013	Finance & Insurance	Financial Markets	0	44,894	44,894
4,352	Finance & Insurance	Financial Markets	0	4,352	4,352
722,000	Transportation and Warehousing	Infrastructure	97,000	0	97,000
27,728	Utilities	Infrastructure	23,517	0	23,517
16,421	Utilities	Infrastructure	10,737	0	10,737
80,000	Industrial & Consumer Products	Manufacturing	20,000	0	3,900
4,800	Professional, Scientific and Technical Services	Telecom & IT	0	4,800	4,800

TABLE C.11 IFC Advisory Services, FY05–11

Project ID	Project Data Sheet Approved Fiscal Year	Project Stage	Project Name	Primary Business Line
23355	2005	COMPLETED	Rio Tinto Brazil	Sustainable Business Advisory
23875	2006	COMPLETED	Recife Transport	Public-Private Partnerships Transaction
23965	2005	COMPLETED	Rio Tinto BR II	Sustainable Business Advisory
24443	2006	COMPLETED	BR 116	Public-Private Partnerships Transaction
24610	2006	UNKNOWN	Pontal 1	Public-Private Partnerships Transaction
25117	2008	PORTFOLIO	Pontal 2	Public-Private Partnerships Transaction
26967	2008	COMPLETED	BA 093	Public-Private Partnerships Transaction
27857	2010	COMPLETED	Bahia Health	Public-Private Partnerships Transaction
502246	2007	OTHER	GEF EFCC Sugar Mill Co-Generation	Sustainable Business Advisory
522777	2006	COMPLETED	Precious Woods Holding Ltd	Sustainable Business Advisory
523602	2006	UNKNOWN	SFMF Bovespa SI	Sustainable Business Advisory
531244	2006	COMPLETED	LKG:Tribanco	Sustainable Business Advisory

Project Status	Project Start Date	Project End Date	Total Project Cost	Prorated Total Funds Managed by IFC	Total Funding Amt
CLOSED	04/14/04		0	0	0
CLOSED	08/10/04	06/30/09	950,000	950,000	100,000
CLOSED	10/12/04	06/30/09	0	0	0
CLOSED	07/21/05	06/30/09	3,240,000	3,240,000	1,240,000
CLOSED	09/13/05	06/30/09	0	0	0
ACTIVE	04/14/06	02/28/13	2,043,250	2,043,250	1,643,250
CLOSED	05/05/08	12/31/10	1,241,610	1,241,610	1,176,610
CLOSED	12/12/08	06/30/10	536,470	536,470	391,470
TERMINATED	07/01/00	06/30/18	4,220,000	4,220,000	4,220,000
CLOSED	04/12/04	03/31/09	262,384	137,384	137,384
CLOSED	06/02/04		0	0	0
CLOSED	09/30/06	12/31/09	0	0	0

continued on page 178

Project ID	Project Data Sheet Approved Fiscal Year	Project Stage	Project Name	Primary Business Line
531500	2006	COMPLETED	Proinfa Wind Projects	Public-Private Partnerships Transaction
531600	2006	UNKNOWN	SFMF FGV Con	Access To Finance
536964	2006	COMPLETED	POEMA-Amazon Paper Project	Sustainable Business Advisory
539763	2006	COMPLETED	São Paulo Simplification of Admin Procedures for Business Registration at the Municipal Level	Investment Climate
540943	2006	COMPLETED	Brazil - Elimination of Administrative Barriers at the Subnational Level (Phase I)	Investment Climate
545484	2007	COMPLETED	Suzano Plastic Cluster in Greater ABC Region	Sustainable Business Advisory
550527	2007	COMPLETED	Improving the Regulatory Environment in Brazil	Investment Climate
552645	2007	COMPLETED	Bovespa ISE II	Sustainable Business Advisory
553067	2008	COMPLETED	Bertin Sustainable Supply Chain	Sustainable Business Advisory
555345	2007	COMPLETED	Brazil HF Pre-Design Assessment	Access To Finance
557825	2008	COMPLETED	CT R-Bauducco	Sustainable Business Advisory
560947	2008	COMPLETED	Srsp Terra Nova	Sustainable Business Advisory

Project Status	Project Start Date	Project End Date	Total Project Cost	Prorated Total Funds Managed by IFC	Total Funding Amt
CLOSED	09/17/04	06/30/08	100,000	100,000	100,000
CLOSED	09/22/04		0	0	0
CLOSED	07/01/05	06/30/07	120,830	120,830	120,830
CLOSED	02/22/06	06/30/11	693,000	678,000	330,000
CLOSED	10/17/05		0	0	0
CLOSED	03/15/07	03/30/09	1,206,068	256,935	256,935
CLOSED	05/03/07	09/30/10	1,624,211	1,561,711	1,497,751
CLOSED			0	0	0
CLOSED	03/10/08	06/30/09	371,855	344,855	310,000
CLOSED	06/15/07	03/15/08	125,000	125,000	125,000
CLOSED	11/15/07	08/01/09	50,772	46,772	46,772
CLOSED	01/25/08	12/30/08	197,000	197,000	197,000

continued on page 180

Project ID	Project Data Sheet Approved Fiscal Year	Project Stage	Project Name	Primary Business Line
562168	UNKNOWN	OTHER	Banco Fibra TA	Access To Finance
565147	2010	PORTFOLIO	CEAPE Maranhao Advisory Services Project	Access To Finance
566027	UNKNOWN	OTHER	AccessBankBrazil	Access To Finance
566227	UNKNOWN	PIPELINE	Sustainable Cattle Ranching Working Group Development of E&S Principles and Criteria	Sustainable Business Advisory
566748	2009	PORTFOLIO	Brazil Frontier States Investment Generation (National-Subnational)	Investment Climate
567287	UNKNOWN	OTHER	ANDE AS	Access To Finance
568527	2010	OTHER	Amazon MFI	Access To Finance
568607	UNKNOWN	PIPELINE	Regulatory Reform and Capacity Building in Brazil	Investment Climate
570588	2009	COMPLETED	Brazil CG Forum	Sustainable Business Advisory
570912	2010	PORTFOLIO	Alianca da Terra	Sustainable Business Advisory
570928	UNKNOWN	PIPELINE	Responsible Soy Production in Brazilian Amazon	Sustainable Business Advisory
575227	UNKNOWN	PIPELINE	Sustainable Forestry in the Brazilian Amazon	Sustainable Business Advisory
579487	2011	PORTFOLIO	BH Primary Care	Public-Private Partnerships Transaction

Project Status	Project Start Date	Project End Date	Total Project Cost	Prorated Total Funds Managed by IFC	Total Funding Amt
TERMINATED	01/11/08		0	0	0
ACTIVE	06/30/10	06/28/13	294,137	269,137	173,521
TERMINATED	02/05/09	03/01/11	1,386,443	1,386,443	718,417
ACTIVE	07/01/10	08/31/13	562,000	250,000	250,000
ACTIVE	05/12/09	10/31/12	1,935,000	1,935,000	0
TERMINATED	08/03/09	01/31/12	932,000	932,000	466,000
TERMINATED	06/01/10	01/15/14	2,715,238	768,000	768,000
CLOSED	04/16/09	09/30/09	107,000	107,000	107,000
CLOSED	11/05/08	11/30/10	280,322	161,822	161,822
ACTIVE	12/21/09	03/31/12	2,275,611	845,000	845,000
CLOSED	11/01/09	06/30/11	480,000	360,000	240,000
ACTIVE	05/15/10	06/30/13	2,650,000	1,650,000	1,650,000
ACTIVE	08/01/10	10/31/12	3,314,419	3,314,419	2,037,419

continued on page 182

Project ID	Project Data Sheet Approved Fiscal Year	Project Stage	Project Name	Primary Business Line
582687	2011	PORTFOLIO	Belo Horizonte Schools	Public-Private Partnerships Transaction
583687	UNKNOWN	PIPELINE	Cerrado Mapping	Sustainable Business Advisory
583707	UNKNOWN	PIPELINE	Responsible Soy - Brazil	Sustainable Business Advisory
587007	2011	PORTFOLIO	Tribanco EE	Access To Finance
595967	UNKNOWN	PIPELINE	Brazilian Airports Project	Public-Private Partnerships Transaction

Project Status	Project Start Date	Project End Date	Total Project Cost	Prorated Total Funds Managed by IFC	Total Funding Amt
ACTIVE	03/20/11	12/31/12	1,555,569	1,555,569	1,037,569
ACTIVE			0	0	0
ACTIVE			0	0	0
ACTIVE	07/01/11	12/31/12	120,000	120,000	70,000
ACTIVE	05/21/12	03/21/13	4,000,000	4,000,000	4,000,000

TABLE C.12 MIGA Projects: FY04–11

Fiscal Year	Project Name	Sector	Gross Exposure	Environment Category
2004	Cefla Capital Services SpA	Services	1.97	C
2004	TermoCabo Ltda	Power	26.76	
2004	Expansion Transmissão Itumbiara Marimbondo Ltda	Power	11	A
2004	Cachoeira Paulista Transmissora de Energia Ltda	Power	17.94	A
2005	Cachoeira Paulista Transmissora de Energia Ltda	Power	15.3	A
2005	Transmissão Itumbiara Marimbondo Ltda	Power	10.3	A
2005	Banco Rabobank International Brasil SA	Capital Markets	66.5	
2006	Munirah Transmissora de Energia SA	Power	9.8	
2006	Artemis Transmissora de Energia SA	Power	21.1	A
2006	Nordeste Transmissora de Energia SA	Power	23.1	A
2006	Sul Transmissora de Energia	Power	10.7	A
2006	Uirapuru Transmissora de Energia	Power	5.7	A
2007	Itumbiara Transmissora de Energia Ltda (ITE)	Power	35.4	A
2007	Porto Primavera Transmissora de Energia Ltda (PPTE)	Power	20.6	A
2007	Vila do Conde Transmissora de Energia (VCTE)	Power	5.4	A
2009	Serra da Mesa Transmissora de Energia SA	Power	33	B

Appendix D
IFC Operations in Brazil, FY04–11

IFC Operational Strategy

IFC's FY04–07 strategy for Brazil followed the four pillars of the CAS. Its primary focus was directed to the competitiveness pillar through private sector development. Its contribution to the other pillars was intended to be indirect and modest. Its sectoral strategy directed investments to the development of financial markets, emphasizing microfinance and housing finance, infrastructure, manufacturing, and agribusiness. It also highlighted the importance of advisory services for environmental and social development.

To respond to major changes in Brazil's economic performance and new priorities, as well as to sharpen its focus on competitiveness, IFC updated its Brazil strategy for the FY06–08 period.[1] This new strategy emphasized expanding IFC's base in target industries by moving investments toward second-tier, sustainable, fast-growing export businesses, infrastructure, and logistics. On the financial sector, "sustainability credit lines" were added to micro, small and medium-size enterprises (SMEs), and housing finance. This update also enhanced the focus on advisory services to PPPs for subnational utilities and for the health and education sectors.

Under the FY08–11 CPS, IFC supported a continued engagement with midsize banks (begun in FY05). The CPS recognized the potentially high development impact of IFC's engagement with midsize banks because these banks (i) make credit available to small and midsized companies, which are typically underserved by larger banks and the capital markets; (ii) help promote competition in the Brazilian banking sector, which is dominated by large public as well as private-sector entities; and (iii) face handicaps compared to larger banks in terms of availability, stability, tenor, and pricing of local currency funding. For the manufacturing and agribusiness sector, IFC completed a mapping exercise and identified 400 second-tier corporate and 4,000 medium-size companies as part of its effort to improve second-tier Brazilian companies' access to financing with longer tenors.

In line with the priorities of the CPS, IFC began taking a more direct role in poverty alleviation. The strategy update in FY10 highlighted the tools IFC could employ to reduce poverty and income inequality in a number of sectors by focusing on people at the bottom of the pyramid and the frontier regions. It also emphasized activities to slow climate change. The FY10 updates maintain the focus on SMEs through engagement with midsize banks, trade finance, and infrastructure investment in the frontier regions.

The limited size of IFC's financing compared to the needs of Brazil's dynamic private sector keeps its projects from generating a countrywide impact. Given the scope of private sector activities, this is even true where its investments were judged relevant to CAS/Country Partnership Strategy objectives and projects were found to be successful.

The availability of other, well-established financing sources, including the National Bank of Economic and Social Development (BNDES), is also an important factor in IFC's role in Brazil. Between 2004 and 2009, BNDES increased its annual disbursement more than fivefold, from $13.8 billion to $71.6 billion, and maintained the high level of annual disbursements at $96.3 billion in 2010 and $82.3 billion in 2011. IFC's disbursements remained modest in comparison—$1.10 billion in FY04–07 and $1.45 billion in FY08–11. In four out of eight years during the period evaluated, IFC disbursements were less than $200 million per year. Even after incorporating IFC's B-loans and other resource mobilization programs (Figure D.1), IFC's disbursements were a small fraction of what BNDES disbursed annually.

To respond to uncertainty of demand under rapidly changing economic conditions, IFC's operational strategy and investments covered a wide variety of industries, including natural

FIGURE D.1 IFC Disbursement in Brazil, FY04–11

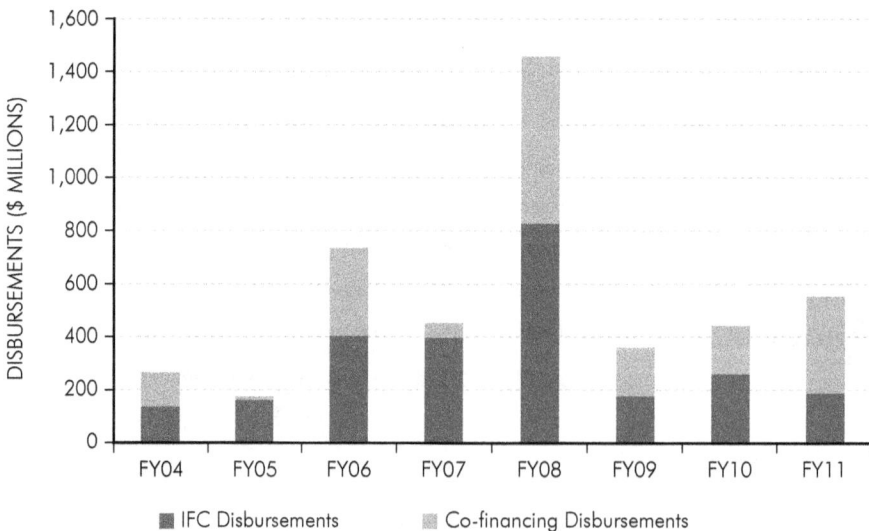

SOURCE: IFC.

resources, agribusiness, manufacturing, infrastructure, social sectors, and financial and capital markets. Attempts were made to focus on second-tier companies to enhance the impact from IFC activities. It built relationships and the portfolio with 14 midsize banks, but the engagement with second-tier companies was not extensive in real sectors.

IFC increased investments on the northeast and Amazon regions in line with the Bank Group country strategies, financing 10 operations in these regions during the FY08–11 period for $389 million in infrastructure, financial services, and manufacturing.[2] However, identifying the right investment opportunities in these regions was a significant challenge. Based on discussions with the top audit firms in Brazil in 2008, only four companies were in the frontier regions of Brazil that were being audited by major international audit firms, making it difficult for IFC to find business opportunities within these regions.

IFC PROGRAM

During FY04–11, IFC had a net commitment of $5.01 billion for 113 investments, making Brazil one of its largest investment portfolios. More than two-thirds (68.5 percent) of IFC commitments between FY04 and FY11 were for the financial market operations, including the Global Trade Finance Program (GTFP), while 12.8 percent supported infrastructure development and 7.3 percent, the agribusiness and forestry sector. During the same period, IFC engaged in 30 advisory service operations. Of these, 6 remain active, 1 was dropped, and 23 were completed as of April 2013. During this period, IFC committed approximately $12.7 million to these operations, of which the public-private partnership (PPP) business line comprised the largest total component at $7.8 million.

Until FY09, the IFC program in Brazil worked under two opposing factors: strong demand for financing in a fast-growing Brazilian private sector, and its own prudential limits to control single-country exposure. Around the time of the FY04–07 CAS discussion, IFC suggested that headroom requirements for Brazil would be determined by the net worth plus general reserves (NW+GR), rather than the more restrictive limit based on the held portfolio. IFC's committed portfolio nearly doubled between FY00 and FY08, and its Brazil exposure reached 15 percent of the NW+GR by FY05 and just under 20 percent in FY08.

During the FY08–11 CPS period, IFC's net commitments more than tripled, to $3.78 billion from $1.22 billion in FY04–07. Much of this increase was due to an expansion of GTFP in Brazil, which accounted for 60 percent of the $2.27 billion in net commitment during the FY08–11 CPS period. The amount of long-term financing of loans and equity investments in Brazil between FY09 and FY11 remained well below the $751.3 million achieved in FY08 (Table D.1).

TABLE D.1 IFC Brazil Annual Commitment: Long-Term and Short-Term Finance

Fiscal Year	Short-Term Finance ($ Millions)	Long-Term Finance ($ Millions)	Annual Net Commitment ($ Millions)
2004	n.a.	24.8	24.8
2005	n.a.	400.3	400.3
2006	45.0	412.6	457.8
2007	122.5	219.0	341.5
2008	249.0	751.3	1,000.3
2009	478.7	48.5	527.2
2010	788.1	353.0	1,141.1
2011	755.2	363.8	1,119.0
Total	2,438.5	2,573.3	5,011.8

SOURCE: IFC.
NOTE: The trade finance program in Brazil started in FY06. n.a. = not applicable.

Between FY04 and FY12, IFC invested approximately $1.7 billion in 56 projects in real sectors (agribusiness, manufacturing and services, health and education, and infrastructure). During the first half of this period, IFC maintained an average annual level of commitments of about $235 million in these sectors, but that fell below $100 million in FY09 and FY10. Real sector investments began recovering in FY11 and reached $350 million in FY12. Throughout the period, real sector investments were dwarfed by rapid growth in loans and guarantees to financial intermediaries, particularly by the trade guarantee programs beginning in 2006. Several factors have likely contributed to this growth. First, financial market transactions typically have a larger size of asset booked per transaction than investment operations in the real sector. They also have shorter processing and portfolio supervision times. In addition, the analyses on credit risk and the IFC role and additionality are often simpler than project financing operations.

During the period evaluated, IFC committed approximately $12.7 million for 30 advisory service engagements in Brazil. These activities supported a wide array of advisory service activities, ranging from sustainable business advice to soya producers and forestry companies to public-private partnership transactions in infrastructure and health and education facilities. IFC also engaged with both federal and state agencies to provide advice to improve the business climate. In connection with the emphasis on frontier regions in the CAS, IFC undertook regional initiatives in Amazon, Para, and Nordeste (supported by specific investment programs). It also participated in environmental and social sustainability studies, with both private business and government agencies, and in efforts to support local and state governments to eliminate administrative barriers to doing business at the subnational level. Toward the end of the period, PPPs became the most important component of advisory services, with the total dollar amount spent on them doubling in FY11.

Overall Development Outcome Ratings

IFC monitors its development outcomes at the partner company level with its Development Outcome Tracking System. The overall development outcome of 22 companies in Brazil, which had transactions with IFC during the period evaluated and had been rated, was 73 percent (Table D.2). This was slightly lower than the Latin America and the Caribbean regional average of 77 percent, but higher than the IFC-wide average of 68 percent. For Financial Performance, Economic Performance, and Environmental and Social Performance subcategories, Development Outcome Tracking System ratings in Brazil were similar to the overall IFC average. However, the rating for Private Sector Development in Brazil was much lower than the IFC-wide average.

During the evaluation period, IEG verified 20 Expanded Project Supervision Reports and undertook three Project Evaluation Summaries of the projects that were approved from FY98 to FY06. Out of 23 projects verified by IEG during the evaluation period, 83 percent were rated mostly successful or better for overall development outcome. Brazil had a higher success ratio than selected middle-income countries (except Colombia at 100 percent), Latin America and the Caribbean (72 percent), and overall IFC (66 percent).

Loan Portfolio

IFC's net commitments in long-term loans in FY04–11 were $2.15 billion, which was larger than a selected group of middle-income countries except India (Table D.3). Long loan tenors was an important strength of IFC support as it was not easy to access long-term international funding in Brazil, sometimes even for top-tier Brazilian companies. The difficulty was particularly acute when Brazil's country risk was considered high for a few years after the crisis in 2002–03. During the period reviewed, IFC had a high level of prepayments by its Brazilian clients: $729.2 million, which is high compared to India and China, which have

TABLE D.2 IFC DOTS Ratings

	Brazil	Mexico	Colombia	Peru	India	China	LAC	IFC-Wide
DOTS Rating								
Overall development outcome (%)	73	52	91	92	60	69	77	68
Number of IFC DOTS ratings	22	23	22	12	94	42	146	361
Financial performance (%)	52	33	77	58	44	52	57	51
Economic performance (%)	70	59	91	67	59	59	64	72
Environmental & social perf (%)	74	61	74	85	80	66	71	70
Private sector development (%)	70	59	91	67	59	59	64	85
XPSR and PSR Ratings								
Number of projects	23	16	11	18	33	34	144	547
Development outcome ratings (%)	83	63	100	83	61	65	72	66

SOURCE: IFC.
NOTE: DOTS = Development Outcome Tracking System; LAC = Latin America and the Caribbean Region; PSR = Project Supervision Report; XPSR = Expanded Project Supervision Report.

$345.6 million and $216.8 million, respectively. With Brazil gaining better access to domestic and international capital markets, IFC's role as a provider of long-term loans became less critical to a number of companies, in particular to the top-tier companies.

The IFC loan portfolio in Brazil generally performed well. At the end of FY11, nonperforming loans were 1.11 percent of total loans, which was lower than the average for the region (3.41 percent) and IFC overall (4.38 percent). In terms of the credit risk rating, IFC's loan portfolio performs much better than the Latin America and the Caribbean Region and IFC-wide averages (Table D. 4). At the end of June 2011, 78 percent of active loan transactions were classified as low risk, compared to that region's average of 59 percent and IFC average of 49 percent.

TABLE D.3 IFC Total Net Loan Commitments of selected Middle-Income Countries, FY04–11

Country/Region	Loan Net Commitments ($ Millions)	Share of Total Commitments with GTFP (%)	Share of Total Commitments without GTFP (%)
Brazil	2,155.0	43.0	83.7
Mexico	999.6	66.7	67.6
Colombia	735.4	59.6	64.3
Peru	831.4	79.7	84.3
India	3,032.4	71.5	71.7
China	1,633.9	53.6	54.7
Latin America and Caribbean Region	8,764.5	57.2	79.0
IFC total	36,593.4	43.0	74.3

SOURCE: IFC.
NOTE: GTFP = Global Trade Finance Program.

TABLE D.4 Credit Risk Status of IFC's Outstanding Loan Portfolio

Loan risk	Brazil	Mexico	Colombia	Peru	India	Indonesia	China	LAC	IFC-Wide
Good	78%	49%	85%	57%	61%	78%	64%	59%	49%
Watch	7%	22%	15%	36%	28%	16%	26%	27%	35%
Poor	16%	29%	0%	7%	11%	6%	11%	14%	16%
Total number of investments	90	45	40	42	114	32	66	462	1837

SOURCE: IFC.
NOTE: Data as of June 2011. LAC = Latin America and the Caribbean Region.

IFC also helped mobilize additional funding across financial and nonfinancial sectors. It mobilized a gross commitment of $2.36 billion during the period evaluated, which is much larger than in some other middle-income countries (China $1.13 billion, Colombia $1.9 billion, and India $1.4 billion). By arranging international syndications for midsize banks in Brazil, IFC introduced these banks to international markets.[3] In some cases, after IFC provided its financing, development finance institutions and commercial banks followed up with their own financing to IFC clients.

Equity Portfolio

The share of equity portfolio in total commitments was small in Brazil, compared to some of the comparable middle-income countries (Table D.5). IFC made net equity investments of $418.3 million, which represented 8.3 percent of total net commitment during the period reviewed. This was lower than for Mexico (32.4 percent with $478.9 million) and Colombia (33.1 percent with $408.1 million). IFC made much larger equity investments in China ($1.35 billion or 44.4 percent of total commitment) and in India ($1.19 billion or 28.3 percent of total commitment).

IFC's major equity investments in Brazil include two investment funds in FY05, one power sector company in FY06, two midsize banks (starting from FY07), and an investment fund for an off-shore oil drilling company in FY11. The largest equity investment was a $103 million

TABLE D.5 IFC Total Equity Commitments of Selected Middle-Income Countries, FY04–11

Country/Region	Equity ($ Millions)	Share of Total Commitments with GTFP (Percent)	Share of Total Commitments without GTFP (Percent)
Brazil	418.3	8.3	16.3
China	1,353.9	44.4	45.3
Colombia	408.1	33.1	35.7
India	1,198.3	28.3	28.3
Mexico	478.9	32.0	32.4
Peru	154.3	14.8	15.7
Latin America and Caribbean Region	2,336.1	15.3	21.0
IFC Total	12,690.1	20.4	25.7

SOURCE: IFC.
NOTE: GTFP = Global Trade Finance Program.

equity investment in an off-shore oil drilling company. In terms of IFC's risk rating, equity investments in Brazil had a profile similar to that of the region and IFC average. At the end of June 2011, 42 percent of 38 active equity investments in Brazil were categorized as low risk, compared to a region average of 43 percent and an IFC average of 39 percent (Table D.6).

Based on interviews conducted for this evaluation, it seems that IFC's equity investment opportunities were hampered by three major factors: (i) constraints caused by the headroom concerns until FY09 before IFC changed its risk calculation from a nominal to a weighted risk-based approach; (ii) increased emphasis on frontier regions, where it is generally more challenging to identify appropriate investment opportunities; and (iii) the cautious approach toward a new sector, particularly during the turbulent years of the Brazilian economy.

Global Trade Finance Program

Short-term trade finance was the dominant financial product for IFC in Brazil during the period evaluated, especially in the last three fiscal years (FY09–11). IFC started the GTFP in Brazil in FY06 and quickly grew to represent 90.8 percent and 69.1 percent of IFC's net commitment in FY09 and FY10 respectively (Figure D.2).

IFC started GTFP in FY06 before the financial crisis. GTFP targeted its assistance to SMEs and energy efficiency-related transactions during the period evaluated. IFC uses the proxy measure of transactions less than $1 million to indicate whether the trade financing is reaching SMEs or not. Between FY06 and FY11, IFC guaranteed a total of 2,013 trade finance transactions in Brazil with a total commitment amount of $2.4 billion. Using this definition, support for SMEs amounted to $452 million (18.6 percent of the GTFP

TABLE D.6 Credit Risk Status of IFC's Outstanding Equity Portfolio

Equity Risk	Brazil	China	Colombia	India	Mexico	Peru	LAC	IFC-Wide
Good	42%	58%	72%	46%	24%	79%	43%	39%
Watch	42%	29%	24%	36%	46%	4%	30%	29%
Poor	16%	13%	4%	18%	29%	18%	28%	32%
Total number of investments	38	113	25	130	41	28	242	1,247

SOURCE: IFC data.
NOTE: Data as of June 2011. LAC = Latin America and the Caribbean Region.

IFC Net Commitment by Financial Products

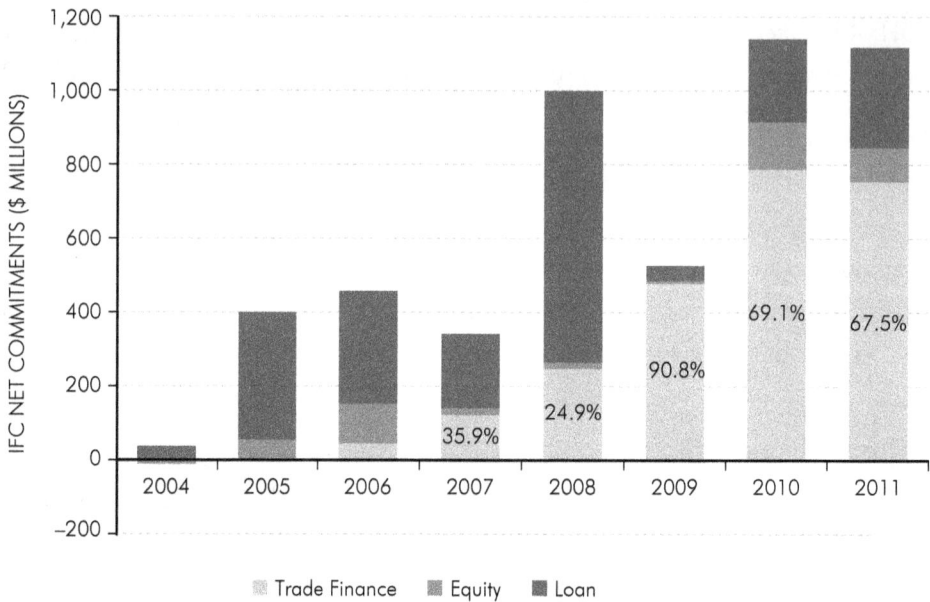

Y-axis: IFC NET COMMITMENTS ($ MILLIONS), ranging from −200 to 1,200

Data labels on bars:
- 2007: 35.9%
- 2008: 24.9%
- 2009: 90.8%
- 2010: 69.1%
- 2011: 67.5%

Legend: Trade Finance   Equity   Loan

SOURCE: IFC.

commitment) and 1,316 transactions (65.4 percent of the GTFP transactions) during this period (Table D.7). However, the recent IEG evaluation on the GTFP (IEG 2013) concluded that additional study is needed to determine whether this definition is a good proxy for the SME status of the emerging market party of a trade transaction. $381.7 million (15.7 percent of the GTFP commitment) and 98 transactions (4.9 percent of the GTFP transactions) were for energy efficiency related transactions.

GTFP was the main product used in IFC's response to the financial crisis. The additionality through GTFP was high at the peak of the financial crisis in 2008–09. IFC played an important role in finding international corresponding banks that were willing to work with midsize banks in Brazil when trade finance lines from international corresponding banks dried up, thereby expanding the correspondent networks and helping to enlarge the pool of available funds for SMEs. However, the GTFP continued to represent a major share of IFC's net commitments (67.5 percent) in FY11, even though much of the impact of the financial crisis had subsided and IFC's additionality had become less clear.[4]

SECTOR PERFORMANCE

This section describes the key trends and directions of the performance of IFC investments and advisory services in major sectors. The findings are based on analyses conducted by

TABLE D.7 IFC Global Trade Finance Program in Brazil during CPE

Fiscal Year	SME ($ Millions)	Share (%)	SMEs (Transactions)	Share (%)	Energy Efficiency ($ Millions)	Share (%)	Energy Efficiency (Transactions)	Share (%)
2006	9.5	21.1	35	67.3	0	0	0	0
2007	52.4	42.8	151	76.3	1.2	1.0	1	0.5
2008	71.2	28.6	201	70.0	1.2	0.5	1	0.3
2009	141.1	29.5	426	74.3	4.6	1.0	7	1.2
2010	88.2	11.2	283	58.4	69.9	8.9	14	2.9
2011	90.0	11.9	220	52.6	304.8	40.4	75	17.9
Total	452.4	18.6	1,316	65.4	381.7	15.7	98	4.9

SOURCE: IFC.
NOTE: CPE = Country Program Evaluation; SME = small and medium-size enterprise.

IEG as well as information collected during interviews undertaken for this evaluation. The discussion is not comprehensive, but it covers the main activities supported by IFC based on the available information.

Financial Sector

During the period evaluated, IFC expanded its financial markets operations. It also shifted focus from the first-tier banks, which have access to domestic deposit funding and international capital market, to midsize second-tier banks, which rely on wholesale funding. The relationship with midsize banks started with the GTFP in FY06. These banks had aggregate assets of $40 billion,[5] which was larger than many of the financial sectors in the Latin America and the Caribbean Region. These banks are important in making credit available to SMEs, which are typically underserved by larger banks and the capital markets in Brazil. Once IFC became more familiar with this market segment, its strategy evolved to provide long-term funding to selected well-managed midsize banks. During the period evaluated, IFC successfully developed relationships with 14 midsize banks.

One of the goals under the FY04–07 CAS and the FY08–11 CPE was SME financing. By supporting midsize banks, IFC aimed to help SMEs increase their access to finance. However, assessing the impact of support for SME financing is difficult.[6] A review of IFC project documents and loan agreements for 23 operations to banking institutions in Brazil also suggests that the conditions regarding the banks' lending to SMEs are not very stringent. In addition, the monitoring of compliance of those conditions may not have been as systematic or thorough over the period evaluated. More specifically, the definitions of "eligible sub-borrower" in nine loan agreements examined in detail leave room to include enterprises that are far larger than those typically considered SMEs.

IFC officially defines a small enterprise as one that meets two of three criteria: (i) number of employees of 10 or more and less than 50; (ii) total assets of $100,000 or more and less than $3 million; and (iii) total annual sales of $100,000 or more and less than $3 million. A medium enterprise is one that meets for two of three criteria: (i) the number of employees of 50 or more and less than 300; (ii) total assets of $3 million or more and less than $15 million; and (iii) total annual sales of $3 million or more and less than $15 million. As IFC's working definition of SMEs uses loan size at origination—$2 million in advanced countries like Brazil—as a proxy, this evaluation could not confirm whether systematic analysis of the increase in the share of loans to SMEs as typically defined are being undertaken within IFC.

During the period evaluated, IFC also supported a new micro and small business financing model with a combination of loan, equity investment, and advisory services. IFC provided a total of $25 million long-term loan and an equity investment of $23.5 million to Banco Triângulo S.A. (Tribanco), a financial intermediary of the major distribution chain Martins Group, which offers financial and management solutions to retail clients that are predominantly family-owned micro and small businesses.[7] IFC complemented its investment with a $200,000 advisory service program to develop Tribanco's internal credit rating capabilities. IEG's evaluation assigned a rating of "excellent" for IFC's role and contribution to Tribanco. IFC's stamp of approval helped Tribanco increase its credit lines[8] and helped foster Tribanco's credibility in the local market by overcoming skepticism about its new business model based on micro and small business financing. Further, IFC's loan proceeds were fully used to provide 4,549 loans to finance capital expenditures and working capital needs of micro and small entrepreneurs.

One of the objectives of the FY08–11 CPS was to help build Brazil's asset-backed securitization market and promote microfinance for low-income individuals. Despite IFC's equity participation from FY05, a securitization firm has yet to reach the scale originally envisaged due to the consolidation of the Brazilian banking sector. For the microfinance sector, IFC has not been able to increase its presence, except in the Tribanco case described above and a small local currency loan of R$3.0 million ($1.7 million) in FY10 to

CEAPE-Maranhão, Brazil's leading microfinance nongovernmental organization. IFC also supported activities related to the issue of sustainability: with IFC's advisory support, Bovespa's Corporate Sustainability Index was launched at IFC International Conference on Sustainable Finance in Emerging Markets, held in São Paulo in December 2005. IFC also established Equator Principles,[9] a voluntary set of environmental and social screening criteria, and Banco do Brasil was the first emerging market bank to adopt this principle in March 2005.

Based on interviews of officials in a number of client banks,[10] IFC has helped these banks address the impact of the 2008–09 global financial crisis with a combination of instruments. In addition to trade finance, IFC provided long-term loans and additional subscription of equity investments to some banks. For instance, during the most acute phase of the global finance crisis in March 2009, Banco Daycoval successfully completed R$410 million ($156 million) of long-term certificates of deposits with IFC and other commercial lenders (IFC committed R$110 million; approximately $42 million). In July 2008, IFC subscribed $10.6 million worth of equity with another client bank, Fibra, and subsequently sent a strong signal to the market that it would continue to support the midsize bank segment throughout the crisis.

Infrastructure

During the period evaluated, IFC supported the infrastructure sector with $641.3 million of commitments in 19 investment projects and PPP advisory services. IFC played a key role by bringing in its international experiences in project finance structuring, setting performance standards, and mobilizing private sector financing. Its development impact extends beyond the transactions it helped to finance or structure. Its infrastructure assistance was also provided at the federal, state, and local government levels.

TRANSPORT: In the port sector IFC had a competitive advantage and provided added value.[11] Seaports are critical to Brazil not only for international trade, but also for domestic transportation. During the review period, IFC financed four port sector projects with a total commitment of $115.63 million. The FY11 Port Santos project was a major activity in which IFC was a lead arranger for syndicated loans totaling $582 million, in addition to its own financing of $97 million. IFC also provided an important stamp of approval for commercial lenders for a new innovative soil washing technique used to recover a site, used for over half a century as a waste dump, into a new terminal. The Port Santos project also demonstrated that a large greenfield port project in Brazil could be structured on a limited recourse project finance basis. In air transport, IFC supported two Brazilian airlines by providing $50 million loans to TAM Airlines in FY05 and GOL Air Transport in FY06.

POWER AND UTILITIES: In FY06, IFC financed the first combined thermal power plant in Ceará with cofinancing of $200 million. In FY08, IFC's investment helped turn around the power utility company, Cemar, in Maranhão with an eight-year local currency financing in a total financing package of $307 million. In FY06, IFC made an equity investment of $50 million to Endesa Brasil, a Brazilian subsidiary of global utility player Endesa Spain. The Expanded Project Supervision Report notes that IFC's additionality was the credibility it added to the company's initial public offering process, as well as its support for Endesa Brazil's implementation of best environmental, social, health and safety practices by incorporating the IFC performance standards. IFC also supported improvement to corporate governance by introducing minority rights related to its investment, which helped Endesa Brasil satisfy the requirements of Novo Mecado for the expected initial public offering.

In the water and sanitation sector, IFC worked closely with the Bank under the joint Subnational Financing Program. In the state of Sergipe, the level of water losses was as high as 50 percent under the management of state-owned water utility company. IFC provided an $11 million local-currency loan to improve the efficiency of the operation in FY11. It also provided a $24 million loan in FY11 to another state-owned water utility company in Santa Catalina to improve its efficiency. Although the subnational lending program is no longer under the joint IFC-World Bank department, IFC and the Bank staff in Brazil continue to cooperate to exchange sector views. Bank sector specialists have also contributed to IFC due diligence of a new transaction for the water and sanitation sector in Brazil. In FY10, IFC approved a $50 million loan to a private water utility company, but this loan was cancelled after the client succeeded in raising large equity funds from the Brazilian public sector investment fund.

Manufacturing

During the period evaluated, IFC approved 10 projects in the manufacturing sector with a net commitment of $193.8 million. Earlier in the period, IFC primarily provided long-term U.S. dollar–based loans to both top-tier and midsized Brazilian companies (except for a small equity transaction in FY05 with Dixie Toga). However, as Brazil's economic landscape changed, the factors determining IFC's role also evolved. In February 2005, IFC arranged a total of $180 million financial package (12-year $35 million loan on its own account and $60 million 10-year and $85 million 8-year B-loans) to Embraer, a world's leading commercial aircraft manufacturer. At the time, because of heightened country risk, it was not easy even for top-tier companies to access loans of more than five years. With the improvement in the market situation, Embraer fully prepaid IFC's loan when it was preparing for a 10-year $500 million corporate bond in November 2011, despite a significant 1.75 percent loan spread reduction.

Similarly, in December 2005, IFC provided a 12-year $200 million loan package to Suzano Petroquímica S.A., one of the largest petrochemical companies in Brazil, including $60 million in its own account. This loan was also fully prepaid in 2010. In August 2005, IFC approved a $150 million loan package to Ipiranga Petroquímica S.A., one of the leading producers of polyolefin in Latin America; this loan was cancelled without disbursements. In contrast, loans to four midsize manufacturing companies approved during the period are still active with no prepayments. IFC had repeated transactions with Brazil's third-largest producer of aluminum cans in FY08, FY11, and FY12, for a total commitment of $170 million with B-loans. The price of aluminum cans and its operations are based on U.S. dollars, and IFC was competitive against alternative funding sources.

Education/Health

EDUCATION: IFC was a pioneer in financing private education projects among development finance institutions. During the period evaluated, IFC invested in six projects in the education sector for a total commitment of $189 million. For its education sector portfolio, Brazil was the largest, with a $135.6 million outstanding portfolio at the end of FY11. IFC's first education sector engagement was a $12 million loan in FY06 to a private equity fund that supports investments in Anhanguera Educacional S.A (AES). AES is a leader in the vocational training, and it provides education for low-income students at an affordable cost. IFC followed up with a seven-year local currency loan to AES in FY10 when it was still difficult to obtain long-term loans from the market even for a successful company like AES. IFC helped raise an additional $23.3 million loan from DEG and Proparco. IFC also offered a local currency loan to another university in FY10 during the financial crisis.

With the number of middle-class families in Brazil growing, AES increased its student enrollments from 10,800 in 2005 to 435,000 in 2012—a compounded annual growth rate of 64 percent—by implementing its aggressive acquisition strategy. Proceeds from two IFC loans were used for the acquisition of universities; however, IFC's financial contribution to this expansion was limited. The university raised over $1.6 billion from the capital market between 2007 and 2012 and IFC's financing to AES was $40.6 million.[12]

HEALTH: In the health sector, IFC approved three investments during the evaluation period for a total net commitment of $47 million. IFC made investments in two hospital chains and one laboratory/diagnostic center. A $20 million loan to Laboratorio Fleury approved in FY04 was not disbursed and was cancelled in FY07 because the company had a larger-than-anticipated cash generation, which reduced the need for debt to fund investments; also, more attractive local currency financing became available for the company. A $50 million loan to Hospital São Luiz in FY08 was followed by another $50 million equivalent local currency loan in FY11 to Rede D'Or, one of the largest networks of independent private hospitals in South America after the acquisition of Hospital São Luiz by Rede D'Or in October 2010.

Agribusiness and Forestry

During the period evaluated, IFC approved 11 transactions with a net commitment of $367.7 million for the agribusiness and forestry sector. The additionality of IFC in the sector has been its assistance to improve environmental and social standards of industry. The results during the period were mixed: according to the Expanded Project Supervision Report, IFC and Amaggi Exportação e Importação Ltda (Amaggi), the global leader in the Round Table on Responsible Soy Association, collaborated in setting a new environmental and social management system. A comprehensive such system was designed to ensure that Amaggi and its prefinanced suppliers did not (i) cultivate soy on illegally deforested land; (ii) employ child and/or forced labor; or (iii) encroach on indigenous lands (the agreement, however, did not cover third party suppliers). This management system established clean procedures and industry best practices for sustainable soy cultivation. Amaggi has also been important in the wider soy sector because it disseminated its experience of applying environment and social practices with its clients, both locally through "field days" with farmers organized as well as globally through the round table. Although IEG rates environmental and social effects partly unsatisfactory, it concludes that IFC made the right decision to finance Amaggi and assist the company to develop an environmental and social management system and pioneering sustainability in the Mato Grosso soy industry by tracking environmental aspects and prohibiting deforestation at its prefinanced suppliers' farms, despite the opposition of some nongovernmental organizations.

IFC faced difficulties in enforcing full compliance of its environment and social standards with five clients in the agribusiness and forestry sector. Noncompliance led to full prepayments of IFC loans by Cosan in January 2010 and by Bertin in April 2010. IFC loans were small portions of long-term debt obligations of these companies (3.0 percent for Cosan and 0.5 percent for Bertin) at the time of prepayments, and both companies also had access to capital markets through listings in stock exchanges. Thus, IFC's financial leverage to improve the environment and social standards of these companies was limited.

Oil, Gas, and Mining

For the oil, gas, and mining sectors, IFC had five projects with a net commitment of $206 million during the period evaluated, including IFC's largest equity investment of $103 million in Constellation, the holding company of Brazilian drilling service group, Queiroz Galvão Óleo e Gás S.A. (QGOG). The engagement with QGOG, which started in 2003, supported the development of the offshore drilling service industry, which was dominated by large international players. IEG validated the successful development outcome of IFC's $50 million loan participation in $810 million in syndicated, limited-recourse project finance to construct the offshore rigs by QGOG. The loan was approved in June 2007 and IEG confirmed that IFC's performance standards were introduced to the new offshore business though this loan. IFC has also helped improve the company's environmental, health, and safety management system through continuous engagement with the company, including site visits and consultations.

Advisory Services

PPP: IFC's PPP advisory service projects had important catalytic effects by setting new standards or providing a new business model for follow-up transactions. During the period evaluated, IFC had nine advisory service projects with a total project cost of $7.7 million. A number of PPP advisory service projects have been financed under the Brazilian Private Sector Partnership Program, a partnership of IFC, BNDES, and the Inter-American Development Bank, which started in October 2007.[13]

For the transport sector, an IFC advisory team engaged in the structuring of two road concession projects. For the first project, IFC succeeded in setting new performance standard requirements for road concession projects in Brazil.[14] These standards were used for the bidding of the 2007 federal government second round of concessions, and also for the 2008 State of São Paulo Government second round of concessions. With its advisory work for another transport project, IFC introduced Equator Principles and its social standards for expropriation and resettlement rules for road concession projects in Brazil. This project was also the first concession of a metropolitan road network with urban tolling.

IFC's involvement was critical in structuring Hospital do Subúrbio project,[15] the first PPP hospital transaction in Brazil. IFC provided international expertise in project finance, assisted in promoting private sector financing, and helped set performance standards for the hospital. The hospital operates more efficiently than public hospitals and has flexibility and speed in hiring employees and procuring medical equipment. It has maintained high standards, as a private hospital operator needs to meet a set of performance standards. Hospital do Suburbio serves the poor community of Salvador in Bahia and provides high-quality care to the community. This innovative PPP hospital project is now being replicated in at least seven other states and municipalities.

IEG's review of this project notes that IFC brought in transparency and independence during the structuring and financial closure of the project. IFC played the "honest broker" role for a road show presentation of this project. Another value added by IFC was that the bidding was overseen by Brazil's stock exchange to have higher transparency. IFC also supported the Municipality of Belo Horizonte in structuring the first education PPP project and mobilized $100 million of private investments by bringing in its global experience in structuring PPP projects in the education sector.

With the success of its private sector partnership program with BNDES and the Inter-American Development Bank, IFC has started a similar program at the state level by working with Banco de Desenvolvimento de Minas Gerais, a state development bank in Minas Gerais. IFC's PPP engagements are based on cost recovery and the receipt of retainer and/or success fees upon successful completion of projects. The private sector partnership program with BNDES and the Inter-American Development Bank has achieved a full cost recovery.

DOING BUSINESS: In 2006, IFC approached 10 municipalities in Northeast Brazil to offer technical assistance to implement regulatory reforms aimed to reduce the paperwork and number of days to open a business and to obtain construction permits and create municipal score cards. Two municipalities (Fortaleza and Teresina) confirmed formal interest in the project via signed cooperation agreements with IFC. For the Municipality of Teresina, there has been progress including (i) the passage of two new municipal laws and decrees to make it easy to issue business licenses and construction permits; (ii) the issuance of business licenses electronically via "Empresa Facil," in three or fewer days; and (iii) an 80 percent reduction in the number of requirements to obtain a business license in Teresina (a decrease of 11 requirements). However, because of overly ambitious design and the lack of clear outcomes, this advisory service project was rated "mostly unsuccessful" by both IFC and IEG for overall development effectiveness.

Endnotes

1 IFC, Latin America and the Caribbean Department, FY06–08 Country Strategy Update, April 19, 2005 (unpublished).

2 IFC has succeeded in further expanding its program in frontier regions. Its frontier program increased to $805 million, consisting of a $545 million long-term loan and $260 million trade finance program.

[3] IFC arranged syndication of a $70 million loan for Banco Daycoval in 2007. This was the first international syndication for the bank.

[4] GTFP remains a major program for these three fiscal years after adjusting for risk. Recent IEG trade finance evaluation recommends risk-based accounting for trade finance, applying different risk factor based on the financial product.

[5] In May 2008 when the CAS was presented to the Board.

[6] According to interviews with seven IFC client banks, as of 2013 the number of SMEs that are part of their portfolios is between 8,500 and 10,000. The loans are mainly for working capital with tenors of less than one year. SMEs in Brazil typically borrow from a pool of three to six banks, which include public sector and both first and second tier private sector institutions. Collateral is always required in various forms including land, receivables, and/or physical goods.

[7] According to IFC's report "Scaling up Inclusive Business: Advancing the Knowledge and Action Agenda" (IFC 2010), Tribanco serves about 150,000 small and micro businesses by offering credit and financial services and issued over 4 million credit cards to these segments with a high repayment ratio of 96.5 percent.

[8] As per the Expanded Project Supervision Report, Tribanco increased its credit lines with local banks from $4.1 million in 2005 (1.4 percent of total nonequity funding) to $67.1 million in 2009 (8.7 percent) after IFC's loan facility commitment in 2005.

[9] Equator Principles are a voluntary set of environmental and social screening criteria and guidelines adopted by major international banks, based on processes established by IFC. The Principles apply globally to development projects with a capital cost of $50 million or more in all industry sectors.

[10] IEG met with seven IFC client banks in March 2013.

[11] Since BNDES, the dominant provider of infrastructure financing in Brazil, cannot finance imported equipment with less than 60 percent domestic content, IFC's loans were used to purchase imported equipment in the port projects. Also, U.S. dollar financing is possible for port projects since the main revenues are in foreign currency terms and IFC can be competitive relative to BNDES for long-term local currency financing.

[12] Anhanguera completed its initial public offering in 2007 and raised a total of R$2,462 (around $1.2 billion) from the Brazilian capital market. It also issued 3 debentures of R$770 million (around $385 million).

[13] The agreement for this partnership was executed on October 19, 2007. This is an example of good partnership among multilaterals and the government. The goal of Brazil PSP was to realize PPP and concession projects to increase the private sector participation in infrastructure financing in Brazil. Another objective of Brazil PSP is to create the capacity of Brazilian government for PPP work.

[14] Although bidding procedures were open to international participation before IFC's engagement with this project, financial and technical requirements created hidden entry barriers to private road concession projects for international and middle-size players.

[15] At the time of IFC's engagement in 2008 for this project, Salvador had not had a new hospital that offered emergency care for 20 years.

References

IEG (Independent Evaluation Group). 2013. *Evaluation of the International Finance Corporation's Global Trade Finance Program, 2006–12*. Washington, DC: World Bank.

IFC (International Finance Corporation). 2010. *Scaling Up Inclusive Business: Advancing the Knowledge and Action Agenda*. Washington, DC: World Bank.

Appendix E
MIGA Operations in Brazil, FY04–11

MIGA's main operation is to provide political risk insurance, which helps ensure greater investor confidence and thus to facilitate foreign direct investment.[1] MIGA's activities over the CPE period were in line with CAS and CPS objectives of supporting a competitive Brazil. MIGA underwrote 16 guarantees in Brazil, with a gross exposure of $314.6 million; most of these (14) were in the power sector ($246 million in gross risk exposure).

MIGA concentrated its activities on the electricity transmission subsector. Except for a two-year guarantee for a diesel power plant project in FY04 issued to ABN AMRO in the Netherlands, 13 of the 14 guarantees were for the transmission subsector for three Spanish investors. MIGA had six transmission projects with one of these investors. Considering MIGA's limited capacity in business development in Brazil, including no field presence, the concentration in the transmission subsector helped consolidate its leverage within the subsector. However, it also negatively affected its ability to maintain its exposures in Brazil when the external environment changed.

The transmission projects MIGA supported were consistent with Brazil's development priorities and the Bank Group's strategic direction. Brazil is a country with the proportions of a continent and most of its energy is produced by hydroelectric dams in the northern Amazon, although major energy consumption centers are in the southeast part of the country. Transmission lines in Brazil cover long distances, so it is important to establish interconnections to ensure efficient and reliable energy delivery.

MIGA's involvement in the transmission subsector in Brazil started in 2003. At the end of FY09, its gross exposure to the subsector had reached $192 million in support of equity investments in 11 projects. The transmission projects guaranteed by MIGA have developed about 2,600 kilometers of high-tension transmission lines and associated facilities such as substations.[2] It also addressed the shortcomings observed in the transmission network during the power crisis in 2001–02 because of regional climatic differences and inadequate transmission interconnections between the northern and southern states. Some research suggested that this power crisis could have been avoided if Brazil had established an adequate interconnection transmission system.

Although the FY03–07 CAS noted that MIGA's capability in Brazil was constrained, as its exposure was approaching its country limit, the actual exposure to Brazil declined throughout the period evaluated, because of cancellations and the absence of new MIGA business after FY09. At the beginning of CPE period, Brazil was one of the largest host countries, with outstanding gross exposures of $625 million and net exposure of $236 million at the end of FY04 (Table E.1). The share of net exposure to Brazil in MIGA's total net exposure declined from 7.3 percent in FY04 to 1.3 percent in FY11 with a net exposure of $67.9 million. In FY11, $132.5 million worth of contracts was cancelled, followed by additional cancellations of $66.1 million contracts in FY12.

Since the cancellation of a $19.2 million guarantee contract for the transmission subsector in December 2012, MIGA has had no guarantee exposure in Brazil. Consolidations in the transmission sector are a major reason that MIGA guarantees were cancelled. After Spanish investors sold their stakes in transmission project companies, a new sponsor considered Brazil's country risk low enough and did not to continue MIGA's political risk coverage. A high concentration of the portfolio with a limited number of sponsors in one subsector has precipitated this decline.

More important, the market environment for MIGA operations in Brazil has become more difficult due to positive improvements in Brazil's country risk. During the CPE period, the sovereign credit rating of Brazil has improved by six notches;[3] the sovereign risk of Brazil was upgraded to above investment grade in April 2008 by S&P and in September 2009 by Moody's. Foreign direct investment flows to Brazil increased to $45.06 billion in 2008, four times more than the 2003 level of $10.14 billion. In the context of improving foreign investor confidence in Brazil, the demand for MIGA's political risk guarantees has apparently declined.

Going forward, MIGA has an opportunity to rebuild its operations in Brazil. With its expanded mandate after the introduction of a new product in April 2009, followed by changes in its Convention in November 2010, MIGA has the potential to undertake risk underwriting business, in particular for the infrastructure sector. MIGA can cover subsovereign credit risk without a federal government guarantee. It can also offer political risk insurance to loans on a stand-alone basis without insuring a portion of the equity investment and also acquisitions of existing infrastructures.

To its four traditional noncommercial risks coverages (transfer restriction, expropriation, war and civil disturbance, breach of contract), MIGA has added nonhonoring of sovereign foreign obligation (NHSFO) coverage with changes in operational regulations approved

TABLE E.1 MIGA Outstanding Exposure (gross exposure, $ millions)

	FY04	FY05	FY06	FY07	FY08	FY09	FY10	FY11	FY12	FY13
Sectoral distribution										
Finance	360.9	248.1	220.9	121.2	50.0	50.0	50.0	50.0	0	0
Infrastructure	115.8	45.4	93.5	155.7	181.5	192.9	168.2	35.7	19.6	0
Mining	0	0	0	0	0	0	0	0	0	0
Oil and Gas	0	101.7	87.1	87.1	1.4	1.4	1.4	0	0	0
Agribusiness, Manufacturing, Services, Tourism	0	47.2	2.0	2.1	2.18	2.6	0	0	0	0
MIGA's risk profile										
Transfer Restriction	576.8	375.9	166.9	177.4	115.3	116.5	108.2	62.3	4.3	0
Expropriation	565.4	357.5	128	123.4	52.6	50.0	50.0	50.0	0	0
War and Civil Disturbance	50.2	24.4	3.4	3.5	3.9	1.4	0	0	0	0
Breach of Contract	29	23.6	97.6	140.1	163.3	166.6	145.4	29.1	15.3	0
MIGA's gross exposure in Brazil	625.7	382.6	227.1	280.4	235.4	244.2	218.2	85.7	19.6	0
Share of MIGA's gross exposure (%)	12.10	7.50	4.20	5.30	3.64	3.35	2.83	0.94	0.20	0.00
MIGA's net exposure in country	236.7	139.3	140	140.8	143.1	162.5	146.9	67.9	9.8	0
Share of MIGA's net exposure (%)	7.30	4.40	4.20	4.40	4.00	4.10	3.42	1.30	0.16	0.00

SOURCE: MIGA.

by the MIGA Board in April 2009. NHSFO provides credit enhancement for transactions involving sovereign and subsovereign obligors. The primary beneficiaries of this coverage are commercial lenders that provide loans to public sector entities for infrastructure and other productive investments. MIGA can protect the lender against losses from nonpayment by the government due to inability or unwillingness to pay. NHSFO also covers a government guarantee obligation of a state-owned enterprise or PPP joint venture.

Brazil will continue to have infrastructure projects at all three levels of government (federal, state, and municipal). For more than three decades, the country underinvested in infrastructure, so investment needs for infrastructure are significant in almost all sectors (except power generation). In addition to new greenfield infrastructure projects, maintenance and upgrading of existing brownfield infrastructure projects require substantial investments because the existing infrastructure stocks deteriorated as a result of past underinvestment. MIGA may be able to find underwriting opportunities in the Brazil infrastructure sector by offering a guarantee to loans for infrastructure projects or facilitating the brownfield acquisition of infrastructure assets by foreign investors. NHSFO coverage will allow MIGA to offer credit enhancements for infrastructure projects at state or municipality level.

Furthermore, Brazil needs to develop a long-term private infrastructure debt market since Brazilian development banks are the main (or almost exclusive) source of long-term infrastructure loans. MIGA will be able to extend the tenor of the commercial infrastructure loans with its NHSFO coverage combined with its new capability to offer coverage for stand-alone debt.

In rebuilding its guarantee underwriting activities in Brazil, MIGA must diversify its portfolio to avoid concentration on a particular infrastructure subsector and an investor country as it had for transmission subsector with Spanish investors during the CPE period.

Endnotes

[1] The new nonhonoring of sovereign foreign obligation coverage offers credit enhancements.

[2] MIGA provided political risk covers for a portion of investments, so MIGA's contribution to the entire project outputs of 2,600 kilometers of transmission line needs to be considered in context.

[3] At the beginning of the review period (July 2004), Moody's foreign currency sovereign rating for Brazil was B2; it improved to Baa2 in June 2011.

Appendix F
Country Partnership Strategy Targets on Forests

TABLE F.1 Country Partnership Strategy Targets, FY08–11

CPS 2008 Target Outcomes	CASCR 2011 Revised Targets
Human Development Index in the Amazon increased from 15% below Brazil average in 2007 to 5% below Brazil average in 2011	Per capita monthly household income: ratio of North to national average 68.1% in 2007, 75.5% in 2011
Annual deforestation rate in the Amazon decreased from 1.4 million hectares in 2005 to 0.7 million hectare in 2011	Reduction in average annual rate of deforestation in the Amazon (2005–07 average annual deforestation rate: 1.48 million hectares; 2011 deforestation rate: 0.7 million hectares

Energy produced from renewable sources or saved by energy efficiency projects supported by BNDES: Zero in 2007; 60,000 terajoules per year in 2011 |
| Area under certified sustainable forest management and/or forest concessions increased from 3 million hectares in 2007 to 8 million hectares by 2011. Increase from 3 million hectares in 2007 to 9 million by 2011 (sic) | Sustainable natural forest management of private and public areas. (2007: 2.7 million hectares in private land—FSC-certified natural forests and zero in public land) (sustainable natural forest management of private and public areas expanded to 5 million hectartes—2011) |

continued on page 210

CPS 2008 Target Outcomes	CASCR 2011 Revised Targets
Protected areas to increase from 100 million hectares in 2007 to 120 million by 2011	Protected areas to increase from 79 million hectares in 2007 to 110 million by 2011
	Mainstreaming of climate change in public and private sector investments (NCCAP not yet approved; no BNDES financed greenhouse gas emission reduction projects) (Planned signed reductions of 20 million tons of CO_2 equivalent per year from actions monitored under NCCAP—including CDM and BNDES—financed projects)
	Improved effectiveness of environmental/social management systems in financial institutions (35% of projects submitted directly to BNDES screened according to the current Institutional Policy—2007) (100% of projects screened and monitored according to the new Environmental and Social Institutional Policy—2010)

SOURCES: World Bank 2008, 2011.
NOTE: BNDES = National Bank of Economic and Social Development; CASCR = Country Assistance Strategy Completion Report; CDM = Clean Development Mechanism; CPS = Country Partnership Strategy; FSC = Forest Stewardship Council; NCCAP = National Climate Change Action Plan.

References

World Bank. 2008. *International Bank for Reconstruction and Development and International Finance Corporation Country Partnership Strategy for the Federative Republic of Brazil for the Period FY2008–2011.* Washington, DC: World Bank.

———. 2011. *International Bank for Reconstruction and Development and International Finance Corporation Country Partnership Strategy for the Federative Republic of Brazil for the Period FY2012–2015.* Washington, DC: World Bank.

Appendix G
World Bank Support for Infrastructure in Brazil, FY04–11

Background

Brazil's government and the Bank have viewed infrastructure investments and related policies and institutions as critical to competitiveness, growth, and poverty reduction. This appendix describes the Bank's engagement in the four main infrastructure sectors—transport, energy, water, and urban development—over FY04–11.

Infrastructure investments in Brazil have declined sharply from more than 5 percent of gross domestic product (GDP) in the 1970s to about 3.6 percent in the 1980s and have remained flat at just over 2 percent ever since (Frischtak and Chateaubriand 2012).[1] The decline was concentrated in 1981–96 and mainly attributable to substantial reductions in public investment that were not offset by increased private investment (World Bank 2007). Though 2 percent of GDP was about average for Latin America by 2005, it has reached 5–7 percent in other regions (World Bank 2012), and several East Asian countries have achieved levels of 9 percent (World Bank 2007). Underinvestment in infrastructure has contributed to the deterioration of the existing stock and has not contributed adequately to either economic growth or to meeting the growing demands of an increasingly middle-income population.[2]

Since 2007, the Brazilian government's Accelerated Growth Program (PAC) has been the most prominent vehicle to increase infrastructure investments. During the initial years of the program (2008–10) those investments rose by an estimated 0.5 percent of GDP. The PAC program entered a second phase in 2010, but in the past two years, public investment in infrastructure has fallen off slightly (to about 1 percent of GDP) and the share of private investment has remained at about 1 percent.

The reduction in infrastructure investment may have affected the capacity of the public sector to plan and execute infrastructure investments. Several stakeholders expressed concerns during this evaluation about limited project cost-benefit analysis and sectoral planning as well as shortcomings in project implementation caused by budgetary rigidities and capacity limitations at all levels.[3] Some noted that because of the decline in past decades, Brazil's public sector had *forgotten how to invest.*

This issue received attention in 2005, when Brazil participated in a pilot program on fiscal space, for which the International Monetary Fund relaxed its fiscal targets to accommodate increased public investment. The Bank participated in this pilot. A key finding of the joint missions with the Fund was the remarkable weaknesses in Brazil's public investment management and the need to install adequate capacities for managing PPP operations. An Institutional Development Fund grant helped improve the quality of public spending and appears to have had some positive impact in one of the core ministries. However, the need to enhance capacity to appraise, execute, monitor and evaluate public sector investment projects remained.

The public sector's role as an enabler of private sector infrastructure investment is also important. As Frischtak and Chateaubriand (and many others) note, private participation or involvement in the management and expansion of infrastructure investments has become an imperative, but private investors continue to face significant barriers. Frischtak and Chateaubriand (2012) and the World Bank (2007) point to regulatory uncertainty, distortions, instability, and lack of transparency in the rules, as well as fragility of regulatory agencies as issues for business. Private investors also require predictability in the cost and speed of processes such as environmental licensing, as well as complementary public investments.

Bank Program for Infrastructure

Bank lending to support infrastructure projects has been substantial during FY04–11 and increased significantly over FY08–11 (Table G.1). However, it remains small relative to Brazil's total infrastructure investments financed by the government budget and other public institutions. For the FY04–11 period, infrastructure projects accounted for nearly half of all new lending operations and over one-third of total commitments, without including the infrastructure components in multisectoral operations.

TABLE G.1 Scale of World Bank Program for Infrastructure

	FY04–07		FY08–11		FY04–11	
	$ Millions	Number	$ Millions	Number	$ Millions	Number
Infrastructure in Brazil	1,320	9	4,430	29	5,750	38
Infrastructure share	26.4%	28.1%	37.5%	59.1%	34.2%	46.9%
All Bank in Brazil	5,000	32	11,801	49	16,801	81

SOURCE: World Bank.
NOTE: Includes additional financing.

The transport sector accounted for the largest share of infrastructure lending volume in each of the two CAS/CPS periods and for the FY04–11 period as a whole (56 percent). It accounted for about 35 percent of the total number of projects (Table G.2). Although each of the four infrastructure sectors received much higher levels of support over FY08–11, the increase was particularly sharp in the transport sector in both volume and number of projects. A substantial part of the increased volume during FY08–11 was extended through additional financing.

Increasingly, the Brazil infrastructure program has included both sectoral Adaptable Program Loans, which enable sustained engagement over time in several operations or horizontal extensions, and SWAps, which allow for financing a slice of the sectoral expenditure program. Both of these instruments have some Development Policy Loan (DPL)-like features, supporting sector programs and quicker disbursements in the case of SWAps.

Some subnational multisectoral operations have significant infrastructure content. Most of the infrastructure content in those was in the transport and water sectors. Some of the integrated (water and urban) and broader multisectoral (Ceará and Minas) operations appear to be generating positive results—in some cases, as in Ceará, the sectoral components in these operations show better results than those in single sector operations implemented in the same state. However, multisectoral projects involve implementation risks from multiple components or implementing agencies and the need for high levels of coordination in the Bank and in-country.

TABLE G.2 Sectoral Composition of the World Bank Program for Infrastructure

	FY04–07		FY08–11		FY04–11	
	$ Millions	Number	$ Millions	Number	$ Millions	Number
Transport	661 (50%)	3 (33%)	2,587 (58%)	10 (35%)	3,249 (56%)	13 (35%)
Energy	0 (0%)	0 (0%)	495 (11%)	1 (3%)	495 (9%)	1 (3%)
Water	103 (8%)	3 (33%)	636 (14%)	8 (19%)	739 (13%)	9 (23%)
Urban Development	556 (42%)	3 (33%)	712 (16%)	10 (42%)	1,268 (22%)	16 (40%)
Total	1,320 (100%)	9 (100%)	4,430 (100%)	27 (100%)	5,750 (100%)	40 (100%)

SOURCE: World Bank.
NOTE: Includes additional financing.

In addition to the lending program, the period evaluated featured considerable related AAA work, both economic and sector work (19 activities) and nonlending technical assistance (14 activities). Urban development had the largest number of tasks, focusing mainly on urban policies and strategies as well as housing and slum upgrading. Work in the energy and transport sectors covered energy security and efficiency, a low-carbon country case study, freight and logistics costs, aviation, the quality of road investments, and a proposed high-speed train project.

Overall, the Bank's infrastructure program addressed issues relevant to Brazil's development challenges. Most of the closed infrastructure projects reviewed by IEG during the period evaluated largely achieved their objectives. The value of the Bank's financing and knowledge, including its project management systems, operational procedures, and fiduciary and safeguard policies, are widely recognized. However, implementation of many infrastructure projects was delayed. The projects were characterized by ambitious objectives and complicated results frameworks that were sometimes not used. In many cases, the objectives were broadly appropriate and relevant, but the projects may have over-reached on sector policy and institutional issues.

Several issues recur across the infrastructure sectors. First, pricing, cost recovery, subsidies, and financial sustainability are of concern to many Brazilian authorities and come up in almost all Implementation Completion and Results Report Reviews. Second, though the Bank has had a positive role in helping to coordinate among agencies and facilitating the decentralization of several sectors, ambiguities and coordination problems linger in and across levels of government, which contributes to project implementation delays. The following sections describe the Bank's operations in the transport, energy, water, and urban development sectors over FY04–11.

Transport

As noted, Bank lending for transport investments accounted for the largest share of lending volume for infrastructure and more than a third of all newly approved projects. These projects, and the eight projects approved earlier that were still active during this period, focused on two areas: roads and highways and urban transportation systems (Table G.3).

ROADS AND HIGHWAYS. The Road Transport Project ($500 million; approved in FY06), the largest of the road projects, has supported the federal road maintenance and rehabilitation program as well as related institutional strengthening activities to improve efficiency and sustainability. It also sought to improve sector policies and institutional development as well as civil works. It followed an earlier operation (Federal Highway Decentralization: $249 million),

TABLE G.3 Composition of Transport Lending, FY04–11

	Commitment ($ Millions)	Number of Projects
Road Projects[a]	1,455	6
Federal	501	1
State	953	5
Share in Total Transport (%)	45	46
Urban Transport[b]	1,794	7
Share in Total Transport	55	54
Totals	3,249	13

SOURCE: World Bank.
a. In addition, there were three earlier road transport operations that closed during the review period.
b. In addition, there were five urban transport operations that closed during the review period.

which closed in FY06, as well as two state road projects (Goias and Rio Grande do Sul), which closed in 2006 and 2007. Five other state-level operations were approved in FY04–11, bringing the total for road transport to nearly $1.5 billion.

These projects appear to be making positive contributions to reducing road transport costs by supporting road maintenance and rehabilitation and institutional innovations to enhance the effectiveness of this program. Performance or output-based management—the Contratos de Reabilitacao e Manutencao system—was first introduced under the federal highway project and the Rio Grande do Sul and Goias state projects. These projects demonstrated that outsourcing maintenance and rehabilitation can reduce administrative costs while achieving results and addressing critical issues related to deteriorating road conditions and high road transport costs. The concept proved attractive and spread across Brazil, often with Bank support (Lancelot 2010). The follow-up federal road transport project (FY06) built on and expanded this experience. It addressed an important unfinished agenda and deepened the results and private sector orientation of the federal road maintenance and rehabilitation program.

Several state-level projects complemented these efforts. The São Paulo Feeder Roads Project (2010 and additional financing in 2011), addressed the efficiency of the road network and related institutional issues (results-based management, planning, PPP capacity). The Bank more recently prepared a new operation, the São Paulo State

Sustainable Transport Project, to further reduce logistics costs, improve environmental management, and address disaster risks and responses.

A number of useful AAA activities undertaken in the road subsector were clearly related to the lending program. Among other things, they analyzed experience with performance-based contracts, PPPs, and improving the appraisal framework for road transport investments and the quality of those investments. Economic and sector work and nonlending technical assistance also considered how to decrease freight logistics costs, aviation, and a proposed high-speed train project.

URBAN/MASS TRANSIT. In urban transport and mass transit systems, a number of large operations were approved during FY04–11 for São Paulo ($1.5 billion) and Rio de Janeiro ($250 million), amounting to about $1.8 billion for the period evaluated. These operations focused on critical mobility and congestion issues, particularly on improving the quality and sustainability of transport services and access for low-income people, through intermodal and tariff integration and financing of new rolling stock and other equipment and related system upgrades and capacity building. The São Paulo operations built on a successful earlier operation that began to address key issues and closed in 2004; the Rio Mass Transit II project built on an earlier operation that closed in 2009 and had additional financing of $600 million approved in FY12.

The outcome of the earlier São Paulo operation was rated highly satisfactory; its achievements included significant steps toward integration of the various systems, pro-poor service improvements, pollution and emissions reductions, as well as support for the private concessioning of São Paulo Metropolitan Train Company's operations and maintenance. Through sustained engagement in subsequent operations in São Paulo, the Bank has contributed significantly to the improved quality, accessibility, and long-term sustainability of urban transport in the São Paulo Metropolitan Region, despite the implementation delays and increased costs that seem to characterize most projects in Brazil.

In particular, external parties consider the completed Metro Line 4 project and private concession particularly innovative; demand projections for the project were exceeded in the first year of operation and the share of metro trips (as well as rail ridership) increased despite rapid growth in motorization. In addition, financial sustainability has been enhanced and accessibility of the low-income population has been improved (most benefits have accrued to low-income families in the periphery of the metro region). One stakeholder interviewed by the evaluation team noted that the Bank-supported operation had transformed the subregion and contributed to social integration and reduced violence, and highlighted the value of the Bank as a partner, not just because of the financial resources it provided but also because of its analysis and advice on key issues (such as on tariff policy).

The Bank's engagement in the Rio mass transit system substantially achieved the objective of improving the quality of urban transport services. The ongoing follow-up operation has contributed to further improvements in service levels and institutional strengthening by financing new trains, related works and equipment, institutional strengthening activities focusing on strategic planning and tariffs, as well as efforts to strengthen regulatory and subsidy policies.

The Bank has also supported gender-related activities, such as enhancing the security of women who did not feel safe in the overcrowded trains and degraded system. In the views of state government officials, the Bank contributed significantly to revitalizing Rio's urban transport system and a number of low-income neighborhoods and provided important advice on critical issues, ranging from tariff structure and financial sustainability to enhancing benefits for the poor to climate impact.

In both São Paulo and Rio de Janeiro, officials stressed that the Bank's financing and procurement procedures had allowed them to obtain equipment of the highest quality at the lowest price. Overall, the Bank's contributions to meeting the challenges of improving urban transport appear to have been positive and significant, despite some shortcomings.

The Bank also engaged in four earlier urban transport operations that closed during 2004–11. These focused on smaller metropolitan areas (Belo Horizonte, Fortaleza, Recife, and Salvador). These projects largely achieved their objectives, although with some shortcomings, such as overly optimistic demand projections and challenges related to decentralization, operating subsidies, tariffs, and delays and increased costs. The exception was the Fortaleza Metro Transport project, where the project scope was sharply reduced and the objectives were only partially met.

Energy

In the energy sector (this review covers electricity but not petroleum/gas), Bank support was less resource intensive than in transport and was provided largely through nonlending activities and a technical assistance loan approved in FY03. At a time when the sector was emerging from a severe crisis and undertaking sector reforms, the Bank responded with both short-term financial and technical assistance support in the period immediately before 2004. The Public-Private Infrastructure Advisory Facility (PPIAF)-funded activity and the longer-term Energy Sector Reform Technical Assistance Loan (ESTAL) proved quite effective in supporting the sector reform program and related decision making. The outcomes were important and much appreciated by the government, including competition and private sector participation in the bidding process for large-scale hydropower, increasing access to energy services for poor populations, revising environmental licensing procedures, and improving long-term expansion planning.

The ESTAL, approved in 2003, was prepared using an extensive participatory process, and its components addressed development of the electricity market and regulation, access and affordability for the poor, environmental management, long-term expansion planning, and institutional strengthening and coordination. As the project was motivated by the major sector crisis in 2001, it also built in flexibility and a mechanism to permit high-level exchange of views between the Brazilian government and the Bank on the implementation of the sector reform program.[4] Although the project had considerable implementation challenges, it was considered highly relevant to a wide range of sector reform issues, as well as contributing to large savings for the government.

In particular, the contribution of this project to the large savings (estimated at $12 billion) that resulted from the shift in the government strategy from noncompetitive negotiated contracts to competitive international bidding in connection with the two large Rio Madeira hydropower plants (Jirau and Santo Antonio) was significant. Its success led to broader adoption of a competitive auction strategy for hydroelectric generation. The project also was instrumental in the adoption of a new phaser-based technology to optimize the operation and dispatch of the power system and the main high-voltage transmission grid, enhancing operational security and saving an estimated $5 billion. The project also contributed significantly to the following: the design of funding mechanisms and affordable lifeline tariffs for poor communities; the environmental review and licensing processes; the sector planning process; and building a strong relationship between the Brazilian authorities and the Bank in the sector and providing advice on a number of other important issues (such as the Angra III nuclear power plant).

Until the ESTAL became effective, a PPIAF grant provided support in a number of important areas, including tariff setting, assessment of the role of the regulatory agency ANEEL, and energy auctions. In addition to the ESTAL and PPIAF support, the Bank undertook a number of AAA activities that were regarded as relevant and of high quality, including the Low Carbon Country Case Study (used by the government in Copenhagen and other climate-related meetings), and several tasks addressing energy security, development, and efficiency. A Global Environment Facility-supported operation that closed in FY06 also focused on supporting Brazil's Energy Efficiency Program.

The only project approved by the Bank during this period was the Eletrobras Distribution Rehabilitation Project (FY10, $495 million), which focused on six weak distribution companies in the North and Northeast. These six distribution companies supply electricity in some of the poorest regions in Brazil and face enormous challenges, including reducing service interruptions and losses and increasing collection rates, as well as institutional weaknesses. The Eletrobras Distribution Rehabilitation project got off to a slow start (a recent Implementation Status Report indicates that an action plan has been prepared and is being monitored closely).

Water

The Bank has had sustained engagement with both water resource management and water supply and sanitation at the federal and subnational levels. It has supported the government with operations aimed at strengthening the water sector's legal and institutional framework and the provision of basic infrastructure investments and services. Several earlier projects were completed immediately before or during the FY04–11 period, including two federal projects (Federal Water Resources and Water Sector Modernization 2) and several state projects (in Bahia, Ceará, and Espirito Santo).

Nine additional projects (amounting to $739 million) were approved during FY04–11. They include operations that combined water resource management and water supply and sanitation at the state level (such as Espirito Santo, Rio Grande do Norte, Pernambuco, and two São Paulo projects, Integrated Water Management and Reagua), a more recent integrated technical assistance operation at the federal level (Interaguas FY11), and a number of municipal operations that were part of a series of horizontal Adaptable Program Loans (São Luis, Teresina, and Uberaba) with significant water content.

The water portfolio in Brazil is quite integrated across subsectors (water resource management and water supply and sanitation, including urban wastewater collection and treatment). It is also well linked with urban development projects in which the water supply and sanitation agenda has often been packaged with municipal operations and slum upgrading components. Rural development and multisectoral operations (for example, in Ceará) also had significant water components with considerable cross-support between the relevant units. Most water projects have had success in increasing access to water supply and sanitation services and addressed the broader water agenda, including support for institutional and financial strengthening, but many challenges persist. The Bank is considered an important partner, helping tackle difficult challenges ranging from environmentally sensitive river basins to deteriorating water quality, sewerage coverage and treatment, utility management, and financial sustainability.

The large Federal Water Resources Management Project (Proagua, $185 million, closed in FY10) focused on both water resource management priority investments (for water storage and conveyance) and institutional development and planning at both state and river basin levels (it initially addressed the semi-arid northeast and was later extended nationally). Similarly, the Bank supported the federal water supply and sanitation agenda through the Water Sector Modernization Projects (closed in FY09) and the earlier Low-Income Sanitation technical assistance project (Prosanear), which aimed to improve the efficiency of the sector by strengthening the sector's weak institutional and regulatory framework, increasing private participation, and providing technical assistance for use in urban upgrading and water supply and sanitation services to the poor.

The Bank's intensive federal engagement made large contributions to both water resource management and water supply and sanitation. Bank-supported investments and related institutional strengthening in water resource management enhanced the management of water resources in priority river basins (in the northeast in particular), improving the reliability and sustainability of water supply for various uses. They also included support for the creation and strengthening of the National Water Agency and the development of water resource management plans in all 26 states (and an atlas of plans for all key municipalities). The broad institutional objectives of the water resource management-focused Proagua were substantially achieved. It prioritized institutional support and promoted learning between states and from other experiences. As one official noted, it contributed to a change in culture, because the Bank has stressed the importance of effective utilization and management of water resource management assets.

Bank support in water supply and sanitation helped expand access or coverage and improve the efficiency of service delivery by encouraging a more competitive and better-regulated environment. It financed a National Information System; supported the formulation of major legislation, policies, and regulations to improve sector performance; introduced private operators for water supply and sanitation; and improved management of water losses, metering, connections, and billing to enhance service quality and efficiency and financial sustainability. More recently, the Bank approved the Federal Integrated Water Sector Project (Interaguas, FY11, $107 million), a technical assistance loan that is helping address the major persisting water sector challenges in Brazil's complex water resource management system. Though Interaguas has just gotten started, a senior official observed that the preparation process itself has already had positive effects by creating and strengthening links between different federal entities and between these and subnational levels. Finally, the Bank has engaged in sector policy dialogue at the national level with specific analytical contributions on key issues (subsidies, utility capacity).

As for state-level operations, earlier projects that closed during this period (Ceará, Espirito Santo, and Bahia) focused on priority investments in water resource management, and to a lesser extent water supply and sanitation, as well as strengthening the institutional and regulatory framework. The projects approved during FY04–11 at the state level focused on resource management infrastructure and institutions as well as increasing coverage and efficiency for supply and sanitation and promoting integrated water resource management, including addressing water quality issues, wastewater collection and treatment, and financial sustainability of water agencies and utilities. The Bank also supported water components in rural and multisectoral operations for an estimated $350 million in additional investments in the sector, a considerable increase in total Bank-supported water investments.

The contribution of Bank-supported operations at the state level varied across states. The projects in Espirito Santo, Rio Grande do Sul, and Ceará have made progress on efficiency and coverage and to some extent on water quality. The project in Bahia has had a more mixed experience, with considerable increases in reliability and access to water as well as some overall progress in integrated river basin management and related investments, but less success in implementing bulk water tariffs, water quality, and institutional and financial reforms.

In Ceará, multisectoral operations have complemented dedicated water projects. They have provided considerable support for the water sector, significantly increasing coverage of water supply and sanitation services as well as the efficiency and financial sustainability of water agencies. Related technical assistance activities focused on important issues such as water quality and tariffs and subsidies. These and other multisectoral projects have also had positive effects on rural water supply and sanitation, and Brazil is regarded as having developed some good practice models for that.

Other state-level water operations approved more recently (Pernambuco, Sergipe) appear to be performing well, with the latter featured in a Smart Lessons piece highlighting the beneficial impact on the water utility of Bank-IFC collaboration (IFC 2010). Building on earlier Bank-supported projects that focused on pollution control and new approaches to water quality in dense urban watersheds, the two São Paulo water operations approved in FY10 are promoting integrated water management in the metropolitan region and water quality in the critical watersheds in the state. Finally some of the city-based operations with considerable water supply and sanitation content, including significant wastewater issues, are reportedly performing well (such as Teresina) while others are not (São Luis), though completion reports are not yet available for these.

Though formal Bank-financed AAA has been limited, the Bank is highly involved in sector dialogue at the national and state levels and in several nonlending technical assistance activities funded by other donors, including a study on subsidies and an assessment of the capacity of state water utilities under the new regulatory environment.

Urban Development

Brazil is a highly urbanized middle-income country with 84 percent of its population living in urban areas. Over 1970–2000, the urban share increased from 56 percent to 82 percent. In addition to the complex issues of urban transport in the largest cities, Brazil has confronted the enormous challenges of providing housing and urban services to a rapidly growing low- and middle-income urban population, while improving urban fiscal and operational management.

The Bank has had a longstanding engagement in the sector, starting with several statewide operations in the 1980s (in Paraná, Rio Grande do Sul, and Santa Catarina) that used municipal development funds to help hundreds of municipalities.[5] These were followed by several statewide operations in the 1990s (Bahia, Ceará, and Minas Gerais), which used a similar design and reached hundreds of municipalities. Two of these included significant slum upgrading and water components (Bahia and Ceará) and closed during 2004–11. In addition, the Recife Urban Upgrading Project (FY03) was the first urban operation that focused primarily on slum upgrading and related infrastructure and institutional issues.

Following the Law of Fiscal Responsibility (2000), the government viewed a Bank offer of further support to all 5,500 municipalities at the start of the FY04–07 period as an attempt to stimulate borrowing that undermined the law. After a hiatus, the Bank resumed its urban lending while respecting the law, and two urban operations were approved during the FY04–07 period (aside from housing, which was a different type of engagement and is discussed later in this section). The Bahia Poor Urban Areas Integrated Development Project (FY06) focused on slum upgrading in poor urban areas as well as related municipal and water infrastructure and institutional strengthening in Salvador and other cities. The Betim Integrated Municipal Project (FY05) was the first project to focus on an individual smaller municipality, with particular emphasis on sewerage and wastewater treatment (this project was technically mapped to the Bank's environment sector and had mixed results).

Urban projects were later approved for a number of small and medium-sized cities as part of horizontal Adaptable Program Loan operations. These focused on municipal strengthening, employment generation, and infrastructure services (including five cities in Rio Grande do Sul, and São Luis, Teresina, and Uberaba), as well as larger projects focusing on Recife (FY08) and Santos (FY10), an urban project focusing on nine small municipalities in Ceará (Regional Development: Ceará Cities, FY09), and two separate operations addressing solid waste management.

Thirteen housing and urban operations were approved in FY04–11, amounting to nearly $1.3 billion in lending commitments, with two large DPLs dominating the commitments (Table G.4). In addition to its traditional focus on urban services, slum upgrading, and municipal strengthening, the Bank introduced a substantial engagement in housing finance. The largest operation during the period reviewed was the $502 million Housing Sector loan, a DPL approved at the end of FY05 and complemented by a small technical assistance loan and a number of related AAA activities. It aimed at improving access to housing for the poor while strengthening and reforming housing sector policy and institutions. This operation was designed to be followed by a second operation that did not materialize.

The other large urban operation in the FY04–11 program was the Rio de Janeiro Metropolitan Urban and Housing DPL (FY11, $485 million), which provided support to the Rio state government for strengthening the planning and management of urban growth in the Rio metropolitan region, promoting the provision of affordable housing and creating integrated social development programs targeted at the urban poor.

TABLE G.4 Urban Sector Lending Operations (FY04–11)

	Commitment Amount		No. of Projects
	$ Millions	Share (%)	
Development Policy Loans (DPLs)	991	78	3
Housing DPL[a]	506	40	2
Rio (DPL)	485	38	1
Other Urban Lending	276	22	10
Total	1,267	100	13

SOURCE: World Bank.
a. This includes the small technical assistance loan ($4 million, FY06).

In addition to lending, there was a considerable amount of AAA linked to housing and slum upgrading, Brazil's urban policy and strategy, city economic growth and competitiveness, and a specific study on São Paulo.

HOUSING. The housing sector loan and the related technical assistance and AAA aimed at supporting the government in its efforts to develop a sound policy and institutional framework for housing strengthen housing credit and savings systems; provide incentives for expansion of the housing market and moving down-market; design and implement a revised housing subsidy system; and reduce the cost of formal land development. This operation preceded, but was consistent with, the government's *Minha Casa, Minha Vida* (My House, My Life) program. It contributed to a significant expansion of housing finance and the strengthening of sector planning and institutional arrangements (Caixa, Ministry of Cities). There were also some shortcomings, including delays in the overall housing plan and subsidy system, limited progress on reducing the cost of land development, lack of evidence of increased access to housing by the poor or consolidation and rationalization of housing subsidies, and no monitoring and evaluation system to track these.

Though the linked technical assistance operation did not successfully complement the DPL and only disbursed $1 million, the related AAA (both economic and sector work and nonlending technical assistance) continued to address critical sector issues and finance strategic studies (housing policy and plan, housing market dynamics, new instruments to raise long-term funds from the capital markets) and made relevant contributions. The overall effectiveness of the DPL and related activities is assessed as moderate and not as far reaching as expected because the dialogue appears to have waned when it became clear that there would not be a second loan.

RIO DE JANEIRO DPL. The other large DPL in the FY04–11 program (Rio Metropolitan Urban and Housing, FY11) covered a wide range of areas in its prior actions and second tranche triggers. Despite the high level of program complexity, there seemed to be no companion technical assistance loan to complement the reform efforts. Based on the latest Implementation Status and Results Report (February 2013), program effectiveness appears to have been mixed, with some areas (planning and management of urban growth) demonstrating good progress and others (affordable housing and integrated social programs) a cause for concern.

With regard to other urban development projects, most of the Bank's operations during FY04–11 were broad city-specific programs in small and medium-sized urban areas. The exceptions were the state-level Bahia Municipal Infrastructure and Poor Urban Areas Projects and the metropolitan-level Recife Urban Upgrading Project. These urban development projects are often highly complex because of many components, subsectors, implementing agencies, and jurisdictions. They also often operate in socially sensitive areas. Despite delays, some appear to have made significant contributions. The large number of broad, integrated projects in smaller cities has required considerable supervision and coordination efforts by the Bank. Several Bank managers and staff have observed that the series of small municipal projects (linked to the horizontal Adaptable Program Loan) may not have been the most strategic choice, as it is unclear whether there are any demonstration effects.

Conclusions and Lessons

Most of the Bank's infrastructure projects were relevant to Brazil's development challenges and effective in achieving their objectives. The authorities appreciate not only the Bank's financing but also the quality of its engagement and advice, including the "embedded knowledge" in its missions and the long-term effects and benefits of learning from the Bank's project management systems and operational procedures (including fiduciary and safeguard policies).

At the aggregate level, however, underinvestment in infrastructure continues. Despite increased financing from the PAC program since 2007, the overall quantity of investment in infrastructure remains insufficient and its quality also appears to be mixed (particularly in view of sector planning and project design weaknesses as well as the PAC's emphasis on disbursements rather than results). The Bank-supported program has had some positive "demonstration effects" at the sectoral level, but the Bank is a relatively small player and has had limited leverage to influence the quantity and quality of infrastructure investments.

The Brazilian authorities are now mainly seeking support for technical assistance at the federal level and investment at subnational levels. The Bank needs to maximize the effectiveness of its technical assistance activities in the infrastructure sectors on addressing key policy, regulatory, and institutional issues and on helping to strengthen capacity at the state and municipal levels. Though the experience with technical assistance loans and technical assistance components in infrastructure has been mixed, they have been important for supporting sector reforms and capacity building in several cases. DPLs are not a substitute for sustained engagement, as shown by the two DPLs in the infrastructure program.

In all the infrastructure sector programs and projects, the Bank has emphasized the importance of focusing on operations and management of infrastructure investments and assets and their financial sustainability, and not just on more works or equipment. In this connection, the Bank has stressed the value of involving the private sector in the process and providing appropriate incentives and regulatory frameworks for this to happen. This has been noted by a number of stakeholders interviewed for this evaluation.

Endnotes

[1] The figures on Brazil's infrastructure investment levels in this section are from Claudio R. Frischtak and Victor Chateubriand, "*Infraestrutura e Desenvolvimento no Brasil,* Inter B." October 12, 2012. They include telecoms (a sector which accounts for an average of 0.6 percent of GDP over this period and where the Bank was not involved so it is not covered in this report). These figures are broadly consistent with those cited in an earlier World Bank report (see World Bank 2007b).

[2] On this and the PAC program see also OECD (2011) and Ter-Minassian (2012).

[3] World Bank (2007b) also mentions this point.

[4] The discussion of the Energy Sector Technical Assistance Loan in this appendix is based on interviews with key government of Brazil officials and World Bank task team leaders, the draft ICR Review dated 01/28/2013 and a paper prepared following a workshop on the project held in Washington, DC, on March 30, 2009; see also De Gouvello (2009).

[5] These early projects are discussed at length in Lee and Gilbert (1999) and IEG (2009c).

References

De Gouvello, Christophe. 2009. *Brazil—Brazil's Energy Services Technical Assistance Loan (ESTAL): Lessons Learned: How Can We Improve the Effectiveness of Technical Assistance Loans?* Washington, DC: World Bank.

Frischtak, Claudio, and Victor Chateubriand. 2012. "Infraestrutura e Desenvolvimento no Brasil." Inter B.

IEG (Independent Evaluation Group). 2009. *Improving Municipal Management for Cities to Succeed.* Washington, DC: World Bank.

IFC (International Finance Corporation). 2010. "Teaming up to Support Sub-National Water Utility in Brazil's Frontier Region." *Smart Lessons.*

Lancelot, Eric. 2010. "Performance Based Contracts in the Road Sector: Towards Improved Efficiency in the Management of Maintenance and Rehabilitation—Brazil's Experience." Transport paper series; no. TP-31. World Bank, Washington, DC.

Lee, Kyu Sik, and Roy Gilbert. 1999. *Developing Towns and Cities: Lessons from Brazil and the Philippines.* Washington, DC: World Bank.

OECD (Organisation for Economic Co-operation and Development). 2011. "Overview of Brazil Economic Survey." OECD, Paris.

Ter-Menissian, Teresa. 2012. "Structural Reforms in Brazil: Progress and Unfinished Agenda." Policy Brief IDB-PB-158, Inter-American Development Bank, Washington, DC.

World Bank. 2007. *How to Revitalize Infrastructure Investments in Brazil (Public Policies for Better Private Participation).* FPSI/LAC Report #36624BR, World Bank, Washington, DC.

———. 2012. *Transformation through Infrastructure: World Bank Group Infrastructure Strategy Update FY2012–2015.* Washington, DC: World Bank.

Appendix H
Subnational DPLs and SWAps: Views from Recipient States

The evaluation team interviewed state officials in Alagoas, Minas Gerais, and Rio Grande do Sul to solicit their views of DPLs and SWAps implemented in those states. The major positive features noted in the interviews are as follows.

- The process of preparing these operations was highly useful, as the Bank team had to harmonize project objectives with the government's priorities. It also encouraged state teams to interact with each other and face common trade-offs and budgetary constraints. It helped focus the internal dialogue and achieve consensus in some difficult areas of reform.

- The identification of eligible expenditure programs and the minimum levels of funding to be protected encouraged sector department officials to articulate priorities and engage the highest state authorities on expenditure allocations. This encouraged strong leadership and ownership from the authorities and helped ensure some continuity. In one case the operation overlapped two administrations, but the second administration continued the original reform program.

- The inclusion of disbursement-linked indicators in SWAp operations and the encouragement of results-based management systems helped create, in the opinion of some officials, some cultural change within the administration that may have effects beyond the project life.

- The associated technical support activities were judged to have been critical to the success of the operations. Other knowledge sharing activities generated important externalities beyond the operation. Seminars and workshops, training programs and courses, and visits within Brazil and abroad were judged by officials to have created important long-term benefits.

- State officials acknowledged the value of an increased dissemination of DPL/SWAp experiences that took place through formal and informal channels.

State officials also noted several areas that call for further attention in future operations:

- Avoid a proliferation of indicators to be monitored and evaluated. They should be simple, well defined, and focused on the essential goals of the program. Cross-sectoral issues indicators should have precedence. Focus on realistic indicators and targets that are under the control of the executive authorities.

- Encourage engagement of the relevant sectoral secretariat from the outset as their participation in defining the results indicators and technical assistance needs will increase their ownership of the program.

- In the case of SWAps, harmonize better the concept of eligible expenditures with the state's expenditure financial programming and payment system to minimize confusion and delays.

- Given the challenge of harmonizing Bank procurement requirements with the Brazilian legislation, more explicit consideration of national consultants would contribute to better project implementation. Allocate more resources to supervision, capacity building, and technical assistance, with special consideration for the poorer states.

- Seek more balanced implementation results between short-term policies (fiscal adjustment, debt restructuring) and structural reforms (state social security, civil service reform, public sector management, poverty reduction); boost implementation technical support to the latter.

Reduce bureaucratic processes in the Bank, especially on procurement related to technical assistance. State officials consider that getting paperwork through Bank procedures faster can considerably increase implementation efficiency.

Appendix I
Brazil: Summary of World Bank Group Program Outcome Ratings

This summary table is derived from the assessments presented in Chapters 3–4 and the achievements against the objectives indicated in the FY04–07 CAS and FY08–11 CPS.

World Bank Group Strategic Goals[a]	Achievement of Associated CAS/CPS Outcomes or Results	World Bank Group Program Outcome Ratings[b]
First Pillar: Towards a more equitable Brazil		**Satisfactory**
This pillar had three major objectives: To reduce extreme poverty and social exclusion by supporting the social assistance programs, enhance skills formation with an emphasis in early childhood and primary education, and improve health care for all communities.		
1. Reduce extreme poverty	*Bolsa Familia*, the main conditional income transfer program for poor families in Brazil, started in 2004 and expanded quickly. By 2010 it provided transfers to almost 12 million families and more than 50 million beneficiaries, about 22 percent of the Brazilian population. Conditions for assistance involve prenatal and natal checkup for mothers, participation in educational health and nutrition seminars, follow vaccine schedules and growth monitoring of children, and school enrollment and minimum attendance by children. The program had an important effect on poverty reduction and school enrolment among participating families. The Bank played a vital role on assisting the government through sustained technical assistance, analytical support, and some financing—a contribution widely acknowledged by Brazilian counterparts.	

continued on page 230

World Bank Group Strategic Goals[a]	Achievement of Associated CAS/CPS Outcomes or Results	World Bank Group Program Outcome Ratings[b]
2. Better knowledge and skills	The main activities of the Bank were in the education sector. A combination of federal and state loans helped increase access to primary education in poor municipalities of the North and Northeast and reduce the difference in performance across schools by establishing pedagogical models. The Bank supported the operations of FUNDEF, a fund that guarantees a minimum per student funding formula and creates incentives for schools to expand enrollment as well as redistributing funds toward poor municipalities. Eventually resources were also distributed for early childhood development programs. This assistance was also helped by advice given in this area to the National Institute of Education. The Bank activities in education gained renewed impetus during the second CAS period by shifting emphasis to the quality of education. It was based on major analytical work and research on the interaction between students and teachers observed at the level of the classroom. Major pieces of work were written on these experiences and disseminated across Brazil. This work helped identify incentives and bonus systems to improve students' outcomes.	
3. Increase accessibility to quality health care for all communities	Over the last decade health outcomes in Brazil have improved markedly, particularly reductions in infant malnutrition and mortality. In part they have been influenced by reforms in several components of the health system. The Bank continued its support to improve disease surveillance. The continuing implementation of the Family Health Extension Project supported the reorganization of primary health care so that health clinics focus not only on maternal and child health, but on families and communities more broadly. Freestanding operation at the federal level focuses on systemic reforms involving federal subnational coordination and reforms at the tertiary level, including medical education and research. A large number of operations had important health-related components, in particular the subnational multisector SWAps and DPLs. These components focus on state-specific health issues. In the poorer and more rural states the attention was on improving maternal and neonatal services. In the wealthier states the components focus on consolidating emergency care and transfer systems between the municipalities and the states. IFC s advisory services assisted in structuring the first PPP hospital transaction in Brazil in the city of Salvador.	

World Bank Group Strategic Goals[a]	Achievement of Associated CAS/CPS Outcomes or Results	World Bank Group Program Outcome Ratings[b]
Second Pillar: Towards a more sustainable Brazil This pillar contained three major objectives: better water quality and water resource management; more sustained land management, forestry, and biodiversity; and more equitable and integrated access to local services, particularly in poor urban and rural communities.		Moderately Satisfactory
1. Better water quality and water resource management	During the FY04–07 CAS period, the emphasis was on the regulatory and management aspects of water systems. Federal projects such as PROAGUA focused on management of water systems at the state and river basin levels. Similarly, the Water Sector Modernization project and the earlier Low-Income Sanitation technical assistance project focused on improving the efficiency of water and sanitation utilities; strengthening the weak institutional and regulatory framework for water supply and sanitation; increasing private sector participation; and providing technical assistance for urban upgrades and water supply services to the urban poor. According to IEG's reviews of completed projects, Bank support helped enhance water resource management in priority river basins—in the Northeast in particular—and strengthen the National Water Agency. However, the impact of operations in states varied. There was limited progress on implementing bulk water supply cost recovery systems and enhancing water quality, though there was significant improvement in the provision of water supply to households. The Bank's convening power was particularly recognized as critical in providing a platform for a multidisciplinary deliberation across sectors and different levels of government.	

continued on page 232

World Bank Group Strategic Goals[a]	Achievement of Associated CAS/CPS Outcomes or Results	World Bank Group Program Outcome Ratings[b]
2. More sustainable land management, forest, and biodiversity	Amazonian deforestation declined dramatically during the last 20 years, partly due to general economic factors but also in response to policy interventions. The Bank has supported the government efforts in a series of areas such as improving infrastructure licensing and safe guards, forest protection, land use regulation, and support for sustainable private sector land management. The clearer contribution of the Bank was in forest protection. Bank projects assisted in the demarcation and recognition of 87 indigenous territories encompassing 37 million hectares of lands and supporting a major expansion of new conservation units in the Amazon region. Harmonization of development and forest conservation remains a challenge however. Attempts to promote poverty reduction in remote forest areas have had limited success; hydropower planning and assessment is not yet on a basin wide basis; and the DPL's value-added to further improve Brazil's environment management system is hard to detect despite the size of the loan.	
3. More equitable access to rural land, housing and local services	Brazil has become increasingly urbanized and about half of the poor live in urban areas. Assisting access to housing and critical services to the poor in a context of fiscal sustainability and capacity constraints of cities is a major challenge. The Bank supported the objectives with a series of integrated urban development and municipal projects supporting city specific programs in many states and metropolitan areas. In some the emphasis was on slums upgrading, in others in supporting basic infrastructure such as water and sanitation. Questions have been raised whether a proliferation of many of these very city specific projects have had sufficient demonstration effects. At the federal level the Bank implemented a policy-based operation accompanied with technical assistance and AAA activities. It suggested up-front transparent budgetary subsidies for social housing instead of subsidized interest rates, but progress in this area has been limited.	

World Bank Group Strategic Goals[a]	Achievement of Associated CAS/CPS Outcomes or Results	World Bank Group Program Outcome Ratings[b]
	In rural areas the Bank made frequent use of community-driven development projects in order to increase the access of rural poor to critical services. The approach projects consisted of a small set of small scale subproject at the local level that are demand driven by the rural communities themselves, relying on their ability to identify priorities and execute these subprojects. The most common services included were water, sanitation and electricity. Many of the CDD projects were complemented by a project to enhance poor farmers' access to land, the *Credito Fundiario* project. Similar projects have been undertaken in the Amazon, taking into account land and forestry sustainable issues faced by poor rural communities. The available evidence shows a mixed success. Projects whose objective has been to expand critical social services have been relatively successful—the community approach seems to be helpful in these circumstances. More problematic have been a new generation of projects aiming at supporting the productivity and entrepreneurial activities of farmers, including access to markets. The sustainability of such projects has been a problem.	

continued on page 234

World Bank Group Strategic Goals[a]	Achievement of Associated CAS/CPS Outcomes or Results	World Bank Group Program Outcome Ratings[b]
Third Pillar: A more competitive Brazil This pillar contains three major objectives: Addressing infrastructure bottlenecks and improving the regulatory framework, including for PPPs; improving the business climate and the environment for competition; and reducing interest rates and the segmentation of financial markets.		Moderately Unsatisfactory
1. Achieving a modern regulatory framework for infrastructure, including a framework for public private partnerships	The strategy was to relieve major infrastructure bottlenecks, improve the capabilities of agencies in managing infrastructure assets, and enhance the incentives for private sector participation in infrastructure with a particular emphasis on PPP arrangements. IFC played an important role in this last area. The Bank used a combination of instruments: first, policy-based lending, ranging from federal DPLs to subnational SWAps and DPLs; second, investment operations in various infrastructure sectors; third, a major piece of AAA in 2007 in the area of private investment in infrastructure in Brazil. Some progress was made in lowering logistic costs by custom reforms and the operation of existing ports and federal roads through outsourcing and result based management of rehabilitation and maintenance. Although PPP legislation created high expectations, progress in PPPs has been slow, except in some specific states such as Minas Gerais. Major mass transport projects (metro and rail) were approved for São Paulo and Rio de Janeiro, with important benefits in reducing commuter time and reduction in pollution. However the opportunity cost in terms of bank lending space has been high—the issue is whether some of the financing could have been mobilized from the markets given the high level of income and creditworthiness of these cities and the possibilities of cost recovery.	

World Bank Group Strategic Goals[a]	Achievement of Associated CAS/CPS Outcomes or Results	World Bank Group Program Outcome Ratings[b]
2. Improving the business climate and the environment for competition	Starting a business, registering property, and paying taxes are high in Brazil relative to many comparator countries and this been documented by IFC doing business. Some states had already started to simplify procedures including "one-stop shops," but in most cases the process remained costly and lengthy. The FY 08–11 CPS committed itself to do more in this area. The main vehicles were components of subnational DPLs and SWAps in Minas Gerais, Ceará, Rio State, and the Rio Municipality. IFC also has had relevant initiatives in municipalities. In 2006, it offered 10 municipalities in Northeast Brazil[1] technical assistance under its advisory service program to reduce the time to open a business and to obtain construction permits, and create municipal scorecards. Cooperation agreements were signed with two municipalities. However, both IFC and IEG judged the development effectiveness of this initiative unsuccessful. The ongoing initiative to develop a comprehensive Doing Business report for Brazil, covering all states and the federal district is timely. In spite of the importance attached to competition and productivity of an open trade regime in the FY04–07 CAS, no AAA was envisaged during the overall evaluation period to investigate the degree of openness of the Brazilian trade regime.	

continued on page 236

World Bank Group Strategic Goals[a]	Achievement of Associated CAS/CPS Outcomes or Results	World Bank Group Program Outcome Ratings[b]
3. Enhance competition in the financial sector	Given the instruments available to the Bank Group, the initial CAS objectives in this area were ambitious: to increase private sector intermediation and long-term investment financing, and nonbank financial services. The main vehicles were a DPL series, a series of technical assistance loans, and AAA examining the sources of high interest rates in Brazil. The provision of credit through financial intermediaries was a major IFC activity at a later point. Some of the reform steps supported by the DPL series were carried out, and some of the impacts on financial intermediation were positive. However the effect of these measures on the level of interest rates and the cost of credit, particularly to SMEs, depended on many variables unaffected by the project. This was recognized by the CAS Completion Report for the period. The FY08–11 CPS proposed a more limited set of activities. First, a Financial Sector technical assistance loan focusing on training on regulation and supervision of the banking system as well as on surveillance and investor protection in the capital markets. The IEG ICR rated the outcomes as moderately satisfactory, the objectives of the project were partly achieved, several studies were cancelled, and the achievements of some subcomponent objectives were rated as modest. Second, analytical work was undertaken to understand the factors behind the high cost of borrowing in Brazil, the extent it is influenced by macroeconomic factors or by market structure such as publicly directed credit crowding out private credit, and whether directed credit was reaching smaller enterprises. These studies have provided a good platform for an exchange of views with the authorities. Trade financing became the predominant IFC financial product in Brazil as a response to the global financial crisis in 2008–09. The volume of trade credit continued to expand beyond the crisis period rather than to restore the pre-crisis proportion of longer-term lending. This is puzzling because after the crisis, the additionality of IFC should have been much higher for long-term financing than for trade credit, particularly if the objective is to serve SMEs. A preliminary examination found the definition of SME to include overly large firms, not necessarily those in most need.	

World Bank Group Strategic Goals[a]	Achievement of Associated CAS/CPS Outcomes or Results	World Bank Group Program Outcome Ratings[b]
Fourth Pillar: Sound macroeconomic and public sector management		Satisfactory
This area is broad and the focus was where the Bank Group has the most comparative advantage. The areas selected were: support specific elements influencing fiscal sustainability, in this case pension reform; and help achieve more efficient public expenditure management systems, including results-based systems. These objectives were to be pursued at the federal and state level.		
1. Contributing to fiscal sustainability	Support for pension reform consisted of closely coordinated DPL lending, analytical work, and technical assistance. Significant background analytical and technical work was undertaken to simulate alternative scenarios and share lessons from other reform experience that could serve as inputs to the Brazilian authorities. At the local level the process was helped by three technical assistance loans that helped in the preparation and implementation of the DPL. The technical assistance loans continued supporting the states and municipalities beyond the lifetime of the DPL, focusing on difficult but critical institutional steps of the pension reforms. Policy dialogue has remained active thereafter taking advantage of the extensive analytical work undertaken. Brazilian counterparts valued highly the knowledge sharing, technical dialogue, and support at the local level. The ICR Review by IEG considers the DPL and associated technical assistance activities an example of good design and relevance.	

continued on page 238

World Bank Group Strategic Goals[a]	Achievement of Associated CAS/CPS Outcomes or Results	World Bank Group Program Outcome Ratings[b]
2. Contributing to a more effective budget and expenditure management including the results based system.	At the federal level the Bank undertook some limited but important analytical activities. In 2005, a pilot program to achieve fiscal space for public investment was launched with the assistance of the IMF to identify projects with a potential for high rates of return. The Bank participated in the project from its inception. Weisman and Blanco (2007) examine the composition of the budget, and suggested reducing earmarking and subsidies though public financial institutions, and enhancing participation of the private sector in infrastructure to complement public investment. The Bank also did some informal analytical work on fiscal federalism and the challenges it presents for taxation, transfers, and subnational indebtedness. Most of the Bank Group assistance in this area took place at the sub-national level. The Fiscal Responsibility Law provided the framework for fiscal sustainability and borrowing to subnational governments and incentives to rationalize and reallocate expenditures. The authorities requested the Bank to assist state government in these areas. The result was a sharp shift toward operations providing budget support to states and municipalities (DPLs and SWAps). States had to identify their policy and expenditure priorities consistent with budget constraints and the borrowing guidelines of the Fiscal Responsibility Law. To facilitate implementation, technical assistance accompanied these operations. Because of their multisectoral nature, these operations were ideal vehicles to address major institutional reforms on the fiscal side that cut across sectors, particularly those requiring difficult steps and a consensus across agencies and different stakeholders. Many were necessary to comply with the Fiscal Responsibility Law and with other reforms that were initiated at the federal level, such as pension reform. Results agreements with the different agencies and secretariats, including tracking of performance, together with efforts at implementing medium-term expenditure frameworks were also prominent in some cases. Interviewed officials acknowledged the importance of the convening role of the Bank in providing a platform for cross-sectoral discussions and the personal involvement of the highest authorities in the state.	

World Bank Group Strategic Goals[a]	Achievement of Associated CAS/CPS Outcomes or Results	World Bank Group Program Outcome Ratings[b]
Overall Bank Group Program Outcome Rating		Moderately Satisfactory

NOTE: AAA = analytic and advisory activity; CAS = country assistance strategy; CDD = community-driven development; CPS = country partnership strategy; DPL = development policy loan; ICR = Implementation and Completion Results Report; PPP = public-private partnership; SME = small and medium-size enterprise; SWAp = sectorwide approach.

a. The goals of Bank Group assistance may be distinct from those of the client country's own development objectives, although the two are usually consistent.

b. The Bank Group program outcome subratings and overall rating assess the extent to which the Bank program achieved the results targeted in the relevant strategy document(s) and/or the documents for individual operations. They do not attempt to assess the extent to which the client country was satisfied with the Bank's program, nor do they try to measure the extent (in an absolute sense) to which the program contributed to the country's development. Equally, they are not synonymous with Bank performance.

Appendix J
Modifications of FY08–11 CPS Outcomes
in Progress Report

During the period evaluated, operational objectives were revised to increase their specificity and facilitate the measurement of results. Of particular interest are the revisions to the FY08–11 CPS results matrix. At the time of the progress report in March 2010 (World Bank 2010b), 21 of the 24 CPS outcomes were modified; 11 of the modifications were minor and primarily to achieve a more precise specification of quantitative targets. Some of the revisions to outcomes in the macroeconomic foundations pillar, particularly those related to public finance objectives, were revised to relate to progress in the specific states where the Bank had been active. The focus on social security spending reductions was replaced by cadastre upgrading to eliminate unwarranted payments—a much more specific objective that is related more directly to the Bank interventions.

These modifications specified more realistic expected outcomes from the country program. Refinement at the time of the progress report was important as the original CPS had intentionally left room for flexibility in responding to unanticipated demand. The enormous uncertainty caused by the 2008–09 global economic crisis further strengthens the rational for these modifications. Most of the adjustments were meaningful in this context, although some outcomes remained broad even after modification. For example, the outcomes aimed to reduce the GDP per capita ratio between the Northeast and the rest of the country by a certain amount or to increase the Human Development Index in the Amazon above the country average by certain percentages were replaced by a single outcome—real per capita disposable income: ratio of Northeast to national average. The link between Bank interventions and the revised outcome remains somewhat tenuous.

In some cases the change involved considerable revision, resulting in substantive departure from the outcomes pursued in the original CPS. For example, a major thematic change and significant narrowing of objectives took place for the city competitiveness outcome. It was replaced by an increase in the volume of waste disposed in environmentally sustainable sanitary landfills with Bank support through the Brazil Integrated Solid Management Project.

TABLE J.1 Examples of Major Revisions in FY08–11 CPS Results Matrix Outcomes

	Original CPS Outcomes	CASCR Matrix Outcomes
Macroeconomic foundations and public sector management	• Increased reliance on reductions in current expenditures (as opposed to increases in taxation) to meet fiscal goals • Federal social security spending/GDP starts to decrease from 12.5% to approximately 12%	• Reduction in ratio of consolidated debt to net current revenues (executive branch) in states where Bank is supporting fiscal programs under the CPS • Number of states participating in cadastre upgrade program to eliminate unwarranted beneficiary payments in all state government branches
Competitive Brazil	• Quality and efficiency of public expenditure in infrastructure is improved by introducing results-based management • Fiscal capacity, management and competitiveness of cities is improved	• Improved effectiveness of government agencies in implementing mandated Brazilian environmental and social management procedures • Increase in volume of waste disposed in environmentally sustainable sanitary landfills with Bank support through the Brazil Integrated Solid Waste Management Project

SOURCE: World Bank 2010.
NOTE: CASCR = Country Assistance Strategy Completion Report; CPS = Country Partnership Strategy.

Also as a result of this revision, a CPS outcome on the quality and efficiency of public expenditure in infrastructure—a critical bottleneck for Brazil's economic growth that was emphasized by the authorities during the original CPS discussions—was dropped. The original objective, "quality and efficiency of public expenditure in infrastructure is improved by introducing results-based management," was replaced by "improved effectiveness of government agencies in implementing mandated Brazilian environmental and social management procedures." Although the quality of public investment is at the core of Brazil's development challenge, the rationale for the revision is not explained clearly (Table J.1).

Reference

World Bank. 2010. *Country Partnership Strategy Progress Report for the Federative Republic of Brazil for the Period FY2008–2011*. Washington, DC: World Bank.

Appendix K
People Met

Public Sector Entities	
Federal Entities	
Baptista da Costa, Francisco Luiz	Director, Transport Planning Department Ministry of Transport
Bicalho Cozendey, Carlos Márcio	Secretary for International Affairs, Ministry of Finance
Collaco de Carvalho, Sergio Henrique	Deputy Director Protected Areas, Ministry of Environment
Ciríaco de Miranda, Ernani	Diretor do Articulação Institucional, Secretaria Nacional de Saneamento Ambiental, Ministério das Cidades
Coelho Saraiva, Bruno Walter	Head of Department, International Affairs Department, Central Bank
Coutinho, Eduardo	Deputy-Secretary, Treasury, Ministry of Finance
da Costa Pinto, Henrique Amarante	Superintendent, Area Project Structuring, the Brazilian Development Bank (BNDES)
da Silva Alves, Iara Cristina	Director of International Projects, Directorate of International Projects of the Executive Secretariat, Ministry of Social Development and Fight Against Hunger, Social Development (Bolsa Familia)
da Silva Júnior, Jarbas Barbosa	Vice-Minister of Health Surveillance, Secretariat of Health Surveillance, Ministry of Health
da Silva Magalhães, Inês	National Secretary of Housing, Ministry of Cities, Urban Development/Low Income Housing

continued on page 244

Public Sector Entities	
de Franceschi, Angelo Luiz	Operations Directorate, National Operator of Electricity System
de Holanda Bessa, Francisco Eduardo	Coordenador-Geral de Recursos Externos, Directoria de Planejamento e Coodenação das Ações de Controle, Secretaria de Controle Interno, Controladoria-Geral da União, Controller
de Oliveira Souza, Filipe	Social Infrastructure area, the Brazilian Development Bank (BNDES)
de Paula Tavares, Rogério	Executive Director, Caixa Economica Federal
Dias Davis, Roberto	National Land Transport Agency
do Prado, Antônio Carlos	Technical Cooperation Coordinator, Secretariat for International Affairs, Brazilian Agricultural Research Corporation (Embrapa)
Ferreria Trindade, Adaílton	National Superintendent, Sanitation and Infrastructure, Caixa Economica Federal
Fonseca Pereira dos Santos, Pablo	Deputy Secretary, Secretariat of Economic Policy, Ministry of Finance
Forattini, Gisela	Director of Environmental Licensing, IBAMA
Gaetani, Francisco	Deputy-Minister, Ministry of Environment
Gomes Costa, José Carlos	Head of Office of the President, Eletrobras
Lacerda, Artur	Ministry of Finance (on leave)
Ladeira de Medeiros, Otavio	Head of Department, Public Debt Strategic Planning Department, Treasury, Ministry of Finance
Lima Soares, Nazaré	Manager of the Territorial Zoning Project, Secretariat of Rural Sustainable Development, Ministry of Environment
Lopes Varella Neto, Paulo	Director, Agência Nacional de Águas (ANA: National Water Agency)

Public Sector Entities	
Machado dos Santos Conea Pereira, Vivian	Manager, International Division, BNDES
Margulis, Sergio	Advisor to the Minister, Ministry of Environment (telephone)
Medeiros de Andrade, Ricardo	Superintendent, National Water Agency
Milhomens, Allan	Manager of the Department of Sustainable Development, Ministry of Environment
Neves Torreão, Marcos	Manager, Area Project Structuring, BNDES
Oliveira, Edélcio	Coordinator, Relations and Financial Analysis of the States and Municipalities (COREM), Treasury, Ministry of Finance
Pires Ferreira, Lúcia Helena	Coordinator, Financial Assets, Treasury, Ministry of Finance
Porto, Marcio C. M.	Head, Secretariat for International Affairs, Brazilian Agricultural Research Corporation (Embrapa), Ministry of Agriculture, Livestock and Food Supply, Agriculture (Embrapa)
Ronaldo Cabral Magalhães	National Land Transport Agency
Santa Rosa, Junia	Director, Ministry of Cities
Siffert Filho, Nelson Fontes	Superintendent, Infrastructure, BNDES
Suarez de Liviera, Daniela America	Director of the Biodiversity and Conservation Department, Ministry of Environment
Tatagiba, Fernando	Chief of Cabinet, Secretariat of Biodiversity and Forests, Ministry of Environment
Timponi Cambiaghi, Cristina	Adviser for International Affairs, President's cabinet, FUNAI (National Foundation for Indigenous Peoples)
Vieira, Rodrigo Martins	General-Coordinator for External Financing, Secretariat for International Affairs, Ministry of Planning, Budget and Management, Planning
Vidotto, Carlos Augusto	Secretary, Secretariat for International Affairs, Ministry of Planning, Budget and Management, Planning

continued on page 246

Public Sector Entities	
Subnational Entities	
Alagoas	
Acioli Toledo, Mauricio	Secretary of Finance
Lages Cavalcanti, Alexandre	Secretary of Public Management
Bahia	
Souza, Mara	Gabinete do Secretário (GASEC), Secretaria de Saúde do Estado da Bahia (SESAB)
Ceará	
Caetano, Alexandre	Regulation specialist, Regulatory Agency for Public Services (ARCE)
Farias de Oliveira, João Lúcio	Director de Planejamento, Companhia de Gestão dos Recursos Hídricos (COGERH)
Fracalossi Júnior, Mário	Secretário Adjunto das Cidades
Holanda, Monica	Secretariat of Hydraulic Resources
Medeiros, Cristina	Planning Secretariat, IPECE
Nottingham, Philipe Theophilo ·	Secretário Adjunto, Secretaria do Planejamento e Gestão
Rodrigues Bezerra, Hugo Estênio	Manager of Project Monitoring, Water Agency (COGERH)
Sobreira, Carlos Eduardo	Secretário Adjunto da Casa Civil
Vital de Siqueira Cruz, Diogo	Director, METROFOR
Espírito Santo	
Bragato, Neivaldo	President-Director, CESAN
Carneiro, Paulo Rui	Former Director, CESAN
Caus, Celso	Former Advisor, CESAN

Public Sector Entities	
Dalbem, José Carlos	Manager, Clean Waters Project
Sossai, Marcos Franklin	Manager, Program Refloresta, IEMA
Tozi, Anselmo	Director of Environmental Issues, CESAN (Companhia Espírito Santense de Saneamento)
Vieira de Melo, Evair	President-Director, INCAPER (state agricultural extension agency) (also, President, National Council of state systems of agricultural research)

Marabá, Pará

Bechara, Jorge	Municipal Secretary of Agriculture
Brito, Carlos	Municipal Secretary of Environment, Municipal Environmental Agency

Minas Gerais

Codo Santos, Eduardo Antonio	Deputy Secretary of State Treasury
Mendonça A. Caldeira, Silvana M.	Assistant Secretary of State Treasury
Noronha, Gabriela	Assistant Secretary for Credit Operations
Ramos Bahia, Bernardo	Superintendent for Investment Financing
Reis, Andre	Undersecretary of Planning and Management
Severino, Arnaldo	PCPR-Rural Poverty Reduction Program
Vilaça, Taise	SCAP-Human Resource Central Management
Vilhena, Renata	Secretary of Planning and Management

Rio Grande do Sul

da Silva, Felipe Rodrigues	Deputy-Secretary of State Treasury

continued on page 248

Public Sector Entities	
Flores, Luciano	Advisor, Finance Secretary and Treasury
Paiva, Andre	Deputy-Secretary of Finance
Ribeiro, Eugenio Carlos	Undersecretary of State Treasury
Rio de Janeiro Municipality	
Costin, Cláudia Maria	Secretária de Educação
La Rocque, Eduarda	Presidente do Instituto Pereira Passos (former Secretary of Finance)
Santos Cardoso, Marco Aurelio	Secretary of Finance
Rio de Janeiro State	
Baptista Lopes, Julio Luiz	Secretário de Estado de Transportes, Secretaria de Estado de Transportes
Costa, Paulo	Superintendent, Secretary of State for Works
Goncalves, Pablo-Villarim	Manager of Resource Mobilization, State Secretariat of Public Works
Kafuri, Sergio	Advisor/Coordinator of World Bank Program, State Secretariat of Transport
Knauer, Andrezza	General Coordinator, State Secretariat of Transport
Lelles Abib Nepomuceno, Daniele Marino	Adviser for Foreign-financed projects, International Relations, Office of Governor
Loureino, Vincente de Paula	Under-Secretary of Urban/Metropolitan Projects, State Secretariat of Public Works
Pessôa, Maurício	Director of Administration and Finance, State Secretariat of Transport
Ribeiro, Suzana Kahn	Sub-secretary, Green Economy, Secretariat of Environment
Silva Lopes, Mario Carlos	Chief Advisor, Communications, State Secretariat of Transport

Public Sector Entities	
Tafner, Paulo	Deputy Secretary, State Finance Secretariat
São Paulo	
Bertoldi, Atílio Gerson	Coordinator of Financing Unit, Secretariat of State Planning
Bissoli, Afonso Celso	Coordinator PMU, Metropolitan Train Company (CPTM)
Campos Jr., Raphael de Amaral	Coordinator of Roads Program, Department of State Roads (DER)
Fernandes, Jurandir F.R.	State Secretary of Metropolitan Transport
Generoso, José Roberto	Director of Planning, Secretariat of State Planning and Regional Development
Granado, Ernesto Augusto	PMU, São Paulo Metro
Monteiro Cremonese, Helcio	Technical Specialist, São Paulo Metro
Guilerane de Araujo, Ricardo	State Water and Sanitation Company (SABESP)
Pollachi, Amauri	Program Coodinator, State Secretariat of Sanitation and Water Resources
Regino, Tassia	Housing Secretary of the Municipality of São Bernardo do Campo, São Paulo
Souza Munhós Jr., Rubens	Department of State Roads (DER)
Tocantins	
Cifuentes, Joaquin Eduardo M.	Superintendent of Research and Ecological-Economic Zoning, Planning Secretariat
Garcia, Lucia Leiko	AGETRANS
Murakami, Andrea	Manager UGP-PDRIS, Planning Secretariat
Sabino, Rodrigo	Director of Economic Ecological Zoning, Planning Secretariat
Santos, Marli	General Director of Forests and Environment of the Secretariat of Environment and Sustainable Development, SEMADES

continued on page 250

Development Partners, Former Policy Makers, Nongovernmental Organizations, and Research Institutes	
Adeodato Veloso, Fernando Augusto	Fundação Getuilo Vargas (FGV)
Appy, Bernard	Director, LCA Consultores
Bacha, Edmar	Director, Casa das Garças Institute for Economic Policy Studies
Barreto, Paulo	Senior Researcher, IMAZON, Belem
Briscoe, John	Gordon McKay Professor of the Practice of Environmental Engineering and Environmental Health, Harvard University (Country Director, Brazil: 2005–08)
Capossoli Armelin, Mauro J.	Superintendent of Conservation, WWF
Castelar, Armando	Coordenador Geral de Pesquisa, Econômica Aplicada, Fundação Getulio Vargas
Costalonga e Gandour, Clarissa	Senior Analyst, Climate Policy Initiative
de Franco, Nelson	Ex-Bank staff (first TTL for ESTAL project)
Duchelle, Amy	Field research coordinator, REDD, CIFOR (International Forest Research Center)
Eisele, Hubert	Senior Project Manager, Tropical Forests, KfW
Ferreira do Amaral Porto, Monica	Professor, University of São Paulo, Hydroaulic Engineering
Frischtak, Claudio	Presidente, Inter.B Consultoria Internacional de Negócios
Gardner, Toby	Rede Amazonia Sustentavel/University of Cambridge
Gomes, Rubens	Director, GTA (Grupo Trabalho Amazonico) (telephone)
Hargrave, Jorge	Former Researcher at Institute of Applied Economic Research (telephone)
Junqueria Assuncao, Juliano	Director of Climate Policy Initiative, Brazil, Climate Policy Initiative

Development Partners, Former Policy Makers, Nongovernmental Organizations, and Research Institutes	
Kelman, Jerson	Private consultant (Former General Director, National Regulatory Agency of the Power Sector)—telephone interview
Lemos de Sa, Rosa	General Secretary of the Fundo Brasileiro para a Biodiversidade, Funbio
Magalhães, Antonio	Advisor, Center for Strategic Studies and Management
Malan, Pedro	Chairman, International Advisory Board, Itaú Unibanco Holding (former Finance Minister)
Martins, Oswaldo Stella	Director of the Climate Change Program, Instituto de Pesquisa Ambiental da Amazonia (IPAM)
May, Peter	Professor, Federal Rural University of Rio de Janeiro (telephone)
Moreira, Teresa	Environmental Governance Specialist, The Nature Conservancy (TNC)
Nepstad, Daniel	Amazon Environmental Research Institute (IPAM) (telephone)
Neto, Belizario Franco	Former Director of the Secretariat of Environment and Water Resources of Palmas (currently in ITEAP)
Novaes, Joao Arnaldo	Director of the Social and Environmental Actions and Territorial Consolidation of the Units of Conservation, Chico Mendes Institute
Portugal, Murilo	Presidente, FEBRABAN
Ramos, Adriana	Adjunct Executive Secretary, Instituto Socioambiental (ISA)
Rocha, Romero	Senior Analyst, Climate Policy Initiative
Rosa, Alexandre	Manager, Infrastructure and Environment Sector, IDB (former Vice-Minister, Planning)
Schneider, Robert	President, Imazon Board of Directors
Soares, Rodrigo	Pontificial Catholic University (PUC)

continued on page 252

Development Partners, Former Policy Makers, Nongovernmental Organizations, and Research Institutes	
Stabile, Marcelo	Researcher, Instituto de Pesquisa Ambiental da Amazonia (IPAM)
Strassburg, Bernardo B.N.	Executive Director, International Institute for Sustainability
Suarez, Sergei	Chefe de Gabinete, Secretaria de Assuntos Estratégicas, Instituto de Pesquisa Econômica Aplicada (IPEA)
Thomas, Vinod	Director-General, Independent Evaluation Department, Asia Development Bank (Country Director, Brazil: 2002–05)
Timmers, Jean-Francois	Superintendent of Public Policies, WWF
Tolmasquim, Mauricio	President, Energy Research Company (EPE)
Wunder, Sven	Principal Economist, CIFOR (International Forest Research Center)
Private Sector	
Bonassa Barros, Bruno	Correspondant Banking, Banco Indusval and Partners
Cezare, Ana Laura	Legal Manager, Latapack-Ball
Chagas, Diego	Financial Analyst, Estacio
Costa, Pedro Moura	Executive President, Bolsa Verde do Rio de Janeiro (telephone)
Dayan, Morris	Executive Director, Banco Daycoval
de Azevedo, Luiz Gabriel	Responsible for Sustainability, Odebrecht (telephone)
De Lima Neto, Antonio	President, Banco Fibra
Del Ciampo, Paulo Celso	Director, BIC Banco
dos Reis Neto, Alexandre	Financial Manager, Bauducco
Forgach, John	Senior Fellow, IISD (telephone)
Gleizer, Daniel	Treasurer, Banco Itau BBA

Private Sector	
Honjo, Cileide	Superintendent International Department, BIC Banco
Masagao Ribeiro, Luz	Banco Indusval and Partners
Miranda, Antonio	President, Rural Producers' Union of Maraba (also an officer of Federation of Agriculture and Ranting of Para)
Motta, Jorge	Medical Director, Hospital do Suburbio
Neto, Yaroslav	Investor Relations, AEGEA
Pereira, Ricardo Simone	CFO, Banco Sofisa
Pinheiro, Sergio Guedes	Managing Director, CIBRASEC
Pini, Vitor	Director for Investor Relations, Anhanguera Educacional
Rodrigues, Jose Miguel	Finance Director, CIBRASEC
Soares, Roberto Emrich	International Financial Institutions and Export Agency Finance Banco Itau BBA
Tokeshi, Helcio	Managing Director, Estruturadora Brasileira de Projetos (EBP)
Venturini, Daniel	Financial Manager, Estacio
Vieira Martins, Carolina	Finance Manager, Latapack-Ball
Von Gal, Cassio	Director, Banco BBM
World Bank Group	
Abicalil, Thadeu	Senior Water Sector Specialist
Alvarado, Oscar	Senior Water and Sanitation Specialist, LCSWS
Alves, Antonio	Principal Trade Finance Officer, Trade and Supply Chain, Business Development, IFC
Amazonas, Fatima	Senior Rural Development Specialist
Aroujo, Jorge	Lead Economist, LCSPE

continued on page 254

World Bank Group	
Batista, Deborah	Operations Officer, Sustainable Business Advisory Service, IFC
Batmanian, Garo	Senior Environmental Specialist
Bianco Darido, Georges	Senior Transport Specialist
Blanco, Fernando	Senior Economist, AFTP4
Bruns, Barbara	Lead Education Economist, LCSHE
Bulmer, William	Director, Environment, Social and Governance Department, IFC
Cabello, Richard	Manager, Public Private Partnership (LAC), IFC
Canuto, Otaviano	Senior Adviser, DECVP
Chen, Guang Zhe	Country Director (Ethiopia) (Sector Manager, Urban and Water: 2008–11)
Chu, Lily	Head, Operations and Knowledge, FPD
Clarke, Roland	Lead Economist and Sector Leader, PREM
Codato, Eleo	Country Manager, AFCMZ (Sector Leader, LAC: 2002–04)
Correa, Paulo Guilherme	Lead Economist, FIEEI
Cortes, Mariano	Lead Financial Sector Economist, Operations and Knowledge, FPD
Coutinho Barreto, Cassia	Consultant
Crawford, Michael	Lead Education Specialist, EASHE
de Gouvello, Christophe	Senior Energy Specialist, LCGEG
Diop, Makhtar	Regional Vice President, Africa (Country Director for Brazil: 2009–12
Dos Santos, Maria Madelena	Consultant
Entwistle, Janet	Senior Operations Officer, LCSHE

World Bank Group	
Evans, David	Senior Economist, AFRCE
Fajnzylber, Pablo	Sector Manager, PREM, AFTP 2 (Sector Leader, PREM, Brasilia: 2009–13)
Ferreira Fonseca Pedroso, Frederico	ET Consultant
Fonseca, Gustavo	Head, Biodiversity, GEF
Garrido, Juliana	Senior Water and Sanitation Specialist
Gichuri, Wambui	Sector Manager, Water, SDN, LAC
Godinho, Joana	Sector Manager, LCSHH
Gomez Ang, Hector	Head, North and Northeast, IFC
Goncalves Pilotto, Rogerio	Senior Investment Officer, Infrastructure, IFC-São Paulo
Guasch, Jose Luis	Former Senior Adviser, Sustainable Development Department, LAC
Guedes, Andrea	Senior Operations Officer, ECSH2
Iijjasz-Vasquez, Ede Jorge	SDN Director, LAC
Irigoyen, Jose Luis	Director, TWI (Sector Manager, Transport, LAC: 2001–08)
Jadeja, Giri	Senior Manager, Global Financial Market, LAC, IFC
Kenyon, Thomas	Senior Private Sector Development Specialist
Kirchner, Lizmara	Senior Water and Sanitation Specialist, LCSWS
Klein, Alzbeta	Director, Portfolio and Operational Risk Department, IFC
Kriss, Paul	Sector Leader, SD
La Forgia, Gerard	Lead Health Specialist, EASHH
Lancelot, Eric	Senior Transport Engineer, LCSTR

continued on page 256

World Bank Group	
Lange, Bernadete	Senior Environmental Specialist
Lindelow, Magnus	Sector Leader, HD
Linden, Frank	Senior Risk Management Officer, MIGA
Lindert, Kathy	Sector Leader, LCC2C (Central American Countries)
Lopez Carlos, Augusto	Director, Global Indicator and Analysis
Lundell, Mark R.	Sector Manager, EASCS (Sector Leader, SDN, LAC: 2006–12)
Marchesini, Luciana M. H.	Research Analyst, Strategy and Coordination, LAC, IFC
Matthan, Rohit	Financial Officer, Finance and Risk Management Group, MIGA
Maurer, Luiz	Principal Industry Specialist, Climate Strategy and Business Development, IFC (Former task team leader for ESTAL)
Mayorga, Carlos Francisco	Manager, Portfolio, Financial Markets, LAC, IFC
Melo Letteiri, Tania	Operations Analyst
Menendez, Aurelio	Sector Manager, Transport, LAC
Monteiro, Emanuela	ET Consultant (Urban Specialist)
Montoliu Munoz, Marisela	Sector Manager, SDN/LAC
Moreira, Adriana	Senior Environmental Specialist
Parandekar, Suhas	Senior Education Economist, EASHE
Petit, Isabelle	Senior Investment Officer, Public Private Partnership (Rio de Janeiro)
Pires, Loy	Senior Manager, IFC
Platais, Gunars	Senior Environmental Economist, LCSEN
Rao, Vijayendra	Lead Economist, DECPI

World Bank Group	
Rebelo, Jorge	Former TTL (Transport)
Rahill, Bilal	Senior Manager, Environment, Social and Governance Department, IFC
Reis, Jose Guillerme	Lead Trade Economist, PRMTR
Rocha, Roberto	Senior Adviser, Financial System Practice, FPD
Rocha Silveira, Ricardo	Former World Bank staff/TTL, Education
Rodriguez, Alberto	Sector Manager, Education, ECSH2
Rodriguez Barbalho, Antonio Alexandre	Sector Manager, Operations Group, MIGA
Rudolph, Heinz	Lead Specialist, Pensions, FCMNB
Sakho, Seynabou	Economic Adviser, OPSPQ
Samuel, Cherian	Lead Evaluation Officer, MIGA
Sara, Jennifer	Sector Manager, EASVS (Sector Leader, FPSI/SDN, LAC: 2004–10)
Smouse, James	Principal Investment Officer, Financial Market
Stein, John	Sector Director, SASSD (Sector Manager, Urban and Water: 2004–07)
Studart, Rogerio	Executive Director, Brazil
Tuck, Laura	Regional Vice President, Europe and Central Asia (Sector Director, ESSD; SDN, LAC: 2006–11)
Utria, Boris	Country Operations Adviser
Valerio, Alexandria	Senior Economist, HDNED
Velez, Carlos E.	Lead Water and Sanitation Specialist

continued on page 258

World Bank Group	
Villar, Daniel	Princial Economist/Credit Risk Head, Corporate Finance and Risk Management
von Amsberg, Joachim	Vice President, CFP (Lead Economist and Sector Leader-PREM, Brazil: 2000–04)
Wahba, Sameh	Sector Manager, Urban (Sector Leader, SDN, LAC: 2010–12)
Wallentin, Eduardo	Senior Manager, Strategy and Coordination, LAC, IFC
Wellenstein, Anna	Sector Manager, Urban and DRM, LAC
Wetzel, Deborah	Country Director
Wise, Bruce	Operations Officer, IFC
Wolf, Gregor	Sector Leader, SD
Zaki, Fares	Senior Manager, MAS Portfolio, LAC, IFC

Appendix L
Comments from Government

MINISTÉRIO DA FAZENDA
Secretaria de Assuntos Internacionais

Brasília, August 16, 2013.

Mr. NICK YORK
Director
Country, Corporate and Global Evaluation
Independent Evaluation Group – World Bank
Washington, D.C.

Re: **Brazil Country Program Evaluation, FY2004-11**

Dear Mr. York,

I am writing with regards to the Independent Evaluation Group's evaluation of the World Bank program in Brazil for the period starting July 2003 to June 2011. I want to express my appreciation to you and your team for carrying out the evaluation, which is of great value for the Government as it contributes to the continuous enhancement of the partnership between Brazil and the Bank Group.

The report provides a comprehensive and insightful analysis of the Bank's engagement with Brazil during a period of shift in focus towards subnational lending. Overall, conclusions and recommendations are balanced and appropriate. I would like, then, to take advantage of this opportunity to comment on some messages conveyed through the evaluation.

The report assumes the single-borrower limit (SBL) as a constraint for the evaluation and recommendations thereof. Brazilian borrowing from the Bank is certainly limited to the current SBL. This notwithstanding, the current SBL should not lay the boundaries for engagement of the Bank with Brazil, nor should it be implied in any way that Brazil is satisfied with the present limitations.

As the report points out, the dollar amount involved in the Bank country program with Brazil may be relatively small compared to the country economy as a whole. Nonetheless, the impact of Bank financial support remains extremely relevant, especially considering current focus on the subnational level.

As you know, Brazil is structured in a federal system, with units of federation (states) and municipalities differing significantly in the level of poverty, institutional strength, infrastructure and public services delivery. There is, therefore, strong demand from subnationals for Bank assistance, both financial and technical. When screening for selectivity, it is acknowledged in the report that in less developed areas the needs may be greater and the value-added of Bank intervention could be high. In these areas, however, challenges for development may be greater and may require even larger resources. Brazil CPS 2008-2011 has innovated in this aspect, providing a way to focus support towards the North and Northeast of Brazil, whose development still falls short compared to other regions.

Flexibility to address client specific circumstances was also an important feature of the Bank engagement plans with Brazil in the period evaluated. Bank support for key federal policies (as the *Bolsa Família Program*) and investment in more developed regions (as São Paulo and Rio de Janeiro states), where challenges are often more complex and the number of poor people is still massive, have contributed to preserving and enhancing the gains in development achieved previously. Bank Group expertise, knowledge sharing and advice, as well as its potential for long-term engagement with the public sector through financing activities – which is the Bank's most distinctive attribute from private advisory and consultancy agencies – has been really valued by counterparts. The importance of the knowledge sharing actions in these more developed regions should not diminish the recognition of the positive results of well executed projects, such as the support for urban mobility projects in the period under examination.

As a matter of fact, we note that the partnership between the Bank and Brazil, while encompassing a character of "dynamic selectivity" being calibrated by the "comparative advantage" of the Bank for the needs of "each client," federal or subnational, is highly aligned with the new World Bank Group Strategy, even though it has been conceived previously. The scope of interventions undertaken have clearly aimed at ending poverty and promoting better distribution of wealth towards the poorest and most vulnerable, in an environmentally sustainable manner, without losing sight of the need for development results to reach all. The confluence of these factors allowed for the optimization of the portfolio and success in our engagement.

Yet, as recommended, some aspects may be enhanced:

- The catalytic role of the World Bank Group to leverage private resources is an avenue for further exploration. For instance, IBRD-IFC analytical and advisory work on business enabling environments, IFC's PPP initiative and MIGA's new product for investment may yield future gains.

- Knowledge products, particularly policy advice, may benefit from exchange of views with Brazilian-based think-tanks and decentralized Bank staff, working on the country, who understand better current and emerging challenges as well as the functioning and priorities of institutions. Closer interaction with authorities may even underpin the forging of stronger engagement and potentially be more able to timely influence policymaking in key areas for reforms. In any circumstance, the potential for better results in this area will be increased if the activities are aligned with the country's objectives and approaches, such as was the case with *Bolsa Família*.

- Decentralization of staff shall also be beneficial for lending activities, especially when incentives are given for the project managers who helped in design to continue throughout implementation, avoiding disengagement and demobilization of teams.

- Attribution of the overall or part of the impact of a public policy to the Bank's efforts merits candid assessment. Clearly identifying the results chain, by linking Bank country program objectives to Bank interventions, as well as streamlining the results matrix might help assess the real contribution of the Bank to the country development outcomes .

I would like to finalize by congratulating you and your team for the report, which I believe will provide useful inputs for the review and design of country partnership strategies of the Bank Group in Brazil. I also hope this review sheds light on the specific circumstances and challenges that middle-income countries may face, helping the World Bank Group strengthen its engagement towards them.

Yours sincerely,

CARLOS MÁRCIO COZENDEY
Secretary for International Affairs
Ministry of Finance
Brazil

Bibliography

Assunção, Juliano, Clarissa Gandour, and Romero Rocha. 2013. "Detering Deforestation in the Brazilian Amazon: Environmental Monitoring and Law Enforcement." Rio de Janeiro: Climate Policy Initiative.

Blanco, Fernando, Fernando de Holanda, Barbosa Filho, and Samuel Pessôa. 2010. "Brazil: Resilience in the Face of the Global Crisis." In *The Great Recession and Developing Countries: Economic Impact and Growth Prospects*, M. Nabi (ed). Washington, DC: World Bank.

Blyde, Juan, Armando Castelar Pinneiro, Christian Daude, and Eduardo Fernández-Arias. 2010. "Competitiveness and Growth in Brazil." Research Notes No IDB-TN-113. Washington, DC: Inter-American Development Bank.

Bowman, Maria S., Britaldo S. Soares-Filho, Frank D. Merry, Daniel C. Nepstad, Hermann Rodriguez, and Oriana T. Almeida. 2012. "Persistence of Cattle Ranching in the Brazilian Amazon: A Spatial Analysis of the Rationale for Beef Production." *Land Use Policy* 29(3): 558–68.

Celentano, Danielle, Erin Sills, Marcio Sales, and Adalberto Veríssimo. 2012. "Welfare Outcomes and the Advance of the Deforestation Frontier in the Brazilian Amazon." *World Development* 40(4): 850–64.

Chomitz, Kenneth M., Joao Carlos Magalhaes, Daniel da Mata, and Alexandre Ywata de Carvalho. 2005. "Spatial dynamics of labor markets in Brazil." World Bank Policy Research Working Paper 3752, Washington, DC.

Chomitz, Kenneth M., Timothy S. Thomas, and Antônio Salazar P. Brandão. 2005. "The Economic and Environmental Impact of Trade in Forest Reserve Obligations: A Simulation Analysis of Options for Dealing with Habitat Heterogeneity." *Revista de Economia e Sociologia Rural* 43(4s): 657–82.

Chomitz, Kenneth M., Keith Alger, Timothy S. Thomas, Heloisa Orlando, and Paulo Vilanova. 2005. "Opportunity Costs of Conservation in a Biodiversity Hotspot: The Case of Southern Bahia." *Environment and Development Economics* 10(3): 293–312.

Frischtak, Claudio, Victor Chateubriand, and Felipe S. Katz. 2011. "Os desafios que os jogos impoem au pais." *Jornal Valor Economico*, April/May.

Giavazzi, Francesco, Ilan Goldfajn, and Santiago Herrera. 2005. "Overview: Lessons from Brazil." In Giavazzi, Francesco, Ilan Goldfajn, and Santiago Herrera (eds.), *Inflation Targeting, Debt, and the Brazilian Experience, 1999 to 2003* (pp. ix–xxii). Cambridge, MA: The MIT Press.

Harris, Nancy L., Sandra Brown, Stephen C. Hagen, Sassan S. Saatchi, Silvia Petrova, William Salas, Mathew C. Hansen, Peter V. Potapov, and Alexander Lotsch. 2012. "Baseline Map of Carbon Emissions from Deforestation in Tropical Regions." *Science* 336(6088): 1573–76.

Macinko, James, Frederico C. Guanais, and Maria de Fátima Marinho de Souza. 2006. "Evaluation of the impact of the Family Health Program on infant mortality in Brazil, 1990–2002." *Journal Epidemiology Community Health* 60:13–19.

Macinko, James, Inês Dourado, Rosana Aquino, Palmira de Fátima Bonolo, Maria Fernanda Lima-Costa, Maria Guadalupe Medina, Eduardo Mota, Veneza Berenice de Oliveira, and Maria Aparecida Turci. 2010. "Major expansion of Primary Care in Brazil Linked to Decline in Unnecessary Hospitalization." *Health Affairs* 29 (12): 2149–60.

Rocha, Romero. 2009. "Programas Condicionais de Transferência de Renda e Fecundidade: Evidências do Bolsa Família." Presented at Sociedade Brasileira de Econometria.

Rocha, Romero, and Rodrigo R. Soares. 2009. "Evaluating the Impact of Community-Based Health Interventions: Evidence from Brazil's Family Health Program." Institute for the Study of Labor, Discussions Papers Series IZA Discussion Paper No. 4119, Germany.

Sátyro, Natália, and Sergei Soares. 2009. "Análise do Impacto do Programa Bolsa Família e do Benefício de Prestação Continuada na Redução da Desigualdade nos Estados Brasileiros—2004 a 2006." Discussion Papers 1435, Instituto de Pesquisa Econômica Aplicada—IPEA.

Thomas, Vinod. 2006. *From Inside Brazil: Development in a Land of Contrasts.* Washington, DC: World Bank.

World Bank. 2012. Project Appraisal Document, Federal Integrated Water Sector Project–INTERAGUAS, Washington, DC, World Bank.